Study Guide
for Crooks and Baur's
Our Sexuality

Seventh Edition

Lauren Kuhn
Portland Community College

Brooks/Cole Publishing Company

I(T)P® An International Thomson Publishing Company

Pacific Grove • Albany • Belmont • Bonn • Boston • Cincinnati • Detroit
Johannesburg • London • Madrid • Melbourne • Mexico City • New York
Paris • Singapore • Tokyo • Toronto • Washington

Senior Assistant Editor: *Faith B. Stoddard*
Editorial Assistant: *Stephanie M. Andersen*
Production Coordinator: *Dorothy Bell*

Cover Design: *Roy R. Neuhaus*
Cover Photograph: *Digital Vision, PhotoDisc*
Printing and Binding: *Patterson Printirg*

For more information, contact:

BROOKS/COLE PUBLISHING COMPANY
511 Forest Lodge Road
Pacific Grove, CA 93950
USA

International Thomson Editores
Seneca 53
Col. Polanco
11560 México, D. F., México

International Thomson Publishing Europe
Berkshire House 168-173
High Holborn
London WC1V 7AA
England

International Thomson Publishing GmbH
Königswinterer Strasse 418
53227 Bonn
Germany

Thomas Nelson Australia
102 Dodds Street
South Melbourne, 3205
Victoria, Australia

International Thomson Publishing Asia
60 Albert Street
#15-01 Albert Complex
Singapore 189969

Nelson Canada
1120 Birchmount Road
Scarborough, Ontario
Canada M1K 5G4

International Thomson Publishing Japan
Hirakawacho Kyowa Building, 3F
2-2-1 Hirakawacho
Chiyoda-ku, Tokyo 102
Japan

Printed in the United States of America

10 9 8 7 6 5 4 3 2

ISBN 0-534-35988-4

To The Student

Crooks and Baur's seventh edition of *Our Sexuality* provides an exciting and informative exploration of the psychological, biological, social, cultural, and historical dimensions of human sexuality. This study guide is designed to assist you in maximizing your learning experience as you read through this text.

Each study guide chapter consists of several different features that, when used together, will help you successfully integrate the factual and conceptual material in the text. Each chapter begins with a brief introductory paragraph. This is followed by a review of key terms and concepts. The chapter overview with fill-ins provides a concise yet thorough summary of material presented in the text that will enable you to actively test your knowledge of the material once you have finished reading the chapter. When appropriate, a matching exercise will follow the chapter overview. In the next section, a series of sample short answer test questions will enable you to elaborate in greater depth on your understanding of the chapter. Subsequent sample multiple choice questions will allow you to test your recall. Finally, at the end of each chapter are several critical thinking and/or personal reflection questions, exercises and/or activities. The purpose of this material is to encourage you to think about and apply what you have read within the framework of your own background, values, and personal experiences.

In order to maximize your study time, you may find it helpful to use the following system. Begin by reading the chapter summary which is at the end of each chapter in the text. This will give you a brief overview of what to anticipate. Then read through the chapter itself, a major section at a time, underlining definitions, key concepts, research conclusions, and summary paragraphs when appropriate. When you have finished, refer to the review of key terms and concepts at the beginning of the study guide chapter to test your recall.

At this point, proceed to the chapter overview with fill-ins. If you have a basic understanding of the overall concepts and definitions of the chapter, you should be able to complete the majority of the fill-ins without referring to your text. If you find yourself struggling with a particular section in the chapter overview, go back and review the corresponding material in your book. Return again to the overview when you feel you understand the material. This process may be repeated at a later time to test your recall. The answers for the fill-ins are located at the end of the chapter.

When you have completed the overview, proceed to the matching exercises, which are included in most, but not all chapters. Following that are the sample short answer test questions, which are listed in the order in which the material is presented in the text. The study guide is designed so that you may write your answers in the book itself, unless you prefer or your instructor requires you to type them on a separate sheet of paper. In many ways, these short answer questions are the "heart" of the study guide. Taking the time to go back, cover up your answers and then recite them aloud is a key part of the learning process which will pay off handsomely for you later.

After completing the short answer questions, you will find a number of multiple choice items. Complete these and check your answers with the key provided at the end of the chapter. Mark the questions you missed, and then go back to the chapter and review the appropriate section.

Finally, there are several critical thinking and/or personal reflection questions and activities, referred to earlier, that you may wish to take the time to answer for yourself.

Prior to your chapter exam, reread the text, paying particular attention to what you have underlined. Review the various sections of your study guide, covering up your answers to test your recall. Once again, remember that recitation is critical to your retention.

Keep in mind that the suggestions above are **guidelines**; variations that are tailored to what works best for you are encouraged.

Taking a human sexuality course can be a very powerful learning experience. There is the potential to expand your knowledge and awareness on a number of levels: intellectually, personally, emotionally, socially, and culturally. You are investing your time, your money, and your energy. Make it count.

Lauren Kuhn

Please note: At the end of the book is a stamped evaluation form for you to return at your convenience. Your comments and feedback are very welcome, and contribute to successful future revisions of this study guide. Thank you.

Contents

1

Perspectives on Sexuality

Introduction

The psychosocial orientation of the text is discussed, and the authors state their opposition to two long-standing sexual themes in Western cultures: sex-for-reproduction and the rigid distinction between male and female roles. The importance of viewing sexual attitudes and behaviors from a cross-cultural perspective is also presented, and a profile of three societies with diverse sexual values and practices exemplifies the range of sexual expression throughout the world. The diversity that exists within the United States is discussed as well. The chapter concludes with an overview of current social and legal trends that affect our sexual decision-making processes.

Review of Key Terms and Concepts

Key terms and concepts are listed and defined below. Refer to the subject index in the back of your textbook for additional information.

1. **psychosocial orientation** — a perspective emphasizing psychological factors and social conditioning as opposed to biological factors

2. **coitus** — penile-vaginal intercourse

3. **foreplay** — usually defined as the touching, kissing, or oral-genital contact that precedes coitus

4. **sociobiological theory** — suggests that sexual interest and behavior is determined by what increases reproductive success

5. **celibacy** — the state of being unmarried (as historically defined); currently defined as not engaging in sexual behavior

6. **sex-for-reproduction legacy** — a perspective rooted in Judaic and Christian tradition that supports engaging in sexual activity solely for procreative purposes

7. **gender-role legacy** — the attitudinal and behavioral expectations that have existed historically for men and women

8. **courtly love** — in medieval times, an unconsummated love affair between a young knight and a married woman of higher rank

9. **"Two Spirit"** (third gender) — in some Native American societies, men and women who pursue the traditional roles of the other sex

10. **polygyny** — practice of having two or more wives at the same time

11. **acculturation** — replacing traditional beliefs and behaviors with those of the dominant culture

12. **revisionism** — a process whereby an ethnic group tries to recapture an aspect of their culture

13. **multiracial** — having predecessors from two or more racial groups

Chapter Overview With Fill-Ins

After reading each of the major sections in the chapter, check your retention by filling in each of the blanks in the corresponding sections below. The answers are provided at the end of the chapter.

The Authors' Perspectives

1. The book has a _____ orientation, reflecting the authors' view that human sexuality is influenced more by social conditioning and psychological factors than by hormones or instincts.

2. A controversial theory on the impact of biology on our sexuality is _____, which suggests that sexual interest and behavior is determined by what increases reproductive success.

3. Two long-standing sexual themes that the authors oppose are: the sex-for-reproduction legacy, which places emphasis on _____-_____ _____, and as a result devalues other kinds of sexual behavior; and the _____-_____ legacy, which limits human potential and produces a negative impact on our sexuality.

The Sex-for-Reproduction Legacy

4. The idea of sex-for-reproduction is associated with both _____ and Christian traditions.

5. Christian writers such as Paul of Tarsus, _____, and Thomas Aquinas contributed to the view of sex as sinful, legitimized only for the purposes of _____ within a marriage.

6. In the sixteenth century, leaders of the Protestant Reformation, such as _____ _____ and John Calvin challenged the view of nonreproductive sex as sinful.

7. In contrast to Western traditions, ancient Taoists, _____ and Islamic cultures placed a high value on sexual behavior within marriage, not just for procreation.

8. Although the availability of modern _____ has allowed people to separate sexuality from procreation to a degree not possible in earlier times, the sex-for-reproduction legacy maintains a powerful influence in twentieth century Western culture.

The Gender-Role Legacy

9. Rigid _____-_____ differences between men and women go far back in Western history.

10. In ancient Hebraic culture, women were required to manage the household, bear _____, and be obedient to their husbands.

11. The writings of _____ in the New Testament emphasized the importance of women being submissive.

12. During the Middle Ages, two contradictory images of women evolved: the pure and unattainable woman revealed in the cult of the _____ _____ and in courtly love; and the evil temptress represented by Eve and by the women persecuted as _____.

13. Women enjoyed increased respect for a brief time in the _____ century.

14. _____ _____ of England wrote a book asserting women's rights, emphasizing the importance of women being well-educated and claiming that women were entitled to sexual satisfaction as well as men.

15. During the _____ era, women were viewed as asexual.

16. The lives of men and women were sharply dichotomized, and men often sought _____ for sex and companionship.

A Cross-Cultural Perspective: Social Norms and Sexual Diversity

17. In China, many men do not know that a woman has a _____.

18. Most married women in China view _____ as the reason for having sex.

19. _____ is the world's fastest growing religion.

20. In the Islamic Middle East, the customs of women wearing veils and _____ _____ are seen as necessary in controlling the inherent power of female sexuality.

21. In _____, sex education, family law and public health services have promoted relaxed and open attitudes toward sexuality and equality for men and women.

Diversity Within the United States

22. Some examples of diversity that exist within the United States include: Asian-Americans, who are generally less likely to engage in _____ intercourse than other subcultures; and Latinos, who endorse sexual exploration for men but value _____ before marriage for women.

23. The degree to which traditional beliefs and behaviors are replaced with those of the dominant culture, known as _____, also creates differences within subcultures.

Sexuality: Personal or Public Domain?

24. The sexual freedoms and responsibilities that men and women currently enjoy are largely the result of psychological, scientific and social advances that have taken place in the _____ century.

25. Many individuals have made contributions in the area of human sexuality, including Alfred _____ , whose research brought greater acceptance of masturbation, homosexuality, and non-marital intercourse as normal expressions of sexuality.

26. The research of Masters and Johnson contributed to a greater understanding of the sexual _____ _____ in men and women.

27. The invention of the _____ _____ _____ in the early 1960s, as well as the increased availability of other reliable contraceptive devices, helped bring sexual decisions even more firmly into the personal realm.

28. In 1973, the U.S. Supreme Court ruled that _____ is a woman's choice, and in the late 1960s and 1970s attitudes regarding another traditional taboo, _____, began to change.

29. The onset of the _____ crisis in the 1980s increased both negative and positive public sentiment toward homosexuality.

30. Although young men and women have more information, contraceptive choices, and medical care available to them than ever before, there has been an epidemic of _____ _____ diseases, an increase in the birth rate among unmarried adolescent women, and extensive confusion regarding personal values.

31. On the other hand, the risk of contracting an often terminal disease — _____ — has prompted many people to be much more cautious and conservative in their sexual behavior.

32. Some people believe _____ choice should be the foundation for decisions related to sexuality, while others believe that personal control should be limited and brought back to the public domain.

Matching

Match the people below with their ideas or contributions.

a. Paul of Tarsus   g. Mary Wollstonecraft
b. Augustine   h. Sigmund Freud
c. Thomas Aquinas   i. Havelock Ellis
d. Martin Luther   j. Theodore Van de Velde
e. John Calvin   k. Alfred Kinsey
f. William Masters and Virginia Johnson

_____1. A reformer who wrote that marital sex was permissible "… to ease the cares and sadness of household affairs, or to endear each other."

_____2. Lived from 1856 to 1939; recognized sexuality in both men and women as natural

_____3. Lived from 353 to 430 AD; formalized the idea that intercourse was for procreation only within the context of marriage.

_____4. Published research that resulted in increased understanding of the sexual response cycle.

_____5. Wrote *Summa Theologica;* maintained that oral-genital sex and anal intercourse was against God's will.

_____6. A contemporary of Freud's who recognized that individuals have different sexual needs.

_____7. Saw celibacy as superior to marriage; his writings were incorporated into the New Testament.

_____8. Lived from 1483 to 1546; recognized the value of sex in marriage.

_____9. Wrote a book in the late 1700s that asserted, among other things, that premarital and extramarital affairs were not sinful.

_____10. Published scientific information that resulted in greater acceptance of masturbation, homosexuality, etc.

_____11. Lived from 1873 to 1937; emphasized the importance of sexual satisfaction and pleasure.

Sample Short Answer Test Questions

1. What is meant by "a psychosocial orientation"?

2. According to sociobiological theory, what explains to whom we are physically attracted?

3. Why do the authors oppose the sex-for-reproduction legacy?

4. What effects do rigid gender-role conditioning have on men and women?

5. How is the sex-for-reproduction legacy related to Judaic and Christian traditions?

6. What were some of the themes in the writings of Paul of Tarsus?

7. How were the philosophies of Augustine and Thomas Aquinas related?

8.   Briefly describe the sexual perspectives of Martin Luther and John Calvin during the Protestant Reformation.

9.   Briefly compare and contrast ancient Taoist, Hindu and Islamic philosophies regarding sexual activity.

10. List four methods of contraception that were used in ancient times.

11. According to the Book of Proverbs, what were the responsibilities of a good wife?

12. Describe the two contradictory images of women that evolved during the Middle Ages.

13. What contributions did Mary Wollstonecraft make regarding equal rights for women?

14. Explain the nature of sex roles for men and women during the Victorian era.

15. List four facts regarding contemporary sexual attitudes and behavior in China.

16. How is female sexuality viewed in the Islamic Middle East?

17. How would you describe the sexual attitudes and behavior in Sweden?

18. How does the practice of oral-genital sex differ between college-educated whites and blacks as well as people with less education?

19. List three developments in the twentieth century that led to greater sexual equality for women?

20. Briefly describe how the works of Sigmund Freud, Havelock Ellis, and Theodore Van de Velde led to new definitions of sexuality.

21. How did the research of Alfred Kinsey contribute to our knowledge and understanding of human sexuality?

22. How did the research of Masters and Johnson contribute to our knowledge and understanding of human sexuality?

Sample Multiple Choice Test Questions

Select the best alternative. Check your answers with the answer key at the end of the chapter.

1. The textbook has a _____ orientation.
   a. biological
   b. sociological
   c. biosocial
   d. psychosocial

2. The notion that our physical attraction to a person may result from our genetically determined desire for a healthy reproductive partner evolves from
   a. sociobiological theory.
   b. psychosocial theory.
   c. sociological theory.
   d. anthropological theory.

3. Which of the following is the **best** example of a potential effect of the **sex-for-reproduction** legacy?
   a. Men may feel compelled to initiate social and sexual interaction.
   b. Women may be more passive sexually.
   c. Men and women may view masturbation as sinful.
   d. Men may feel obligated to be sexually knowledgeable.

4. Which of the following cultural themes would **most likely** result in men feeling pressure to initiate social or sexual interaction?
   a. sex-for-reproduction legacy
   b. the gender-role legacy
   c. "sex" is synonymous with penile-vaginal intercourse
   d. goal-oriented sexual expression

5. Which of the following is **not** associated with Paul of Tarsus?
   a. viewing celibacy as superior to marriage
   b. explaining why women should be submissive
   c. writing his *Summa Theologica*
   d. associating sex with sin

6. During the Protestant Reformation, _____ disagreed with church doctrine on celibacy and chastity.
   a. Martin Luther
   b. Thomas Aquinas
   c. Augustine
   d. Paul of Tarsus

7. The writing of Mary Wollstonecraft
   a. emphasized sex for procreation.
   b. elaborated on courtly love.
   c. asserted women's rights.
   d. discussed women's roles during the Victorian era.

8. A woman who feels guilty because she is sexually more knowledgeable and experienced than her male partner is a victim of
   a. the equal rights movement.
   b. rigid gender-role conditioning.
   c. a psychosocial orientation.
   d. the sex-for-reproduction legacy.

9. Compared to European settlers, Native American sexual customs
   a. were quite similar.
   b. were more restrictive.
   c. were more permissive.
   d. were very similar in some respects but radically different in others.

10. In the Islamic Middle East, women wear veils and female circumcision
    a. is practiced to demonstrate female devotion to Allah.
    b. is imposed upon women who have dishonored their husbands by having extramarital affairs.
    c. is deemed necessary to control the power of female sexuality.
    d. is practiced in order to ward off evil spirits that can damage female physical and emotional well-being.

11. What was the focus of Masters' and Johnson's research?
    a. a broad survey of people's sexual attitudes and behaviors
    b. a study of adolescent sexuality
    c. sexual response patterns in men and women
    d. case studies of atypical sexual behavior

12. The individual who has provided an explanation for the shift in power from female deities to male deities over the course of history is
    a. Merlin Stone.
    b. Havelock Ellis.
    c. Theodore Van de Velde.
    d. Alfred Kinsey.

13. The term "Two Spirit" most accurately refers to a
    a. shaman.
    b. native American transvestite.
    c. native American person with homosexual orientation.
    d. third gender.

Critical Thinking/Personal Reflection

Throughout this course and as you read the assigned chapters in the text, you will have the opportunity to examine your values regarding a range of issues related to human sexuality. The following exercise is designed to help you begin this "values clarification" process. The topics below represent some of the more sensitive and controversial issues you will be addressing as you read this book. The questions beneath each topic are designed to stimulate your thoughts related to the subject, but they are not comprehensive, so feel free to digress on your own. In addition, for each topic, ask yourself:

1. What is my knowledge base regarding this subject? What facts do I have to support my view?

2. How have my values evolved on this issue? Have they always been the same, or have they changed over time? If there has been a shift in my attitude over time, what factors have contributed to that?

3. To what extent am I open to exploring my values on this topic as I progress through this course?

Sex education

To what extent do I feel this should be taught at home, if at all? Why? What are some specific ways parents might assume more responsibility for sex education at home? To what extent do I feel sex education should be taught in school, if at all? Why? If I support sex education in school, at what grade level should sex education begin? What topics should be addressed in a sex education curriculum in grade school? Junior high school? High school?

Premarital sexual intercourse

How do I feel about this **for me**? Under what circumstances or conditions is this acceptable? Unacceptable? Why? How do I feel about my partner having experience with premarital sexual intercourse? Why?

Masturbation

How do I feel about this **for myself**? What are the benefits and drawbacks? Do I feel this is more acceptable at some age levels than others? Would I feel comfortable with this practice for myself or my partner if we were married or living together? Under what circumstances would I be or am I uncomfortable with this practice?

Cohabitation

Under what circumstances would I consider living with a partner, if at all? What do I perceive as the benefits and drawbacks? Do I feel that living together would result in a potentially more successful marital relationship? Why or why not?

Homosexuality

How do I feel about people with a homosexual orientation? Why? Do I feel that sexual orientation can be altered or changed? Do I believe that people with a homosexual orientation should have the same rights and freedoms as people with a heterosexual orientation? Why or why not?

Abortion

Under what circumstances would I consider having an abortion or support my partner in having one, if any (e.g., contraceptive failure, in cases of rape or incest, high risk of birth defects, etc.)? How do I feel about abortion being available to women in the community? Under what conditions or circumstances, if any? How do I feel abortion should be funded?

Love and sex

How do I feel about the relationship between love and sex? Are they related? If so, in what way? Is it or would it be possible **for me** to have a good sexual relationship without being in love? Under what circumstances, if at all? Do I think men and women perceive the relationship between love and sex in similar or different ways? Elaborate.

Extramarital sexual intercourse

Under what circumstances, if any, would extramarital sex be acceptable for me or my partner (e.g., different values or priorities regarding sex, prolonged illness, extended absence, etc.)? Have my partner or I ever experienced this, now or in a previous relationship? What impact did it have?

Pornography

How do I define "pornography"? To what degree, if at all, have I been exposed to pornography? Do I feel that it does or would enhance my sexual experience — alone or with a partner? Or detract from it? Do I think that viewing pornography would affect sexual attitudes and behavior — for myself or for others? Why or why not?

Sexual harassment

Have I ever experienced sexual harassment as a perpetrator and/or victim? How do I feel about the increased focus on this subject in recent years? What impact has that had on my attitudes and behavior, if any?

- You may wish to expand the list of issues above as you proceed through the course.

- You may wish to do this assessment again after you have finished reading the text and/or completed the class to see how your values have changed, if at all.

- As a variation on this activity, after completing it alone, you may wish to sit down with a partner, friend, group of friends or family members to discuss your values with one another. It can be especially challenging if you select people whose values you know are different than your own. The ground rules are:

  1. Listen to each other with the intent to more fully **understand** each other's view, **not** to attempt to **change** it.

  2. Ask questions to get more information to help you better understand how and why the person happens to view the issue in a certain way, **not** to challenge the person's position or to make the person defend his or her view.

Chapter Overview With Fill-In Answers

1. psychosocial
2. sociobiology
3. penile-vaginal intercourse; gender-role
4. Judaic
5. Augustine; procreation
6. Martin Luther
7. Hindu
8. contraception
9. gender-role
10. children
11. Paul of Tarsus
12. Virgin Mary; witches
13. eighteenth
14. Mary Wollstonecraft
15. Victorian
16. prostitutes
17. clitoris
18. procreation
19. Islam
20. female circumcision
21. Sweden
22. premarital; chastity
23. acculturation
24. twentieth
25. Kinsey
26. response cycle
27. oral contraceptive pill
28. abortion; homosexuality
29. AIDS
30. sexually transmitted
31. AIDS
32. personal

Matching Answers

1. e   2. h   3. b   4. f   5. c   6. i   7. a   8. d
9. g   10. k   11. j

Sample Multiple Choice Answers

1. d   2. a   3. c   4. b   5. c   6. a   7. c   8. b
9. c   10. c   11. c   12. a   13. d

2

Sex Research: Methods and Problems

Introduction

Understanding how sex research is conducted and becoming familiar with several classic research studies will help lay the groundwork for integrating and appreciating much of the information presented in the text. This chapter describes four research methods used in studying sexuality and outlines advantages and limitations of each. The impact of feminist scholarship or sex research is also discussed. Finally, the authors explore the reliability of sex research reported in the popular media.

Review of Key Terms and Concepts

Key terms and concepts are listed and defined below. Refer to the subject index in the back of your textbook for additional information.

1. **survey** — a research method in which a sample of people are questioned about their attitudes or behaviors, either through their response to a written questionnaire or a face-to-face interview

2. **representative sample** — a type of research sample in which every person in the total population about which one wishes to draw a conclusion has an equal chance, or probability, of being included

3. **random sample** — a type of survey sample that is selected by indiscriminate or random procedures; this sample may or may not be the same as a representative sample

4. **nonresponse** — the number of people who choose NOT to participate in survey research, and the problems this creates in interpreting the results of the survey

5. **self-selection** — the degree to which research results may be distorted by the individuals who choose to participate in a study as opposed to those who do not

6. **demographic bias** — research in which the survey samples contain a disproportionately higher number of one group of individuals as opposed to another

7. **sexology** — the study of sexuality

8. **case study** — a research method that involves in-depth study of one or more subjects who are examined individually

9. **direct observation** — a research method in which subjects are observed as they go about their activities

10. **experimental research** — a research method in which the subject's reactions and behaviors can be reliably measured under controlled laboratory conditions

11. **penile strain gauge** — a device used in sex research that can measure even the slightest changes in penis size as the result of sexual arousal

12. **vaginal photoplethysmograph** — a device used in sex research to measure the increases in vaginal blood volume that occurs as a woman becomes sexually aroused

13. **independent variable** — a condition of the experiment that is under the control of the researcher

14. **dependent variable** — the outcome that the experimenter observes but does not control

Chapter Overview With Fill-Ins

After reading each of the major sections in the chapter, check your retention by filling in each of the blanks in the corresponding sections below. The answers are provided at the end of the chapter.

The Goals of Sexology

1. Sexologists share certain goals with scientists in other disciplines and these include understanding, _____ and controlling events that are the subject matter of their fields.

Nonexperimental Research Methods

2. A _____ _____ examines either a single subject or small group of subjects, each studied individually and in depth.

3. Most of our information about human sexuality has been obtained by a second research method, the _____ , in which people are asked about their sexual attitudes or experiences.

4. The above method may take the form of face-to-face _____ or written _____.

5. Researchers strive to select a _____ sample, in which various subgroups are represented proportionate to their incidence in the target population.

6. Another kind of sample, called a _____ sample, is selected by randomization procedures, but this does not necessarily ensure a representative sample.

7. A common problem encountered in sex survey research is that of _____ , the refusal to participate in a research study.

8. Even if the researcher has been careful in selecting the sample population, _____-_____ , also called "volunteer bias", may distort the sample.

9. Another problem that affects sex surveys is _____ bias, which occurs when one group of people is disproportionately represented.

10. Because survey respondents may consciously or unconsciously distort information regarding their sexual experiences, _____ of information is still another problem that plagues sex research.

11. A very well-known example of sex survey research is the work conducted by _____ _____ and his associates in the late 1940s and early 1950s on male and female sexuality.

12. The single best sex survey ever conducted on adult sexual behavior to date is the _____

13. A third method for studying human sexual behavior is _____ _____ , where researchers observe and record responses of participating subjects.

14. A classic research study using the method above is the work of _____ and _____ , who observed the physiological changes that men and women experience during sexual arousal.

The Experimental Method

15. A fourth method, _____ research, involves presenting subjects with certain specific stimuli under controlled conditions so that their reactions can be reliably measured.

16. The _____ method is the best suited for exploring cause and effect relationships.

Feminist Theory and Sex Research

17. Feminist scholars would like to see sex research include more emphasis on the _____ experience of sexuality for women and men, rather than the current primary emphasis on quantitative aspects.

Popular Media and Sex Research

18. The majority of _____ surveys fail to use scientific methodology.

Evaluating Research: Some Questions To Ask

19. When evaluating a particular piece of research, first determine the _____ of the researchers, and note the type of _____ in which the results were published.

20. Examine the type of _____ used, by checking the sample size of the group and by considering the possibility of _____ in the selection of subjects.

Matching

Match the research method below with the appropriate description.

      a. survey method
      b. case study method
      c. direct observation
      d. experimental research

_____1. Sexual response patterns were studied in this way by Masters and Johnson.

_____2. The National Health and Social Life Study used this method.

_____3. Questionnaires or interviews are two ways in which this method may be used.

_____4. This method is being used with increasing frequency to study human sexual behavior.

_____5. If this method is used, it is difficult to make generalizations about the rest of the population.

_____6. This is the way in which most of our information regarding human sexuality has been obtained.

_____7. This method allows sex to be studied under controlled conditions.

_____8. Using this method, cause-and-effect relationships may best be explored in detail.

_____9. Kinsey used this method.

_____10. Much current information about transsexuals and sex offenders has been obtained through this approach.

Sample Short Answer Test Questions

1. List and briefly describe three goals of sexology.

2. When did the field of sexology originate? Who conducted the first extensive survey of American sexual behavior?

3. In what kinds of research would use of the case study method be most appropriate? Cite an example of research that has used the case study method.

4. List the advantages and disadvantages of the case study method.

5. List the two types of survey methods and describe advantages and limitations of each.

6. Define and give an example of a representative sample.

7. Summarize recent research findings on self-selection.

8. Explain how demographic bias was reflected in Kinsey's research.

9. Briefly describe how the problems of nonresponse and self-selection bias were reflected in the *Redbook* survey.

10. Briefly describe the nature of Kinsey's research:

    a. Who were the subjects of his study?

    b. Was Kinsey's study population considered a representative sample? Why or why not?

    c. What research method did he use?

11. In the National Health and Social Life Survey, what percentage of the sample subjects agreed to participate?

12. What is considered the best sex survey ever conducted in the United States to date?

13. How did the findings of the NHSLS contradict what was widely believed?

14. Summarize the survey findings of Demur, et. al. regarding use of pornography as it relates to the likelihood of committing rape or using sexual force.

15. Briefly describe the nature of Masters and Johnson's research:

    a. What was the purpose of their research?

    b. Describe the sample population.

    c. What research method did they use?

    d. What stimulus situations were used to observe sexual response?

16. List advantages and limitations of the direct observation method of research.

17. What method is being used with increasing frequency in studying human sexual behavior? Why?

18. In the Malamuth and Check experiment, what was the independent variable?

19. When measured **physiologically**, how does alcohol consumption affect sexual arousal?

20. Cite three examples of sex research in which female behavior or experience has been limited or ignored.

21. Why are magazine surveys often not very reliable?

22. Briefly list seven criteria to consider in evaluating a piece of research.

23. Briefly describe several ethical and legal considerations in conducting research on human sexuality.

24. Name two devices used to measure penile tumescence and describe how they work.

25. How does a vaginal photoplethysmograph work?

Sample Multiple Choice Test Questions

Select the best alternative. Check your answers with the answer key at the end of the chapter.

1. Sexual behavior became the subject of serious study
    a. in the late 17th century.
    b. mid 18th century.
    c. mid 19th century.
    d. in the 20th century.

2. Which of the following statements regarding the survey method is **true**?
    a. The researcher is able to explore cause and effect relationships.
    b. Masters and Johnson used this method in their research.
    c. This would be a good method to use in studying the physiological effects of alcohol consumption on sexual arousal.
    d. Most of our scientific knowledge of human sexuality has been obtained by this method.

3. The ideal sample is called a/an _____ sample.
    a. random
    b. representative
    c. survey
    d. equivalent

4. In conducting a survey, a researcher may choose to conduct interviews rather than administer a survey because interviews are
    a. cheaper.
    b. more anonymous.
    c. more flexible.
    d. easier to administer.

5. Self-selection is another term for
    a. volunteer bias.
    b. demographic bias.
    c. ethnocentrism.
    d. the primacy effect.

6. Disproportionate representation of certain groups of people (i.e., college students, white-collar workers) illustrates the problem of
    a. geographic discrimination.
    b. demographic bias.
    c. data discrimination.
    d. ethnocentrism.

7. A limitation of the case-study method is that
    a. data gathering procedures are very structured.
    b. generalizations can rarely be drawn to the rest of the population.
    c. it does not allow for in-depth exploration of a person or social group.
    d. cause-and-effect relationships cannot be explored.

8. A penile strain gauge
    a. measures the slightest change in penis size.
    b. is a flexible "ruler" that is attached to the penis and measures changes in length during arousal.
    c. measures the time between arousal and orgasm.
    d. measures subjective reports of sexual arousal in men.

9. Which of the following is a limitation of the direct observation method of research?
    a. data falsification through memory deficits
    b. having to rely on subjective reports of past experiences
    c. inability to see and measure sexual behavior firsthand
    d. the degree to which a subject's behavior may be influenced by an observer

10. The studies cited on the effects of alcohol on sexual arousal as measured **physiologically** used which research method?
    a. survey
    b. case study
    c. direct observation
    d. experimental

11. Which of the following statements concerning experimental research is **false**?
    a. This method is being used with increasing frequency in studying human sexual behavior.
    b. The studies cited on how alcohol consumption affects physiological sexual arousal used this method.
    c. Cause-and-effect relationships cannot be explored when using this method.
    d. This method allows the researcher to control variables thought to influence the behavior being studied.

12. Two devices for measuring sexual arousal include
    a. a penile strain gauge and vaginal photoplethysmograph.
    b. a tumescent thermometer and vaginal photoplethysmograph.
    c. a penile strain gauge and vaginal dilator.
    d. a tumescent thermometer and vaginal dilator.

13. If you wished to do an in-depth study of individuals seeking sex-change surgery, which of the following research methods would probably be **most** appropriate?
    a. experimental research
    b. direct observation
    c. case study
    d. survey

14. A _____ variable is a condition of the experiment that is under control of the researchers.
    a. dependent
    b. independent
    c. representative
    d. random

15. Which of the following groups of people were **omitted** from Kinsey's survey?
    a. better-educated, city-dwelling Protestants
    b. older people
    c. people living in rural communities
    d. blacks

16. The National Health and Social Life Survey underrepresented which of the following groups of people?
    a. Native Americans and Hispanic Americans.
    b. African Americans and Hispanic Americans.
    c. Asian Americans and Native Americans.
    d. African Americans and Jews.

17. Masters and Johnson's research has made a major contribution to the understanding of
    a. men's and women's sexual values, attitudes and behavior.
    b. the sexual behavior of adolescent males and females.
    c. the effects of alcohol on sexual arousal.
    d. physiological changes that occur during sexual arousal.

18. A group of college men is exposed to films with nonviolent sexual themes. A second group is exposed to R-rated films in which men commit sexual violence against women. Several days later, all men complete an attitude questionnaire. The results demonstrate that the second group of men is more accepting of violence toward women than the first group. What is the independent variable in this study?
    a. the degree of violence in the films observed
    b. the first group's response to the questionnaire
    c. the second group's response
    d. the attitude questionnaire

19. One of the **more controversial** ethical issues in human sexual research involves
    a. potential physical harm to subjects.
    b. potential psychological harm to subjects.
    c. the issue of deception.
    d. the issue of anonymity.

20. Feminist scholars would like to see sex research, with its primary emphasis on _____ data collection, expanded to include _____ data collection as well.
    a. quantitative; qualitative
    b. qualitative; quantitative
    c. survey; experimental
    d. experimental; survey

Critical Thinking/Personal Reflection

1. Peruse a variety of popular magazines at a local library, book or grocery store. Find two articles in two of these magazines that deals with sex. Evaluate each article in terms of the seven criteria discussed in your test at the end of chapter two.

2. Assume that you are a researcher who is interested in gathering information on childhood sexuality (i.e., the level of sexual knowledge and awareness that children possess at various ages, sources of sexual information, masturbatory activity in which children might engage, orgasmic response, sex play with siblings or other children, etc.). What method(s) would you choose to obtain this information? What problems might you encounter in doing this type of research? How might you deal with them?

Chapter Overview With Fill-In Answers

1. predicting
2. case study
3. survey
4. interviews; questionnaires
5. representative
6. random
7. nonresponse
8. self-selection
9. demographic
10. accuracy
11. Alfred Kinsey
12. National Health and Social Life Survey (NHSLS)
13. direct observation
14. Masters; Johnson
15. experimental
16. experimental
17. qualitative
18. magazine
19. credentials; media
20. methodology; bias

Matching Answers

1. c   2. a   3. a   4. d   5. b   6. a   7. d   8. d
9. a   10. b

Sample Multiple Choice Answers

1. d   2. d   3. b   4. c   5. a   6. b   7. b   8. a
9. d   10. d   11. c   12. a   13. c   14. b   15. d   16. c
17. d   18. a   19. c   20. a

3

Gender Issues

Introduction

This chapter examines the complex process whereby our maleness and femaleness are determined and the extent to which they influence our social and sexual behavior. Both the biological and social-learning aspects of gender-identity formation are discussed as well as some of the variations that may occur as a result of abnormal prenatal differentiation. Finally, the authors explore a number of gender-based societal stereotypes and how these may inhibit our growth and development.

Review of Key Terms and Concepts

Key terms and concepts are listed and defined below. Refer to the subject index in the back of your textbook for additional information.

1. **Tchambuli of New Guinea** — a society in which traditional masculine and feminine behavior patterns are complete opposites of those that characterize American society

2. **sex** — our biological maleness or femaleness, two aspects of which are genetic sex (determined by sex chromosomes) and anatomical sex (the physical differences between males and females)

3. **gender** — the psychosocial aspects of being masculine or feminine

4. **gender assumptions** — beliefs regarding how people are likely to behave based on their maleness or femaleness

5. **gender identity** — how one psychologically perceives oneself as being either male or female

6. **gender role (sex role)** — a collection of attitudes and behaviors that are considered normal and appropriate in a specific culture for people of a particular sex

7. **chromosomal sex** — the first level of sex differentiation, whereby our biological sex is determined by the sex chromosomes (XX or XY) present in the reproductive cells at the moment of conception

8. **sperm** — male reproductive cell

9. **ovum** — female reproductive cell

10. **autosomes** — the 22 pairs of human chromosomes that do not significantly influence sex differentiation

11. **sex chromosomes** — a single set of chromosomes that influences biological sex determination

12. **testes** — male gonads inside the scrotum that produce sperm and sex hormones

13. **gonadal sex** — the second level of sex differentiation, whereby the presence of TDF triggers the transformation of the gonads into testes, and the absence of TDF causes the gonads to develop into ovaries

14. **gonads** — the reproductive organs (testes in men and ovaries in women)

15. **ovaries** — female gonads that produce ova and sex hormones

16. **hormonal sex** — the third level of sex differentiation, whereby the testes secrete androgens, causing development of male sex structures. Without androgens, female structures develop.

17. **endocrine system** — several ductless glands located throughout the body that produce hormones. The major endocrine glands include the pituitary, gonads, thyroid, parathyroids, adrenals, and pancreas.

18. **estrogens** — ovarian hormones, the most important of which is estradiol, which influence the development of female sex characteristics and help regulate the menstrual cycle

19. **progestational compounds** — ovarian hormones, most importantly progesterone, which help regulate the menstrual cycle and stimulate the development of the uterine lining in preparation for pregnancy

20. **androgens** — the primary hormone products of the testes, most importantly testosterone, which influences both the development of male physical sexual characteristics and sexual motivation

21. **Müllerian ducts** — a pair of ducts in the embryo that develop into female reproductive organs

22. **Wolffian ducts** — the internal duct system of the embryo that develops into male reproductive organs

23. **Müllerian inhibiting substance (MIS)** — a substance secreted by the fetal testes that causes the Müllerian ducts to shrink rather than develop into internal female structures

24. **dihydrotestosterone (DHT)** — a hormone in the fetal bloodstream that stimulates the labioscrotal swelling to become the scrotum, and the genital tubercle and genital folds to differentiate into the penis

25. **hypothalamus** — a brain structure that plays a major role in controlling the production of sex hormones and the regulation of fertility and menstrual cycles through its interaction with the pituitary gland

26. **cerebral hemispheres** — the left and right sides of the cerebrum, the largest part of the brain

27. **bed nucleus of the stria terminalis (BST)** — an area of the hypothalamus that contains estrogen and androgen receptors and plays an essential role in the sexual behavior of non-human animals

28. **true hermaphrodites** — a very rare condition in which individuals have both ovarian and testicular tissue and a mixture of male and female external genitals

29. **pseudohermaphrodites** — more common than true hermaphrodites, they possess ambiguous internal and external reproductive anatomy but their gonads match their chromosomal sex

30. **Turner's Syndrome** — a rare chromosomal abnormality characterized by the presence of only one sex chromosome, an X

31. **Klinefelter's Syndrome** — a chromosomal abnormality that results when an atypical ovum is fertilized by a Y-bearing sperm, creating an XXY individual

32. **androgen insensitivity syndrome** — a condition resulting from a genetic defect that causes chromosomally normal males to be insensitive to the action of testosterone and other androgens, which results in the development of normal-looking female external genitals

33. **fetally androgenized female** — chromosomally normal female, who, as a result of excessive exposure to androgens during prenatal sex differentiation, develops external genitalia resembling those of a male

34. **DHT-deficient males** — a chromosomally normal (XY) male who develops external genitalia resembling those of a female as a result of a genetic defect that prevents the prenatal conversion of testosterone into DHT

35. **interactional model** — the perspective whereby gender identity is considered to be a result of both biological and social learning factors

36. **transsexual** — a person whose gender identity is opposite to his or her biological sex

37. **gender dysphoria** — another term for transsexualism, the condition in which an individual's gender identity is opposite to his or her biological sex

38. **stereotypes** — a generalized notion of what a person is like based only on that person's sex, religion, ethnic background or similar criterion

39. **socialization** — the process whereby society conveys behavioral expectations to the individual

40. **androgyny** — possessing behavioral characteristics of both sexes; also used to describe gender role flexibility

41. **SRY** — the maleness (testis determining) gene

Chapter Overview With Fill-Ins

After reading each of the major sections in the chapter, check your retention by filling in each of the blanks in the corresponding sections below. The answers are provided at the end of the chapter.

Male and Female, Masculine and Feminine

1. _____ refers to our biological maleness or femaleness.

2. There are two aspects of biological sex: _____ sex, which is determined by our sex chromosomes, and _____ sex, the obvious physical differences between males and females.

3. _____ refers to the psychosocial meanings added to our biological maleness or femaleness.

4. _____ _____ refers to our subjective sense of being male or female.

5. Gender _____ refers to the attitudes and behaviors that are appropriate in a specific culture for people of a particular sex.

Gender-Identity Formation

6. Gender-identity formation involves both _____ and social-learning factors.

7. Our physical maleness or femaleness is the result of processes that occur at six different levels of sexual differentiation: chromosomal sex, _____ sex, hormonal sex, sex of the internal reproductive structures, sex of the external genitals, and sex differentiation of the _____.

8. At the first level of differentiation, our biological sex is determined by the chromosomal makeup of the _____ (male reproductive cell) which fertilizes an _____ (female reproductive cell).

9. Fertilization of the ovum by a Y-bearing sperm produces an XY combination, resulting in a _____ child.

10. Fertilization by an X-bearing sperm results in an XX combination and a _____ child.

11. The _____ chromosome must be present to ensure the complete development of internal and external male sex organs.

12. During the first few weeks of prenatal development, the _____ — structures that will become the reproductive organs — are the same in males and females.

13. Differentiation begins about _____ weeks after conception.

14. The ovaries produce two classes of hormones: _____ and progestational compounds.

15. The primary hormone products of the testes are the _____, the most important of which is testosterone.

16. The appropriate amount of androgens, secreted by the _____, stimulates the development of male structures.

17. In the absence of male hormones, the fetus develops _____ structures.

18. At about eight weeks after conception, internal reproductive structures begin to differentiate from two paired internal duct systems, the Müllerian ducts and the _____ ducts.

19. If the embryo is chromosomally male, and if the gonads have previously differentiated into testes, the testes will begin secreting two substances: _____-_____ substance, which causes the Müllerian ducts to shrink, and androgens (testosterone), which stimulate the development of the _____ ducts into internal male reproductive structures.

20. If the Müllerian ducts are not suppressed by MIS and testosterone, they develop into internal _____ structures.

21. When testosterone begins circulating in the bloodstream of males, it is converted in some tissues into a hormone called _____ which causes the tissues to differentiate into male genitals.

22. In the absence of _____, the external female genitals evolve.

23. Research suggests that important functional and structural differences exist in the _____ of human males and females that result in part from prenatal sex differentiation.

24. These differences appear to involve at least two major brain areas: the _____, and the left and right _____ hemispheres.

25. Sex differences in the structure of the two cerebral hemispheres suggest a possible biological basis for differences in the _____ and spatial abilities of males and females.

26. However, other theorists argue that these differences are largely due to _____ factors.

27. _____ hermaphrodites are very rare and have both (true) ovarian and testicular tissue in their bodies.

28. _____ hermaphrodites are more common, and unlike the above, have gonads that match their chromosomal sex.

29. Five examples of pseudohermaphrodites are: Turner's Syndrome; _____ Syndrome; _____ insensitivity syndrome; _____ androgenized females; and DHT-deficient _____.

30. In addition to the biological explanation for the formation of gender identity, there is also the _____-_____ interpretation that suggests that gender identity results from social and cultural models and influences we are exposed to during our early development.

31. In addition to other research, _____ studies of other cultures also support the social-learning interpretation.

32. Margaret Mead studied three societies in _____ _____, two of which demonstrated minimal differences between the sexes, while another, the _____, demonstrated a reversal of our typical masculine and feminine roles.

33. The research of _____ _____ and his colleagues has also provided evidence in support of the social-learning perspective.

34. Today most researchers and theorists support the _____ model of gender-identity formation, which acknowledges both biology and experience in the development of gender identity.

35. A person whose gender identity is opposite to his or her biological sex is called a _____; this condition is also referred to as _____ _____.

36. There are several steps involved for the individual who wants to pursue sex reassignment surgery: extensive screening _____; living a lifestyle consistent with their gender _____ (dress and behavior patterns); _____ therapy; and finally, the surgical procedure itself.

Gender Roles

37. A _____ is a generalized notion of what a person is like based only on the person's sex, race, religion, etc.

38. _____ is the process by which individuals learn society's expectations for behavior.

39. _____ play a role in the socialization of gender roles in their children by the behaviors they encourage or discourage, the roles they model, and how they interact with their children on the basis of their sex.

40. In addition to parents, the _____ _____ is influential in the socialization of gender roles, particularly during the adolescent years.

41. Other agents of socialization include schools, television and _____.

42. The authors discuss several _____ _____ assumptions that are common in our society and the effects that these assumptions have on our intimate relationships with one another.

43. One assumption, women as _____, men as _____, makes it difficult for women to openly acknowledge their sexual interest for fear of being labeled "slut," "sleaze," etc.

44. In a second gender-role assumption, men as _____, women as _____, men may feel the constant pressure to initiate social and sexual interaction, while women, due to their more passive role, lack opportunities to take control of their social or sexual relationships.

45. The pressure on men to be sexually knowledgeable and experienced is a result of another gender-role assumption, men as "_____".

46. A woman who feels she must constantly control her partner's raging sexual lust, and in the process of doing that may suppress her own sexual feelings, is a victim of the gender stereotype of women as _____, men as _____.

47. The last stereotype discussed, men as unemotional and strong, women as _____ and _____, makes it difficult for men to develop emotionally satisfying relationships and women may find their role rather tiresome, especially when there is little reciprocity.

48. _____ is a term used to describe flexibility in gender roles.

Matching

Match each term below with the appropriate numbered description. Note that each term below may be used more than once, and there may be more than one term for each description.

    a. transvestites
    b. fetally androgenized females
    c. individuals with androgen-insensitivity syndrome
    d. DHT-deficient males
    e. transsexuals
    f. individuals with Klinefelter's Syndrome
    g. individuals with Turner's Syndrome

_____1. the problem is usually discovered when menstruation fails to commence

_____2. their external genitals begin to appear at puberty

_____3. individuals who cross dress for the purpose of sexual arousal

_____4. an example of abnormal prenatal differentiation

_____5. chromosomally normal; as infants, external genitals resemble those of a male to varying degrees

_____6. prenatal exposure to excessive amounts of male hormones may precipitate this condition

_____7. these individuals experience gender dysphoria

_____8. there is currently no definitive explanation for what causes this condition

_____9. social-learning factors appear to be significant in determining how these individuals behave

_____10. sociocultural factors appear to facilitate gender identity change in these individuals at puberty

_____11. chromosomal sex is XO; normal external genitals; sterile

_____12. chromosomal sex is XXY; undersized external genitals; sterile

Sample Short Answer Test Questions

1. Distinguish between the terms "sex" and "gender."

2. Distinguish between the terms "gender identity" and "gender role."

3. List the six different levels of sexual differentiation.

4. Briefly explain what occurs at the level of chromosomal sex differentiation under normal conditions.

5. What is the function of SRY and DHT?

6. Identify the following:

    a. endocrine system

    b. estrogens

    c. progestational compounds

    d. androgens

7. Briefly describe how the Müllerian and the Wolffian ducts may develop into internal female or male structures.

8. Name the homologous male equivalents to each of the following: clitoris, labia minora, labia majora, ovaries, Skene's ducts, and Bartholin's glands.

9. How does the BSTc vary between men and women? What may this suggest?

10. How do men and women compare on tests for verbal and spatial skills?

11. Distinguish between true and pseudohermaphrodites.

12. Briefly describe the characteristics of an individual with Turner's Syndrome.

13. Briefly describe the characteristics of an individual with Klinefelter's Syndrome.

14. What are the effects of androgen insensitivity syndrome?

15. In females who are fetally androgenized, what are two possible sources of the androgen?

16. What are the effects of excessive prenatal androgen exposure in females?

17. Summarize Money and Ehrhardt's findings (1972) regarding fetally androgenized females.

18. When males are DHT-deficient, what is the result?

19. What is a possible explanation for why the individuals in the Dominican study of DHT-deficient males converted to a male identity?

20. How may the apparent inconsistencies in the results of the studies of hormone-based differentiation errors be explained?

21. Most children have developed a firm sense of their gender identity by what age?

22. Describe the gender-role behaviors of males and females in the following New Guinea cultures studied by Margaret Mead.

    a. Mundugumor

    b. Arapesh

    c. Tchambuli

23. According to Money's research, what kind of gender identity did children develop whose assigned sex did not match their chromosomal sex?

24. John Money studied two twin boys, one of whom experienced a circumcision accident at eight months. What did long term follow-up of this individual reveal?

25. Describe the interactional model of gender identity.

26. How is transvestism different from transsexualism?

27. Currently, how many men as opposed to women seek sex-reassignment surgery?

28. Are transsexuals biologically normal?

29. Briefly discuss two theories of the causes of transsexualism.

30. List the stages an individual must go through in order to have a sex change.

31. Summarize the recent research findings on the postoperative follow-up of transsexuals' lives.

32. What country has taken the lead in promoting sex-reassignment surgery during the teenage years?

33. How is orgasmic capacity affected in postoperative transsexuals?

34. According to a recent research study, how do parents treat boys and girls similarly or differently?

35. During adolescence, how do peers influence gender-role socialization?

36. Briefly describe how each of the following contribute to gender-role socialization.

    a. schools

    b. television

    c. religion

37. Of the various ethnic groups described in the "Sexuality and Diversity" box, which has tended to be more egalitarian, socially and economically?

38. Briefly summarize how the following gender-role assumptions may limit men and women regarding their social and sexual behavior.

    a. women as undersexed, men as oversexed

    b. men as initiators, women as recipients

    c. men as "sexperts"

    d. women as controllers, men as movers

    e. men as unemotional and strong, women as nurturing and supportive

39. Define "androgyny."

40. Summarize research findings regarding how androgynous people tend to differ from people who are strongly gender-typed.

Sample Multiple Choice Test Questions

Select the best alternative. Check your answers with the answer key at the end of the chapter.

1. Gender refers to
    a. having characteristics of both sexes.
    b. our biological maleness or femaleness.
    c. flexibility in male/female roles.
    d. the psychosocial concept of our maleness or femaleness.

2. _____ refers to our own personal, subjective sense that "I am a male" or "I am a female."
    a. Gender
    b. Gender assumptions
    c. Gender identity
    d. Gender role

3. Six-year-old Felipe believes that men become doctors and women become nurses. This demonstrates that Felipe has already acquired a knowledge of traditional
    a. gender roles.
    b. gender types.
    c. sexual norms.
    d. gender identities.

4. Biological sex is determined by the _____ present in the reproductive cells at the moment of conception.
    a. autosomes
    b. chromosomes
    c. hormones
    d. DHT

5. To ensure the complete development of external male sex organs, _____ must be present.
    a. the X chromosome
    b. the Y chromosome
    c. DHT
    d. the primary autosome

6. _____ appears to be responsible for initiating the development of male gonads.
   a. The testis-determining gene (SRY)
   b. Androgen
   c. Estrogen
   d. Dihydrotestosterone (DHT)

7. The structures that contain the future reproductive cells are called
   a. gonads.
   b. bipotential chromosomes.
   c. genes.
   d. Müllerian ducts.

8. Hormones stimulate the development of the Wolffian ducts into
   a. internal female reproductive structures.
   b. internal male reproductive structures.
   c. external female sexual structures.
   d. external male sexual structures.

9. The labia minora in the female is homologous to the _____ of the male.
   a. shaft of the penis
   b. scrotal sac
   c. prostate gland
   d. glans of the penis

10. In a female-differentiated hypothalamus, sex hormones are released
    a. at random.
    b. steadily.
    c. in a cyclic fashion.
    d. once every three months.

11. Money's study of genetic males with androgen-insensitivity syndrome who were raised as girls revealed that most of them were
    a. interested in traditionally masculine activities.
    b. interested in traditionally feminine activities.
    c. androgynous in their attitudes and behavior.
    d. interested in changing their sex.

12. _____ helps regulate the menstrual cycle and stimulates development of the uterine lining in preparation for pregnancy.
    a. Estrogen
    b. Progesterone
    c. Androgen
    d. Müllerian-inhibiting substance

13. Which of the following **least** supports the importance of social-learning factors in gender identity formation?
    a. Margaret Mead's research on cultures in New Guinea
    b. John Money's research on children whose assigned sex didn't match their chromosomal sex
    c. Rubin's research on how parents respond to their newborn babies
    d. Money's research on fetally androgenized females

14. Androgen insensitivity syndrome is the result of
    a.   a rare genetic defect.
    b.   a chromosomal abnormality.
    c.   steroid abuse.
    d.   gender dysphoria.

15. A person whose gender identity is opposite to his or her biological sex is called a/an
    a.   transvestite.
    b.   bisexual.
    c.   androgynous person.
    d.   transsexual.

16. Which of the following statements regarding transsexualism is **true**?
    a.   Most transsexuals have the appropriate XX or XY chromosomes.
    b.   There are currently more women than men requesting sex change surgery.
    c.   It is becoming increasingly clear that transsexualism is caused by social learning experiences.
    d.   Most transsexuals have malformed or nonexistent internal reproductive structures.

17. **Most** female-to-male transsexuals would desire a sexual relationship with a
    a.   lesbian.
    b.   heterosexual woman.
    c.   gay man.
    d.   heterosexual man.

18. Which of the following statements regarding male-to-female transsexuals is **false**?
    a.   Intercourse is not possible after surgery.
    b.   Surgical procedures for these individuals are more effective than female to male transsexuals.
    c.   Many report postsurgical capacity to experience arousal and orgasm.
    d.   The majority of these individuals are sexually attracted to heterosexual men.

19. The majority of researchers today support a _____ explanation for how gender identity is acquired.
    a.   biological
    b.   social learning
    c.   biological and social learning
    d.   sociobiological

20. Which of the following statements regarding stereotypes is **false**?
    a.   Stereotypes do not take individuality into account.
    b.   There is strong evidence that gender-role stereotypes are pervasive in our culture.
    c.   "Women are aggressive" is an example of a stereotype.
    d.   Research suggests that women may be less entrenched in gender-role stereotypes than men.

21. The process whereby society conveys behavioral expectations to the individual is called
    a.   imprinting.
    b.   gender identification.
    c.   stereotyping.
    d.   socialization.

22. Which of the following is **not** one of the gender-role assumptions discussed by the authors?
    a. women as controllers, men as movers
    b. women as undersexed, men as oversexed
    c. women as initiators, men as recipients
    d. women as nurturing, men as unemotional

23. A man feels pressure to demonstrate sexual interest in a woman early on in the relationship, in spite of his personal inclination to take his time and go more slowly. This man is a victim of which of the following gender-role assumptions?
    a. men as initiators, women as recipients
    b. men as "sexperts"
    c. women as controllers, men as androgynous
    d. men as unemotional and strong, women as nurturing and supportive

24. Androgyny refers to
    a. flexibility in gender role.
    b. an asexual orientation.
    c. a condition where people have both male and female genitalia.
    d. gender dysphoria.

25. Research on androgyny has demonstrated that
    a. androgynous males demonstrate better overall emotional adjustment than masculine-typed males.
    b. androgynous college professors exhibit less job-related stress than those who are more gender-typed.
    c. among college students, masculine personality characteristics were more closely associated with being versatile than was the trait of androgyny.
    d. gender-typed individuals have more positive attitudes toward sexuality than androgynous individuals.

Critical Thinking/Personal Reflection

1. What messages did you receive as you were growing up regarding specific expectations or behaviors appropriate to your gender? Think in terms of academic/career expectations, social and sexual behavior, emphasis on competition (in sports or in school), household chores required of you, recreational activities in which you participated, etc.

2.   If you had siblings of the other sex, how were they treated differently, if at all? Think in terms of household chores required of you, curfew limits, messages regarding appropriate social or sexual behavior, educational and/or career goals, etc.

3.   You have seen how your father/mother has lived his/her life as a man/woman. What would you do differently? What would you want to remain the same? Cite specific examples.

4.   How do you feel that your life would be different, if at all, if you were a member of the other sex? Think in terms of your recreational interests, education, work/career interests, relationship involvement, parenting experiences, etc. Do you think the rewards, pressures, fears, and anxieties would be the same?

5.   How do you view your current relationships with men and women? Do you perceive your behavior as more gender-typed or more androgynous? Give specific examples. Do you have attitudes or behaviors regarding gender roles that you would like to change? If so, what are they?

Chapter Overview With Fill-In Answers

1. Sex
2. genetic; anatomical
3. Gender
4. Gender-identity
5. role
6. biological
7. gonadal; brain
8. sperm; ovum
9. male
10. female
11. Y
12. gonads
13. six
14. estrogens
15. androgens
16. testes
17. female
18. Wolffian
19. Müllerian-inhibiting; Wolffian
20. female
21. dihydrotestosterone
22. testosterone
23. brains
24. hypothalamus; cerebral
25. verbal
26. psychosocial
27. True
28. Pseudo
29. Klinefelter's; androgen; fetally; males
30. social-learning
31. anthropological
32. New Guinea; Tchambuli
33. John Money
34. interactional
35. transsexual; gender dysphoria
36. interviews; identity; hormone
37. stereotype
38. Socialization
39. Parents
40. peer group
41. religion
42. gender-role
43. undersexed; over-sexed
44. initiators; recipients
45. sexperts
46. controllers; movers
47. nurturing; supportive
48. Androgyny

Matching Answers

1. c	2. d	3. a	4. b–d, f, g	5. b	6. b
7. e	8. e	9. c, d, e	10. d	11. g	12. f

Sample Multiple Choice Answers

1. d	2. c	3. a	4. b	5. c	6. a	7. a	8. b
9. a	10. c	11. b	12. b	13. d	14. a	15. d	16. a
17. b	18. a	19. c	20. c	21. d	22. c	23. a	24. a
25. c							

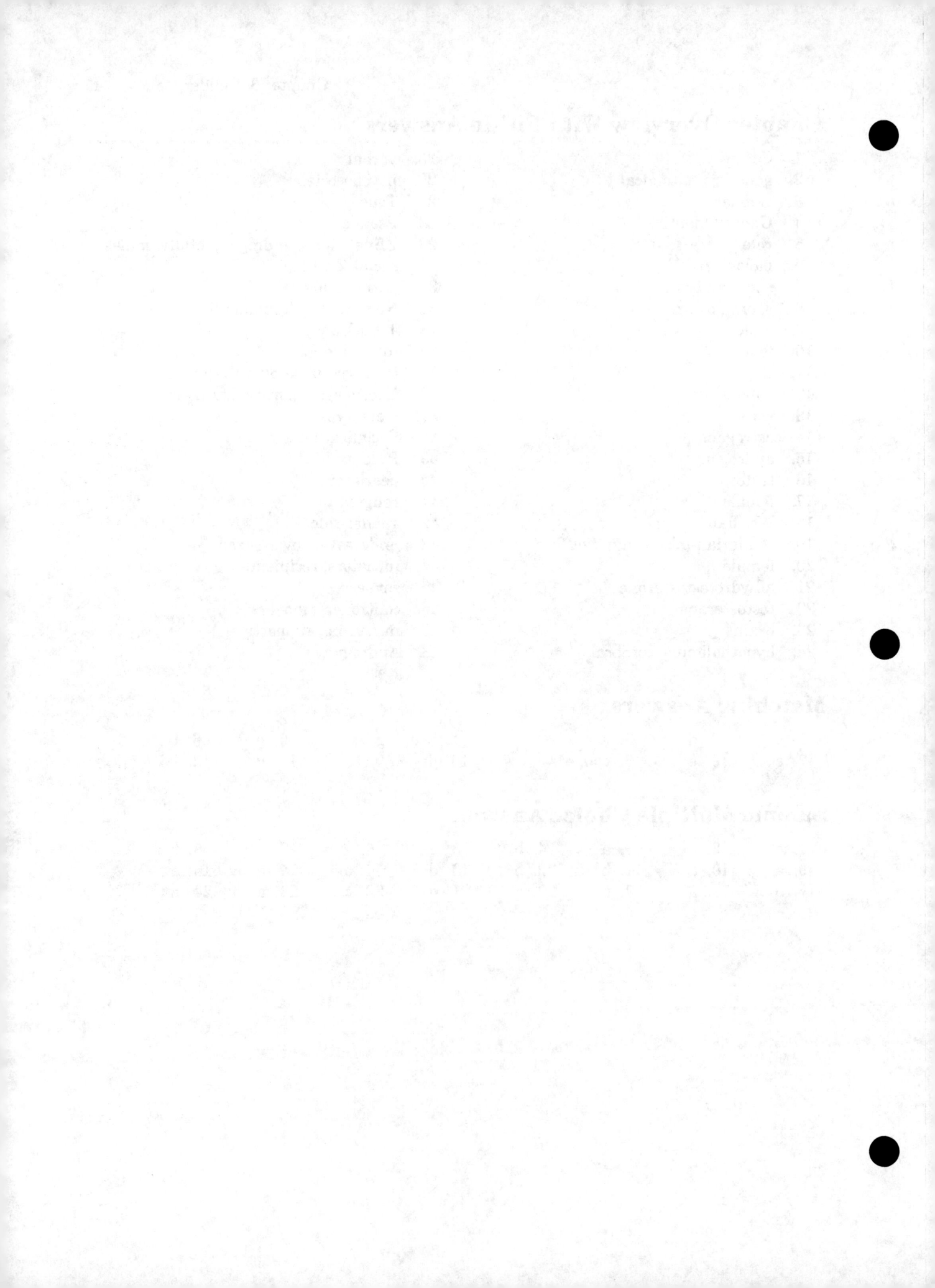

4

Female Sexual Anatomy and Physiology

Introduction

Becoming more aware of our bodies and how they function helps us in taking a more active, responsible role in our health care, as well as feeling more comfortable with ourselves and with our partners. This chapter deals with female sexual and reproductive structures and functions, with an emphasis on relevant health care concerns.

Review of Key Terms and Concepts

Key terms and concepts are listed and defined below. Refer to the subject index in the back of your textbook for additional information.

1. **gynecology** — the medical specialty for female sexual and reproductive anatomy

2. **vulva** — all external female genital structures

3. **mons veneris** — literally "mound of Venus"; refers to the pads of fatty tissue covering the pubic bone

4. **labia majora** — the outer lips that extend downward from the mons on each side of the vulva; they surround the labia minora and urethral and vaginal openings

5. **labia minora** — the inner lips, located within the labia majora, that consist of hairless folds of skin that join at the clitoral hood

6. **prepuce** — clitoral hood, or skin that covers the clitoris

7. **clitoris** — a highly sensitive structure of the female external genitals, the only purpose of which is sexual pleasure

8. **clitoral shaft** — the length of the clitoris between the glans and the body

9. **clitoral glans** — the head of the clitoris, richly endowed with nerve endings

10. **crura** — the innermost tips of the cavernous bodies that connect to the pubic bones

11. **smegma** — genital secretions, skin cells, and bacteria which may accumulate under the clitoral hood

12. **cavernous bodies** — the two small spongy structures in the shaft of the clitoris that engorge with blood during sexual arousal

13. **vestibule** — the area of the vulva inside the labia minora where both the urinary and vaginal openings are located

14. **urethra** — the short tube connecting the bladder to the urinary opening, located between the clitoris and the introitus

15. **introitus** — the opening of the vagina, located between the urinary opening and the anus

16. **hymen** — a fold of tissue partially covering the vaginal opening

17. **imperforate hymen** — in rare instances, when the hymen completely covers the vaginal opening

18. **perineum** — the area of smooth skin between the vaginal opening and the anus

19. **episiotomy** — an incision that is sometimes made in the perineum to prevent the ragged tearing of tissues that may occur during the birth process

20. **vestibular bulbs** — two bulbs, one on each side of the vaginal opening, that engorge with blood during sexual arousal

21. **Bartholin's glands** — two small glands located on each side of the vaginal opening that secrete a few drops of fluid during sexual arousal

22. **Kegel exercises** — a series of exercises developed by Arnold Kegel that strengthen the muscles underlying the external male or female genitals

23. **vagina** — an expandable canal in the female that opens at the vulva and extends about four inches into the pelvis, consisting of mucous, muscle and fibrous tissue

24. **mucosa** — the layer of mucous membrane that a woman feels when she inserts a finger inside her vagina

25. **rugae** — the soft, moist, folded walls of the vagina

26. **vasocongestion** — the engorgement of blood vessels in particular body parts in response to sexual arousal

27. **Grafenberg spot** — the system of glands and ducts surrounding the urethra which can be located by stimulating the anterior wall of the vagina below the urethra

28. **douching** — rinsing out the vagina with plain water or solutions; usually unnecessary. Excessive douching may result in vaginal irritation.

29. **vaginitis** — inflammation of the vaginal walls caused by a variety of vaginal infections

30. **speculum** — an instrument used to hold open the vaginal walls during a gynecological exam

31. **cervix** — the small end of the uterus, located at the back of the vagina

32. **os** — the opening in the cervix that leads to the interior of the uterus

33. **Pap smear** — a screening test for cervical cancer

34. **uterus** — a pear-shaped organ inside the female pelvis, within which the fetus develops

35. **myometrium** — the smooth muscle layer of the uterine wall

36. **perimetrium** — the thin membrane covering the outside of the uterus

37. **endometrium** — the tissue that lines the inside of the uterine walls

38. **fallopian tubes** — two four-inch tubes that extend from the uterus in the pelvic cavity where the egg and sperm travel

39. **fimbriae** — fringe-like ends of the fallopian tubes into which the released ovum enters

40. **ovaries** — female gonads that produce ova and sex hormones

41. **ovulation** — the release of a mature ovum from the graafian follicle of the ovary

42. **oophorectomy** — the surgical removal of the ovaries

43. **mammary glands** — milk glands in the female breast

44. **areola** — the darkened circular area surrounding the nipple of the breast

45. **secondary sex characteristics** — the physical characteristics other than genitals that indicate sexual maturity, such as body hair, breasts, and deepened voice

46. **hysterectomy** — the surgical removal of the uterus

47. **breasts** — secondary sex characteristics, composed of fatty tissue and mammary glands

48. **nipple** — the central pigmented area of the breast, which contains numerous nerve endings. In women, the nipple also contains the milk ducts

49. **mammography** — a highly sensitive x-ray test for the detection of breast cancer

50. **cysts** — a common, benign, fluid-filled lump that may occur in the breasts

51. **malignant tumor** — a lump made up of cancer cells that may occur in the breasts

52. **fibroadenomas** — a common, benign, solid, rounded tumor which may occur in the breasts

53. **menarche** — the initial onset of menstrual periods in a young woman

54. **proliferative phase** — the phase of the menstrual cycle in which the ovarian follicles mature

55. **menstrual phase** — the phase of the menstrual cycle when menstruation occurs

56. **secretory phase** — the phase of the menstrual cycle in which the corpus luteum develops and secretes progesterone

57. **menstruation** — the sloughing off of the built-up uterine lining that takes place if conception has not occurred

58. **menstrual synchrony** — the development of congruent menstrual cycle timing that sometimes occurs among women who live in close proximity

59. **follicle stimulating hormone (FSH)** — a pituitary hormone secreted by a female during the secretory phase of the menstrual cycle that stimulates the development of ovarian follicles

60. **luteinizing hormone (LH)** — the hormone secreted by the pituitary gland that stimulates ovulation in the female

61. **corpus luteum** — a yellowish body that forms on the ovary at the site of the ruptured graafian follicle and secretes progesterone

62. **premenstrual syndrome** — physical and/or psychological symptoms that women may experience before each menstrual period

63. **dysmenorrhea** — pain or discomfort that occurs before or during menstruation

64. **prostaglandins** — hormones produced by body tissues that cause the muscles of the uterus to contract

65. **endometriosis** — a condition in which cells from the uterine lining adhere to the fallopian tubes or other parts of the abdominal cavity

66. **amenorrhea** — the absence of menstruation

67. **toxic shock syndrome** — a disease caused by toxins produced by the bacterium staphylococcus aureus that may induce a person to go into shock, occurring most commonly in menstruating women

68. **climacteric** — physiological changes that occur during the transition period from fertility to infertility in both sexes

69. **menopause** — cessation of menstruation due to the aging process or surgical removal of the ovaries

70. **hot flashes** — a common symptom associated with menopause whereby the fluctuating levels of hormones rapidly dilate the blood vessels, causing a woman to feel a momentary rush of heat

71. **hormone replacement therapy (HRT)** — the use of supplemental hormones during and after menopause

72. **osteoporosis** — abnormal bone loss

Chapter Overview With Fill-Ins

After reading each of the major sections in the chapter, check your retention by filling in each of the blanks in the corresponding sections below. The answers are provided at the end of the chapter.

Genital Self-Exam

1. _____ is the medical specialty for female sexual and reproductive anatomy.

2. Genital self-exam serves at least two purposes: to help women learn about and feel more comfortable with themselves, and to augment routine _____ care.

The Vulva

3. The _____ refers to the female external genital structures.

4. The vulva includes the _____ _____, which is the area covering the pubic bone; the _____ _____, or large outer lips; the _____ _____, or inner lips that join at the prepuce, or clitoral hood; the clitoris, which is composed of the external shaft and _____, and the internal crura; the _____ which is the area of the vulva inside the labia minora that includes the urinary and vaginal openings; and the _____, located between the clitoris and the vagina.

5. The _____ is a fold of tissue partially covering the _____, or vaginal opening.

6. The _____ is the smooth area of skin located between the introitus and the anus.

Underlying Structures

7. The _____ _____ are located on each side of the vagina, and they fill with blood during sexual arousal, causing the vagina to increase in length.

8. The _____ glands are located on each side of the vaginal opening, and they typically produce a drop or two of fluid just prior to orgasm.

9. Pelvic floor muscles can be strengthened by doing _____ exercises, which were developed in the early 1950s as a way of helping women gain control of _____ after childbirth.

10. An added benefit is that women usually report an increase in _____ sensitivity as a result of practicing these exercises.

Internal Structures

11. In its nonaroused state, the _____ is three to five inches in length.

12. It contains three layers of tissue: _____, muscle, and fibrous tissue.

13. Vaginal lubrication is the result of _____, the blood engorgement that occurs in the pelvic area.

14. The Grafenberg spot is located within the _____ wall of the vagina.

15. It consists of a system of glands and ducts that surround the urethra, and is believed to be the female counterpart to the male _____ _____.

16. The _____ is the small end of the uterus and is located at the back of the vagina.

17. The opening in the center of the cervix is called the _____.

18. The _____, or womb, is a thick, pear-shaped organ.

19. Fertilization usually occurs in the _____ _____, and then the united sperm and egg, called the _____, travel down and become implanted in the uterus.

20. The fallopian tubes extend from the _____ into the pelvic cavity.

21. Fringe-like projections called _____ at the outside end of each tube wave the newly released egg inside.

22. Fertilization occurs while the egg is still close to the _____.

23. The _____ are endocrine glands that produce two classes of sex hormones.

24. Egg maturation and release, or _____, occurs as a result of the complex chain of events known as the menstrual cycle.

Gynecological Health Concerns

25. About _____ out of every five women will have a urinary tract infection in her lifetime.

26. There are a number of routine precautions that may prevent urinary tract infections, two of which are _____ immediately after intercourse and drinking lots of _____ juice.

27. A vaginal infection or _____ results when the natural chemical valance of the vagina is disturbed.

28. A number of factors increase a woman's susceptibility to vaginal infections, including a diet high in _____ and the use of _____.

29. The screening test for cervical cancer is called the _____ _____.

30. Treatments for cervical cancer include _____ (freezing of tissues), removing malignant tissue by means of a _____, or in more severe cases, a complete _____ (surgical removal of cervix and uterus).

The Breasts

31. The breasts are _____ sex characteristics.

32. They are composed of _____ _____, which accounts for variation in breast size among women, and _____ _____, which produce breast milk after childbirth.

33. The nipple is the center of the _____, which contains oil-producing glands that help lubricate the nipples during breast feeding.

34. _____ is an X-ray screening test for cancerous breast lumps.

35. Cysts and _____ are benign tumors, and they are the most common breast lumps.

36. A third type of lump, a _____ tumor, is cancerous.

Menstruation

37. The first menstrual bleeding is called the _____.

38. Cycle length can vary from _____ to _____ days, depending upon the woman.

39. When women who live together develop similar menstrual cycles it is referred to as menstrual _____.

40. There are three stages in the menstrual cycle: the menstrual phase, the _____ phase, and the secretory phase.

41. The cycle is regulated by hormonal interaction among the hypothalamus, the _____ gland, the adrenal glands, the ovaries and the uterus.

42. During the menstrual phase, the uterus sheds the _____ , which is discharged as menstrual flow.

43. During the proliferative phase of the menstrual cycle, the pituitary gland increases production of _____-_____ hormone.

44. _____ causes the endometrium to thicken.

45. When the level of ovarian estrogen reaches a peak, the pituitary gland depresses the release of FSH and stimulates the production of _____ hormone.

46. Approximately _____ days before the onset of the next menstrual period, ovulation occurs.

47. Some women experience _____, a twinge, pain or cramping in their abdomen at ovulation.

48. During the secretory phase, the ruptured follicle develops into a yellowish bump called the _____ _____, which secretes progesterone.

49. Progesterone, combined with _____ produced by the ovaries, causes the endometrium to thicken and engorge with blood in preparation for _____ of a fertilized egg.

50. If implantation does not occur, the _____ gland responds by shutting down production of FSH and LH.

51. This causes the _____ _____ to degenerate, and estrogen and progesterone production decrease.

52. This reduction of hormone levels triggers the sloughing off of the endometrium, initiating the _____ phase once again.

53. Premenstrual syndrome refers to the _____ and _____ symptoms that occur before each menstrual period and are severe enough to interfere with some aspects of life.

54. While there is speculation that fluctuations in sex hormones may affect this condition, at this time the causes of PMS are _____.

55. Painful menstruation is called _____.

56. Primary dysmenorrhea occurs during menstruation and is usually caused by the overproduction of _____.

57. Secondary dysmenorrhea occurs prior to or during _____ and is characterized by lower abdominal pain that can extend to the back and thighs.

58. Another common menstrual difficulty is _____, the absence of menstruation.

59. _____ _____ is the failure to begin to menstruate at puberty.

60. _____ _____ involves the disruption of an established menstrual cycle, with the absence of menstruation for three months or more.

61. _____ _____ syndrome is a rare disease that is associated with the use of tampons and is most likely to occur in menstruating women.

Menopause

62. The term _____ refers to the physiological changes that occur during the transition period from fertility to infertility.

63. _____, one of the events of the female climacteric, refers to the cessation of menstruation.

64. For many women menopause brings a range of symptoms that are caused by the decline in _____.

65. _____ _____ therapy (HRT) involves taking supplemental estrogen and progesterone to compensate for the decrease in natural hormone production that occurs during the climacteric.

66. HRT has a number of benefits as well as potential _____.

Identification

Label the various parts of the female sexual anatomy indicated below. Check your answers with the key at the end of the chapter.

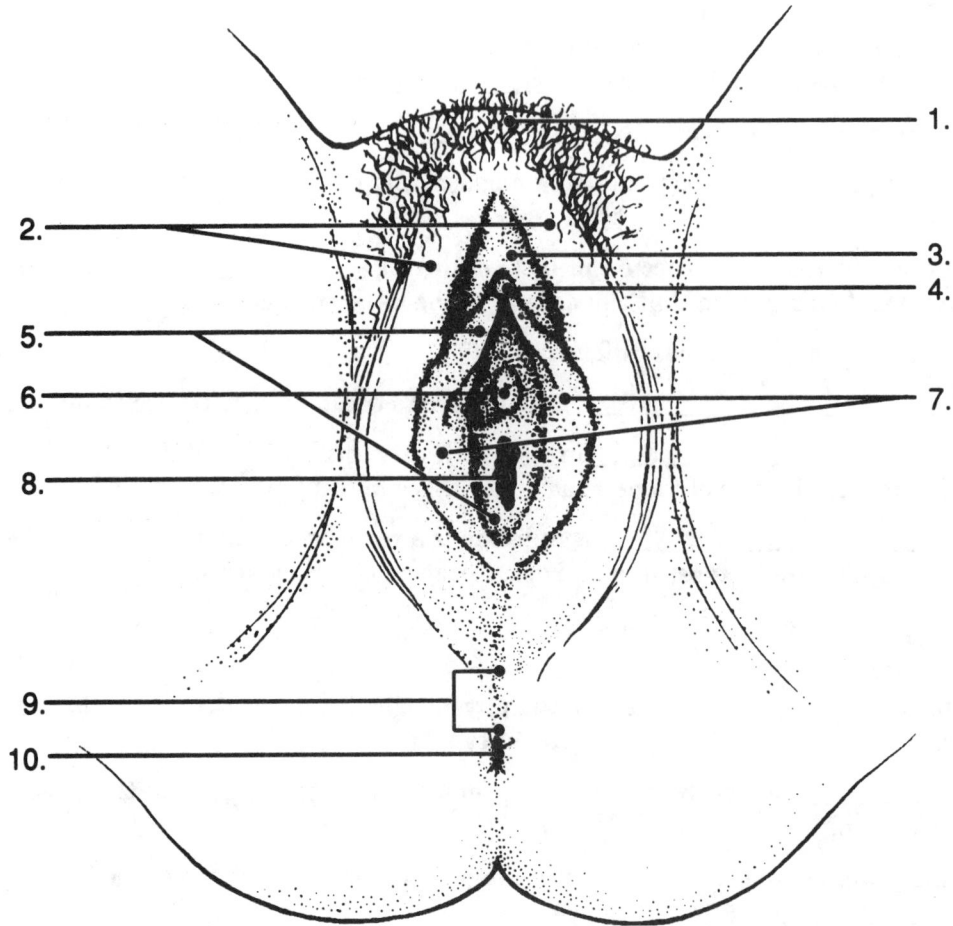

1. _____

2. _____

3. _____

4. _____

5. _____

6. _____

7. _____

8. _____

9. _____

10. _____

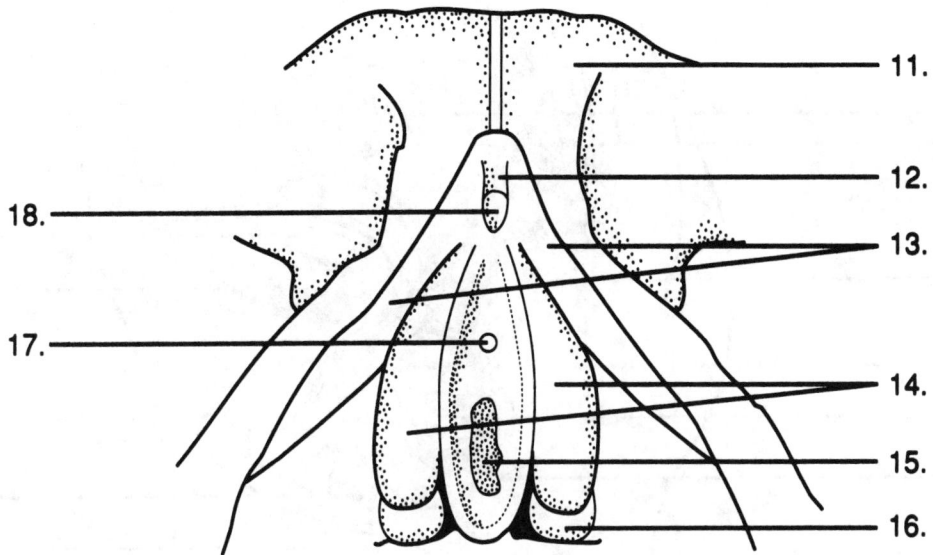

11. _____

12. _____

13. _____

14. _____

15. _____

16. _____

17. _____

18. _____

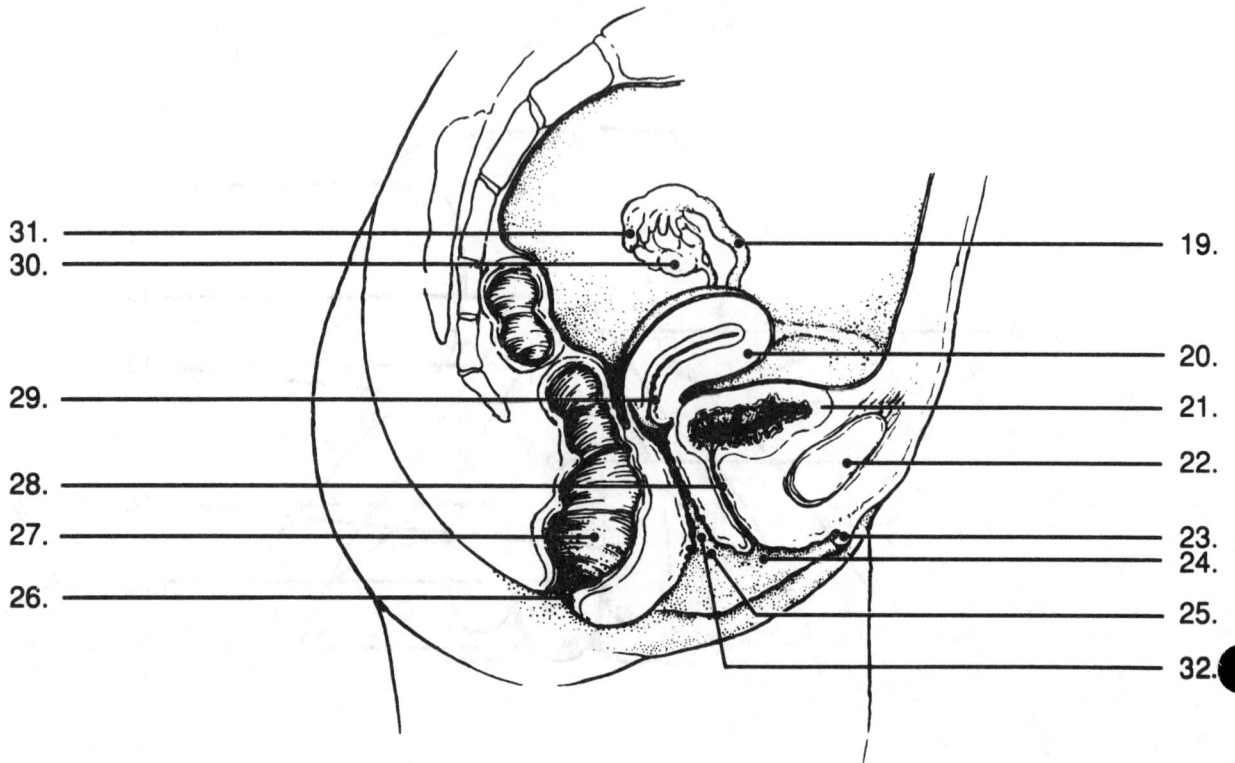

31.

30.

29.

28.

27.

26.

19.

20.

21.

22.

23.
24.

25.

32.

19. _____

20. _____

21. _____

22. _____

23. _____

24. _____

25. _____

26._____

27._____

28._____

29._____

30._____

31._____

32._____

Sample Short Answer Test Questions

1. List some of the reasons for doing a genital self-exam.

2. List and briefly describe eight structures of the vulva.

3. What role does the clitoris play in sexual arousal and orgasm?

4. Name two structures that are located within the vestibule.

5. What is an imperforate hymen? How is this condition treated?

6. What changes in the vestibular bulbs and the Bartholin's glands occur during sexual arousal?

7. List and describe the three layers of vaginal tissue.

8.   What is the source of vaginal lubrication that occurs during sexual arousal?

9.   List the two functions of vaginal lubrication.

10. What may inhibit vaginal lubrication?

11. What is the Grafenberg spot and where is it located?

12. Describe the natural chemical balance of the vagina and how douching may affect this.

13. What is the opening in the center of the cervix called?

14. Briefly describe the structure of the uterus.

15. Where does fertilization occur?

16. Briefly explain the structure and function of the ovaries.

17. What are some symptoms of urinary tract infections?

18. List at least eight factors that may contribute to urinary infections in women.

19. List six factors that increase susceptibility to vaginitis.

20. List six ways that vaginitis might be prevented.

21. Briefly describe the procedure for a Pap smear. How frequently should this procedure be done?

22. Identify three treatments for cervical cancer.

23. List five factors that increase the risk of developing cervical cancer.

24. Describe the effects of hysterectomy on a woman's sexuality.

25. What accounts for the difference in size in women's breasts?

26. When is the best time to do a breast self-exam?

27. What is a mammogram and when is it recommended?

28. What percent of women may develop breast cancer from flaws in a gene?

29. List and describe the three types of breast lumps.

30. List three factors that may minimize fibrocystic breast disease.

31. Name at least eight high risk factors for breast cancer.

32. List several forms of treatment for breast cancer.

33. List three factors associated with the timing of menarche.

34. What appears to be the trigger for menstrual synchrony?

35. Describe the role of the hypothalamus in the menstrual cycle.

36. Briefly explain what occurs in each of the following phases of the menstrual cycle.

    a. menstrual phase

    b. proliferative phase

    c. secretory phase

37. List several examples that indicate how other cultures have viewed menstruation.

38. What does research conclude regarding the relationship between sexual activity and the menstrual cycle?

39. Define premenstrual syndrome. What causes it and how is it treated?

40. What is the difference between primary and secondary dysmenorrhea?

41. List three conditions in which women might experience secondary amenorrhea.

42. List five suggestions that may help minimize menstrually-related problems.

43. Name three types of genital mutilation. What are the various reasons for performing these mutilations?

44. What causes the range of symptoms women may experience during menopause?

45. What causes hot flashes to occur?

46. List eight symptoms of menopause.

47. List the risks and benefits of hormone replacement therapy.

Sample Multiple Choice Test Questions

Select the best alternative. Check your answers with the answer key at the end of the chapter.

1. The term for the female external genital structures is the
   a. vestibule.
   b. vagina.
   c. vulva.
   d. mons veneris.

2. Which of the following statements regarding the labia minora is **false**?
   a. They are hairless.
   b. They are surrounded by the labia majora.
   c. They have nerve endings and fatty tissue similar to that of the mons.
   d. They join at the prepuce over the clitoris.

3. The clitoris
   a. is comprised of the external shaft and glans, and internal crura.
   b. has several different reproductive and sexual functions.
   c. is located in the vestibule.
   d. has very few nerve endings.

4. The formation of _____ can be prevented by drawing back the hood while washing the vulva.
   a. Bartholin's glands secretions
   b. smegma
   c. venereal discharge
   d. clitoral adhesions

5. Smegma
   a. is released from the Bartholin's glands.
   b. may accumulate in the urethra.
   c. can be surgically removed by a physician if necessary.
   d. may cause pain during sexual activity if allowed to accumulate.

6. The _____ is the short tube connecting the bladder to the urinary opening.
   a. introitus
   b. urethra
   c. vestibular bulb
   d. vagina

7. A (an) _____ _____ completely covers the vaginal opening.
   a. introital membrane
   b. perineal adhesion
   c. imperforate hymen
   d. clitoral transudate

8. The _____ _____ engorge with blood during sexual arousal, causing the vagina to increase in length.
   a. Bartholin's glands
   b. Kegel muscles
   c. labia majora
   d. vestibular bulbs

9.   Which of the following is **not** part of the vulva?
     a. clitoris
     b. labia minora
     c. mons veneris
     d. pelvic floor muscles

10. _____ is one option for treating cervical cancer in which the cancerous cells are removed from the cervix by freezing the tissue.
     a. Cryosurgery
     b. Laparoscopy
     c. Hysterotomy
     d. Colposcopy

11. The vagina
     a. contains mucous, muscle, and fibrous tissue.
     b. is approximately twelve inches long in its nonaroused state.
     c. has a high concentration of nerve endings in the back near the cervix.
     d. is a part of the vulva.

12. Vaginal lubrication
     a. helps to make the chemical balance of the vagina more acidic.
     b. occurs within five to ten minutes after effective stimulation begins.
     c. is derived primarily from the Bartholin's glands.
     d. prepares the vagina for entry of the penis.

13. Which of the following statements regarding the Grafenberg spot is **false**?
     a. It consists of a system of glands and ducts that surround the perineum.
     b. It can be stimulated through the anterior wall of the vagina
     c. It is believed to be the female counterpart of the male prostate gland.
     d. Some women ejaculate following Grafenberg spot stimulation.

14. Which of the following may increase susceptibility to vaginitis?
     a. a high protein diet
     b. using a sterile lubricant during intercourse
     c. wearing cotton underwear
     d. using antibiotics

15. Which of the following may help prevent urinary tract infections?
     a. having a woman's partner wash hands and genitals before sexual contact
     b. wiping from back to front after urination and defecation
     c. using intercourse positions that gently massage the urethral wall
     d. drinking coffee or tea on a regular basis

16. The _____ is located at the back of the vagina and contains mucous-secreting glands.
     a. Grafenberg spot
     b. cervix
     c. endometrium
     d. perineum

17. Which of the following statements regarding the cervix is false?
     a. It is located at the back of the vagina.
     b. The opening to the cervix is called the os.
     c. It contains many nerve endings which make it sensitive to touch.
     d. Cells are removed from the cervix when a Pap smear is taken.

18. A woman who has had genital warts as well as a large number of sexual partners may be at increased risk for developing
    a. fibroadenomas.
    b. cervical cancer.
    c. endometriosis.
    d. clitoral adhesions.

19. Cryosurgery, biopsy and hysterectomy are all treatments for
    a. fibroadenomas.
    b. myometriosis.
    c. cervical cancer.
    d. cystitis.

20. Increased risk of cervical cancer has been associated with all of the following **except**
    a. high-fat diet.
    b. smoking cigarettes.
    c. having a husband who has occupational contact with toxic materials.
    d. having had genital warts.

21. Which of the following statements regarding the uterus is **false**?
    a. It is suspended in the pelvic cavity by ligaments.
    b. It is normal for the uterus to be in different positions, depending upon the woman.
    c. The top area of the uterus is called the fundus.
    d. It is where fertilization occurs.

22. Which of the following statements regarding hysterectomy is **false**?
    a. It does not affect sexual response.
    b. It refers to the removal of the uterus.
    c. It is the most frequently performed major surgery for women in the United States.
    d. It may be used to treat cervical cancer.

23. All of the following are types of lumps that can occur in the breasts **except**
    a. cysts.
    b. mammary adhesions.
    c. fibroadenomas.
    d. malignant tumors.

24. Which of the following places a woman at lower risk for breast cancer?
    a. no pregnancies
    b. menopause after 50
    c. early onset of menstruation (before age 12)
    d. low-fat diet

25. All of the following may contribute to benign breast lumps **except**
    a. eating red meat.
    b. drinking caffeine.
    c. eating chocolate.
    d. drinking cranberry juice.

26. Research indicates that sexual adjustment is better following _____ than _____ mastectomy.
    a. partial; radical
    b. radical; partial
    c. aspirated; cauterized
    d. cauterized; aspirated

27. _____ percent of women may develop cancer from flaws in a gene.
    a. Five to ten
    b. Fifteen to twenty
    c. Twenty five
    d. Thirty five

28. Menarche refers to
    a. painful menstruation.
    b. absence of menstruation.
    c. pain at ovulation.
    d. the first menstrual bleeding.

29. Which of the following statements regarding menstruation is **false**?
    a. The average cycle length is 21 to 35 days.
    b. Women who live together may develop similar menstrual cycles.
    c. Time differences in cycle length occur in the phase after ovulation.
    d. The menstrual cycle is divided into three phases.

30. The hypothalamus stimulates the _____ to release hormones.
    a. pituitary gland
    b. corpus luteum
    c. endometrium
    d. fimbriae

31. The corpus luteum
    a. develops during the proliferative phase.
    b. produces the hormone progesterone.
    c. produces FSH.
    d. causes the endometrium to thicken.

32. Which of the following occurs during the proliferative phase of the menstrual cycle?
    a. The corpus luteum develops.
    b. Ovulation occurs.
    c. The amount of estrogen and progesterone are at low levels.
    d. Menstruation occurs.

33. Around ovulation there is an increase and change in cervical mucous secretions due to increased levels of
    a. progesterone.
    b. estrogen.
    c. FSH.
    d. LH.

34. To date, studies regarding the relationship between menstrual cycle changes and sexual behavior
    a. show no significant variations in arousal at different points in the cycle.
    b. indicate an increase in sexual feelings and behavior during ovulation.
    c. indicate an increase in sexual feelings and behavior prior to and during menstruation.
    d. Different studies demonstrated all of the above.

35. Which of the following is **not** a symptom of PMS?
    a. depression
    b. irritability
    c. fever
    d. breast tenderness

36. _____ causes premenstrual syndrome.
    a. Hormonal imbalance.
    b. Vitamin deficiency.
    c. High-stress lifestyle.
    d. The cause of PMS is unknown.

37. The average age of menarche in the United States is _____ years old.
    a. 10
    b. 12
    c. 14
    d. 16

38. Overproduction of prostaglandins is usually the cause of
    a. mittelschmerz.
    b. amenorrhea.
    c. primary dysmenorrhea.
    d. secondary dysmenorrhea.

39. Endometriosis refers to
    a. a condition in which cells from the uterine lining implant in the abdominal cavity.
    b. chronic infection of the reproductive organs.
    c. benign tumors present in the uterus.
    d. a type of ovarian cancer.

40. Which of the following statements regarding amenorrhea is **false**?
    a. It may be caused by an imperforate hymen.
    b. It is more common among athletes than the general population.
    c. Primary amenorrhea is a normal condition during pregnancy and breast feeding.
    d. It may be caused by hormonal imbalances or problems with the reproductive organs.

41. Which of the following is **not** a type of female genital mutilation?
    a. clitoridectomy
    b. vulval extraction
    c. circumcision
    d. genital infibulation

Critical Thinking/Personal Reflection

For Women:

1. Have you ever taken the time to leisurely touch and explore your body with the goal of becoming more knowledgeable and accepting of your body and how it functions? If not, why not? In considering the possibility of doing so, what thoughts or feelings come up for you? If you have taken the time to do some body exploration, what was your experience in doing so? What were the benefits? The drawbacks?

2a. Set aside an hour or more when you can have some uninterrupted time alone. Take a leisurely bath or shower, and then select some lotion or massage oil that is pleasing to you. As you apply the lotion or oil to all parts of your body, experiment with different types of pressure, rhythm and touch. Explore your face, neck, arms, hands, breasts, abdomen, buttocks, legs, feet and toes. Notice what kinds of touch your body responds to. Notice what parts of your body you appreciate or find attractive as well as the parts you criticize or find unattractive. How have you developed the relationship you have with your body? Are you comfortable with that relationship or is it something you would like to change? What are your personal standards for health and attractiveness? What do you base them upon? Are they realistic?

b. Using a mirror, touch and explore all the different parts of your vulva: the mons, clitoris, inner and outer lips, urethral and vaginal openings. What words do you use to refer to your vulva or to your vagina? Are you comfortable using these words? In looking at and touching your vulva, what thoughts or feelings come up for you as you do this? What are the sources of these thoughts or feelings? How do they affect your sexual self-esteem, the way in which you care for your body, and your relationship with a partner or potential partner?

c.   Is there anything you would like to change regarding the way in which you think or feel about your body, or are you comfortable just as you are? List specific things you do or could do to enhance the acceptance, comfort and pleasure you feel in relationship to your body.

For women and men:

1.   In addition to self-exam, how might women be encouraged to become more comfortable with and accepting of their bodies, and more specifically, their genitals? Think in terms of messages and information provided by parents, teachers, the media, health care providers, and partners.

2.   A substantial percentage of young men and women receive inadequate information regarding menstruation. What might parents and educators do to change this? Discuss at what age and in what type of format and environment this information would be most effectively transmitted.

3.   If you had to do it over again, how would you change or improve the way in which you learned about female genital anatomy? What factors might have contributed to more awareness or comfort with this subject?

Chapter Overview With Fill-In Answers

1. Gynecology
2. medical
3. vulva
4a. mons veneris
4b. labia majora
4c. labia minora
4d. glans
4e. vestibule
4f. urethral opening
5. hymen; introitus
6. perineum
7. vestibular bulbs
8. Bartholin's
9. Kegel; urination
10. genital
11. vagina
12. mucous
13. vasocongestion
14. anterior
15. prostate gland
16. cervix
17. os
18. uterus
19. fallopian tube; zygote
20. uterus
21. fimbriae
22. ovary
23. ovaries
24. ovulation
25. one
26. urinating; cranberry
27. vaginitis
28. carbohydrates; antibiotics
29. Pap smear
30a. cryosurgery
30b. biopsy
30c. hysterectomy

31. secondary
32. fatty tissue; mammary glands
33. areola
34. Mammography
35. fibroadenomas
36. malignant
37. menarche
38. 21; 35
39. synchrony
40. proliferative
41. pituitary
42. endometrium
43. follicle-stimulating
44. Estrogen
45. luteinizing
46. 14
47. mittelschmerz
48. corpus luteum
49. estrogen; implantation
50. pituitary
51. corpus luteum
52. menstrual
53. physical; psychological
54. unknown
55. dysmenorrhea
56. prostaglandins
57. menstruation
58. amenorrhea
59. Primary amenorrhea
60. Secondary amenorrhea
61. Toxic shock
62. climacteric
63. Menopause
64. estrogen
65. Hormone replacement
66. risks

Identification Answers

1. mons veneris
2. labia majora
3. clitoral hood or prepuce
4. clitoris
5. vestibule
6. urethral opening
7. labia minora
8. introitus
9. perineum
10. anus
11. pubic bone
12. clitoral shaft
13. crura of clitoris
14. vestibular bulbs
15. introitus
16. Bartholin's glands
17. urethral opening
18. clitoral glans
19. fallopian tubes
20. uterus
21. bladder
22. pubic bone
23. clitoris
24. urethral opening
25. introitus
26. anus
27. rectum
28. urethra
29. cervix
30. ovary
31. fimbriae
32. vagina

Sample Multiple Choice Answers

1. c	2. c	3. a	4. b	5. d	6. b	7. c	8. d
9. d	10. a	11. a	12. d	13. a	14. d	15. a	16. b
17. c	18. b	19. c	20. a	21. d	22. a	23. b	24. d
25. d	26. a	27. a	28. d	29. c	30. a	31. b	32. b
33. b	34. d	35. c	36. d	37. b	38. c	39. a	40. c
41. b							

5

Male Sexual Anatomy and Physiology

Introduction

The key structures of male sexual anatomy are discussed, including explanations of how these structures affect sperm, hormone, and seminal fluid production. Both the physiological and psychological aspects of erection, ejaculation, penis size, and circumcision are also addressed. Finally, male genital health concerns are discussed and regular genital self-exams are encouraged as a way to assume more responsibility for health care.

Review of Key Terms and Concepts

Key terms and concepts are listed and defined below. Refer to the subject index in the back of your textbook for additional information.

1. **penis** — a male sexual organ consisting of the internal root and external shaft and glans

2. **root** — the portion of the penis that extends internally into the pelvic cavity

3. **shaft** — the external, pendulous portion of the penis, excluding the head

4. **glans** — the smooth, acorn-shaped head of the penis

5. **cavernous bodies** — the structures in the shaft of the penis that engorge with blood during sexual arousal

6. **spongy body** — an internal chamber that forms a bulb at the base of the penis, extends up into the penile shaft and forms the penile glans

7. **foreskin** — a covering of skin over the penile glans

8. **frenulum** —a highly sensitive, thin strip of skin that connects the glans to the shaft on the underside of the penis

9. **corona** — the rim of the glans of the penis

10. **Kegel exercises** — a series of exercises that strengthen the muscles underlying the external female or male genitals

11. **scrotum** — the pouch of skin of the external male genitals that encases the testicles

12. **tunica dartos** — the second layer of the scrotal sac, composed of smooth muscle fibers and fibrous connective tissue

13. **testes** — male gonads inside the scrotum that produce sperm and sex hormones

14. **spermatic cord** — a firm, rubbery tube that contains the vas deferens and from which a testicle is suspended

15. **inguinal canal** — during fetal development, the route the testes take from inside the abdomen to the scrotum

16. **cryptorchidism** — a condition in which the testicles fail to descend from the abdominal cavity to the scrotal sac

17. **cremastic reflex** — involuntary contractions of the major scrotal (cremasteric) muscle, causing the scrotum to draw closer to the body

18. **epididymis** — the structure along the back of each testicle in which sperm maturation occurs

19. **seminiferous tubules** — thin, highly coiled structures in the testicles in which sperm are produced

20. **interstitial cells** — (Leydig's cells) cells located between the seminiferous tubules that are the major source of androgen in males

21. **vas deferens** — a sperm-carrying tube that begins at the testicle and ends at the urethra

22. **vasectomy** — male sterilization procedure that involves removing a section from each vas deferens

23. **ejaculatory duct** — two, short ducts located within the prostate gland

24. **seminal vesicles** — two, small glands adjacent to the terminals of the vas deferens that secrete an alkaline fluid conducive to sperm motility

25. **cilia** — hairlike filaments that line the inner walls of the vas deferens

26. **prostate gland** — a gland located at the base of the bladder whose secretions comprise about 30 percent of the seminal fluid released during ejaculation

27. **urethra** — the tube through which urine passes from the bladder to the outside of the body

28. **prostatitis** — inflammation and enlargement of the prostate gland as a result of various infectious agents

29. **Cowper's glands** — (bulbourethral glands) two pea-sized glands located alongside the base of the urethra in the male that secrete an alkaline fluid during sexual arousal

30. **urology** — the medical specialty that focuses on male reproductive structures

31. **erection** — coordinated by the autonomic nervous system, the process whereby the three erectile chambers of the penis engorge with blood causing it to increase in size

32. **ejaculation** — the process whereby semen is expelled through the penis to the outside of the body

33. **emission phase** — the first stage of male orgasm, in which the seminal fluid is gathered in the urethral bulb

34. **circumcision** — surgical removal of the foreskin of the penis

35. **urethral bulb** — the portion of the urethra between the urethral sphincters in the male

36. **expulsion phase** — the second stage of male orgasm, during which the semen is expelled from the penis by muscular contractions

37. **retrograde ejaculation** — process by which semen is expelled into the bladder instead of out of the penis

38. **nocturnal emissions** — involuntary ejaculation during sleep, also known as a "wet dream"

39. **phimosis** — a condition characterized by an extremely tight penile foreskin

40. **semen** — a fluid ejaculated through the penis that contains sperm and fluids from the prostate, seminal vesicles, and Cowper's glands

41. **prostatitis** — when the prostate gland becomes enlarged and inflamed, usually as the result of an infectious agent

42. **benign prostatic hyperplasia** — when the prostate gland increases in size as a man ages

43. **prostate-specific antigen (PSA)** — a marker for prostate cancer that can be detected by a blood test

Chapter Overview With Fill-Ins

After reading each of the major sections in the chapter, check your retention by filling in each of the blanks in the corresponding sections below. The answers are provided at the end of the chapter.

Sexual Anatomy

1. The penis consists of nerves, blood vessels, fibrous tissue, and three parallel cylinders of tissue: two _____ bodies and one spongy body.

2. The _____ of the penis is the part that extends into the pelvic cavity.

3. The external, pendulous portion (excluding the head) is called the shaft, and the head of the penis is called the _____.

4. Some of the skin covering the penile shaft folds over the glans, and this is called the _____, or prepuce.

5. _____ involves the permanent removal of this sleeve of skin.

6. The greatest concentration of nerve endings in the penis is in the _____.

7. Two areas in particular are sensitive to stimulation: the _____, or rim of the penis; and the _____.

8. Men may strengthen the network of muscles surrounding the root of the penis by doing _____ exercises.

9. The _____ is a loose pouch of skin that is an outpocket of the abdominal wall in the groin area.

10. Inside the scrotal sac are two separate compartments, each of which contains a single _____.

11. Each testis (or testicle) is suspended within the compartment by the _____ cord, which contains the _____ _____ (sperm-carrying tube), as well as other blood vessels, nerves, and fibers.

12. The testicles have two major functions: the secretion of male sex _____ and the production of _____.

13. Sometimes one or both of the testes fail to descend into the scrotum, a condition known as _____.

14. Self-examination of the genitals is encouraged in order to prevent or provide early treatment for _____ cancer, sexually transmitted diseases, and other infections.

15. Within and adjacent to the testes are two separate areas involved in the production and storage of _____.

16. The first of these, the _____ _____, is where sperm production takes place.

17. The _____ cells, or Leydig's cells, are located between the tubules and are the major source of _____.

18. The second important area for sperm processing is the _____, a C-shaped structure that adheres to the back of each testicle.

19. The sperm move through the epididymis and drain into the _____ _____, a long thin duct that travels up through the scrotum inside the spermatic cord.

20. This is where the male sterilization procedure, _____, takes place.

21. The _____ _____ are two small glands adjacent to the terminals of the vas deferens.

22. The seminal vesicles secrete an alkaline fluid that constitutes up to _____ percent of seminal fluid.

23. The _____ gland is a structure about the size of a walnut and is located at the base of the bladder.

24. The ejaculatory ducts and the _____ pass through the prostate gland.

25. The _____ glands, or bulbourethral glands, are located on each side of the urethra just below where it emerges from the prostate gland.

26. When a man is sexually aroused, the Cowper's glands secrete an _____ fluid that helps buffer acidity of the urethra and provides lubrication for the flow of seminal fluid through the penis.

27. The _____ that is ejaculated through the opening of the penis comes from the seminal vesicles, the prostate, and the Cowper's glands.

Male Sexual Functions

28. An _____ is a process coordinated by the autonomic nervous system.

29. Nighttime erections occur during the _____-_____ movement, or dreaming, stage of sleep.

30. _____ is the process whereby the semen is expelled through the penis to the outside of the body.

31. Ejaculation occurs in two stages: the _____ phase and the expulsion phase.

32. Some men experience _____ ejaculation, in which the semen is expelled into the bladder rather than through the penis.

33. Sometimes a man will experience orgasm without direct genital stimulation, an occurrence which is usually referred to as a _____ _____, or "wet dream".

Some Concerns About Sexual Functioning

34. Historically, there has been a preoccupation with the _____ of a man's penis.

35. For many men, penis size has played a part in defining their _____ or worth as a lover.

36. From a physiological standpoint, the nerve endings in a woman's vagina are concentrated in the _____ portion, and while some women do find pressure and stretching deep within the vagina to be pleasurable, it is not usually essential for female sexual gratification.

37. _____ is the surgical removal of the foreskin, and there are arguments for and against this procedure.

Male Genital Health Concerns

38. _____ is the medical specialty that deals with reproductive health and genital diseases of the male and urinary tract diseases in both sexes.

39. The glands located in the foreskin secrete an oily, lubricating substance, and if these secretions are allowed to accumulate they combine with sloughed-off dead skin cells to form a substance called _____.

40. Routine _____ can prevent this substance from accumulating.

41. There are a number of risk factors associated with _____ cancer, a rare malignancy that if left untreated can destroy the entire penis and potentially be fatal.

42. _____ cancer is one of the more common malignancies that occur in men ages 15 to 34.

43. _____, a condition in which the prostate may become inflamed as a result of various infections, may occur in men at any age.

44. About 50% of men between ages 50 and 60 experience _____ _____ _____, a condition in which the prostate gland becomes enlarged.

45. Some men may also develop _____ _____, the second leading cause of cancer death among men in the U.S.

Matching

Match each term below with the appropriate description. Each term is used only once.

a. inguinal canal
b. cremasteric muscle
c. seminiferous tubules
d. interstitial cells
e. epididymis
f. vas deferens

g. seminal vesicles
h. prostate gland
i. Cowper's glands
j. seminal fluid
k. cavernous and spongy bodies

_____1. a C-shaped structure that serves as a storage chamber for sperm

_____2. the major source of androgen

_____3. their secretions constitute a major portion of seminal fluid

_____4. its amount is influenced by the length of time since last orgasm, among other factors

_____5. the area through which the testes descend

_____6. they often secrete an alkaline fluid when a man is sexually aroused

_____7. the coils found within the testes where sperm production occurs

_____8. they engorge with blood when a man gets an erection

_____9. located at the base of the bladder, it is checked for cancer by means of a rectal exam

_____10. sudden fear may cause it to contract

_____11. the duct that carries sperm from the scrotal sac and is severed during a vasectomy

Identification

Label the various parts of the male sexual anatomy indicated below. Check your answers with the key at the end of the chapter.

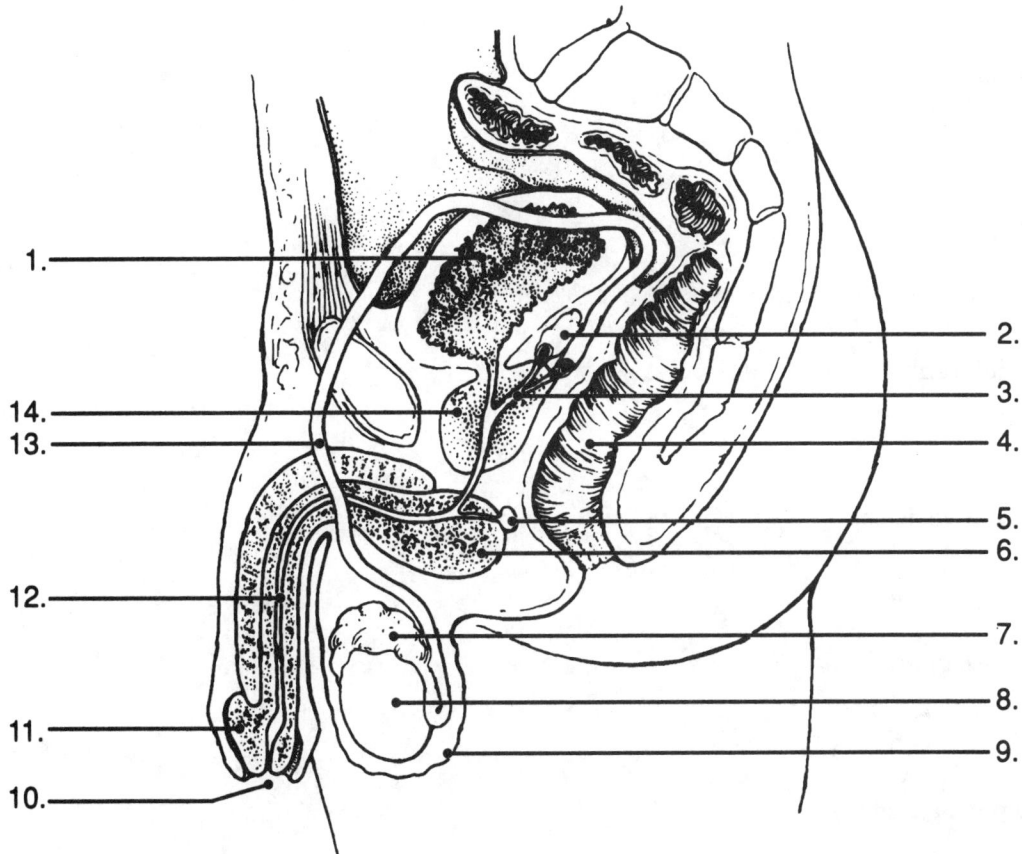

1. _____   8. _____

2. _____   9. _____

3. _____   10. _____

4. _____   11. _____

5. _____   12. _____

6. _____   13. _____

7. _____   14. _____

Sample Short Answer Test Questions

1. Briefly describe the **structure** and **function** of the following:

    a. penis

    b. scrotum

    c. testes

    d. vas deferens

    e. seminal vesicles

    f. prostate gland

    g. Cowper's glands

    h. semen

2. Identify the two areas of the glans of the penis that are most responsive to stimulation.

3. What are three potential benefits men may experience as a result of practicing Kegel exercises?

4. Define cryptorchidism. How is it treated? What may happen if it is not treated?

5. How may scrotal temperature be related to male infertility?

6. Name three types of stimuli that will provoke the cremasteric reflex.

7. List three factors that influence the amount of seminal fluid a man ejaculates.

8. When do night-time erections occur?

9. List several nonsexual stimulus situations that cause erections in men.

10. List and briefly describe the two stages of ejaculation.

11. What is retrograde ejaculation? Under what circumstances does it occur?

12. How may a man experience orgasm without direct penile stimulation?

13. Explain how the size of a man's penis may affect his female partner's sexual pleasure during intercourse.

14. List the arguments for and against circumcision.

15. What are the differences in sexual responsiveness between men who are circumcised and those who are not?

16. List and briefly describe **three** types of male genital modification/mutilation.

17. Briefly discuss the sexual self-health practices that a man may utilize in the preventive care of his penis.

18. Physiologically, what does a penis fracture involve? How can this happen and how might it be prevented?

19. List seven risk factors associated with penile cancer.

20. How common is testicular cancer? What are some of the symptoms?

21. Define prostatitis and list some of the symptoms.

22. How common is prostate cancer? At what age should men start being examined for this?

23. List six risk factors with prostate cancer.

24. List three ways in which prostate cancer might be diagnosed.

25. List eight treatment alternatives for prostate cancer.

26. What is currently the most favored treatment strategy for prostate cancer outside the U.S.?

Sample Multiple Choice Test Questions

Select the best alternative. Check your answers with the answer key at the end of the chapter.

1. The _____ is a loose pouch of skin that is an outpocket of the abdominal wall in the groin area.
    a. foreskin
    b. epididymis
    c. scrotum
    d. vas deferens

2. Which of the following is not associated with the testicles?
    a. sperm production
    b. Cowper's glands
    c. inguinal canal
    d. storage of sperm

3. Which of the following statements concerning cryptorchidism is **false**?
    a. This is a condition where one or both testicles fail to descend from the abdominal cavity.
    b. As many as 15 percent of boys may demonstrate this condition at birth.
    c. This condition may result in infertility.
    d. This condition may be associated with increased risk for developing testicular cancer.

4. The cremasteric reflex
    a. is characterized by the strain and pressure of the testicles when they are exposed to extreme heat.
    b. is revealed by the movement of the testes away from the body when the room temperature increases.
    c. is manifested as an upward movement of the testes toward the body wall when the inner thighs are stroked.
    d. is manifested as a scream of pain when a male falls on the crossbar of a bike.

5. The _____ are thin, highly coiled structures where sperm production takes place.
   a. seminal vesicles
   b. Cowper's glands
   c. interstitial cells
   d. seminiferous tubules

6. The epididymis
   a. is where sperm processing takes place.
   b. is the major source of androgen.
   c. is where sperm production takes place.
   d. is located at the base of the prostate gland.

7. Which of the following statements concerning the vas deferens is **false**?
   a. It is located inside the spermatic cord.
   b. It is the tube that is severed in a vasectomy.
   c. It is the tube through which urine passes from the bladder to the outside of the body.
   d. Sperm drain into it from the epididymis.

8. The prostate gland
   a. is the major source of seminal fluid.
   b. releases alkaline secretions that combine with other secretions to form the seminal fluid.
   c. is a C-shaped structure located along the base of the vas deferens.
   d. is a source of male sex hormones.

9. All of the following are symptoms of prostatitis **except**
   a. pain in the pelvic area
   b. a mass within the testicle
   c. a burning sensation while urinating
   d. a cloudy discharge from the penis

10. Which of the following **best** describes the function of Cowper's glands secretions?
    a. buffers the acidity of the urethra and facilitates flow of semen through the urethra
    b. facilitates flow of semen through the urethra and helps to lubricate the vagina
    c. helps to lubricate the vagina and buffers the acidity of the urethra
    d. buffers the acidity of the urethra and makes up the largest portion of the fluid in semen

11. All of the following are factors in the amount of seminal fluid a man ejaculates **except**
    a. the length of time since last orgasm
    b. the duration of arousal time prior to ejaculation
    c. a man's age
    d. how physically fit a man is

12. Which of the following is found in the penis?
    a. the seminal vesicles
    b. extensive muscular tissue
    c. a cylinder-shaped bone
    d. three chambers of spongy tissue

13. The _____ and _____ are two places on the glans of the penis that many men find especially responsive to stimulation.
    a. prepuce; corona
    b. shaft; frenulum
    c. corona; frenulum
    d. shaft; prepuce

14. All of the following are benefits that men may experience as a result of doing Kegel exercises **except**
    a. stronger, more pleasurable orgasms
    b. better ejaculatory control
    c. increased pelvic sensation during sexual arousal
    d. shorter refractory period

15. _____ is a medical specialty that focuses on the male reproductive structures.
    a. Urology
    b. Gonadotology
    c. Gynecology
    d. Proctology

16. On rare occasions during intercourse, too much weight is placed on the penis when attempting to gain or regain vaginal penetration. This may result in a
    a. glans decapitation.
    b. penile fracture.
    c. coronal collapse.
    d. frenulum fissure.

17. The first stage of ejaculation is the _____ phase while the second stage is called the _____ phase.
    a. emission; expulsion
    b. expulsion; emission
    c. REM; nocturnal emission
    d. nocturnal emission; REM

18. Which of the following statements concerning retrograde ejaculation is **false**?
    a. It results from a reversed functioning of the two urethral sphincters.
    b. This condition sometimes occurs in men who have had prostate surgery.
    c. This condition is potentially fatal if not treated.
    d. Certain tranquilizers can cause this reaction.

19. Nocturnal emissions
    a. are also known as "wet dreams."
    b. occur when semen is expelled into the bladder.
    c. occur during the emission stage of ejaculation.
    d. refer to Cowper's glands secretions that occur during sleep.

20. The size of a man's penis tends to be related to
    a. the length of his fingers.
    b. his race.
    c. his body build.
    d. none of the above

21. Circumcision is the surgical removal of the
    a. frenulum.
    b. foreskin.
    c. tunica dartos.
    d. scrotal sac.

22. Smegma
    a. may harbor organisms that can cause infections in women.
    b. is a watery gray discharge.
    c. may accumulate in the vas deferens.
    d. may result in urethral constriction.

23. Which of the following statements concerning circumcision is **true**?
    a. Recent research has suggested that the incidence of ovarian cancer is more frequent in women who have sex with uncircumcised partners.
    b. Circumcision is widely practiced in Europe and Africa.
    c. Circumcision is widely practiced throughout the world for religious or hygienic reasons.
    d. It appears that urinary tract infections occur more frequently among circumcised boys.

24. Generally speaking, a circumcised male responds
    a. more quickly during intercourse than an uncircumcised male.
    b. less quickly during intercourse than an uncircumcised male.
    c. about the same during intercourse as an uncircumcised male.
    d. Research results regarding the role of the foreskin in sexual performance have not been conclusive.

25. Sperm production in the male requires a temperature that
    a. is higher than body temperature.
    b. is lower than body temperature.
    c. is the same as body temperature.
    d. varies from high to low temperatures from day to day.

Critical Thinking/Personal Reflection

For Men:

1. Have you ever taken the time to leisurely touch and explore your body with the goal of becoming more knowledgeable and accepting of your body and how it functions, as well as to explore the feelings and sensations in various parts of your body without the goal of orgasmic release? If not, why not? In considering the possibility of doing so, what thoughts or feelings come up for you? If you find yourself feeling disgusted, embarrassed, defensive, or confused at the prospect of doing so, why do you think that is? If you have taken the time to do some body exploration, what was your experience in doing so? What were the benefits? The drawbacks?

2.   Set aside an hour or more when you can have some uninterrupted time alone. Take a leisurely bath or shower, and then select some lotion or massage oil that is pleasing to you. As you apply the lotion or oil to all parts of your body, experiment with different types of pressure, rhythm and touch. Explore your face, neck, arms, hands, chest, nipples, abdomen, buttocks, legs, feet and toes. Notice what kinds of touch your body responds to. Notice what parts of your body you appreciate or find attractive as well as the parts you criticize or find unattractive. How have you developed the relationship you have with your body? Are you comfortable with that relationship or is it something you would like to change? What are your personal standards for health and attractiveness? What do you base them upon? Are they realistic?

3.   Touch and explore the different parts of your genitals: the glans and shaft of your penis, your scrotum, and the perineum (the area between the scrotum and the anus). What words do you use to refer to your genitals? What words would you prefer your partner or potential partner to use? In doing this exercise, what thoughts or feelings come up for you? How do you feel about the size, shape or color of the various parts of your sexual anatomy? What are the sources of these feelings? How do they affect your sexual self-esteem, the way in which you care for your body, and your relationship with a partner or potential partner? Are you comfortable with these thoughts and feelings? If not, what would you like to change?

For Men and Women:

1.   If you had it to do over again, how would you change or improve the way in which you learned about male sexual anatomy and function? What factors might have contributed to more awareness or comfort with this subject? Give specific examples.

2.   If you had a newborn son, would you choose to have him circumcised? Why or why not?

3.   From your perspective, how important is penis size to a woman's sexual satisfaction? Think in terms of coital satisfaction as well as psychological stimulation. Has penis size been an issue for you and/or for your partner? How have you dealt with that?

Chapter Overview With Fill-In Answers

1. cavernous
2. root
3. glans
4. foreskin
5. Circumcision
6. glans
7. corona; frenulum
8. Kegel
9. scrotum
10. testicle
11. spermatic; vas deferens
12. hormones; sperm
13. cryptorchidism
14. testicular
15. sperm
16. seminiferous tubules
17. interstitial; androgen
18. epididymis
19. vas deferens
20. vasectomy
21. seminal vesicles
22. 70
23. prostate
24. urethra
25. Cowper's
26. alkaline
27. semen
28. erection
29. rapid-eye
30. Ejaculation
31. emission
32. retrograde
33. nocturnal emission
34. size
35. masculinity
36. outer
37. Circumcision
38. Urology
39. smegma
40. hygiene
41. penile
42. Testicular
43. Prostatitis
44. benign prostatic hyperplasia
45. prostate cancer

Matching Answers

1. e   2. d   3. g   4. j   5. a   6. i   7. c   8. k
9. h   10. b   11. f

Identification Answers

1. bladder
2. seminal vesicle
3. ejaculatory duct
4. rectum
5. Cowper's gland
6. root of penis
7. epididymis
8. testis
9. scrotum
10. urethral opening
11. glans of penis
12. urethra
13. vas deferens
14. prostate gland

Sample Multiple Choice Answers

1. c   2. b   3. b   4. c   5. d   6. a   7. c   8. b
9. b   10. a   11. d   12. d   13. c   14. d   15. a   16. b
17. a   18. c   19. a   20. d   21. b   22. a   23. c   24. d
25. b

6

Sexual Arousal and Response

Introduction

Our sexual arousal and response are influenced by a myriad of psychological, cultural, and biological factors. In this chapter, the focus is on the biological aspects of arousal and response: hormones, brain functions, sensory processes, foods, drugs, and chemicals. In addition, the physiological changes that men and women experience throughout sexual arousal and response are also discussed.

Review of Key Terms and Concepts

Key terms and concepts are listed and defined below. Refer to the subject index in the back of your textbook for additional information.

1. **castration** — surgical removal of the testes or ovaries.

2. **orchidectomy** — the surgical procedure for removing the testes

3. **antiandrogens** — drugs that reduce the amount of testosterone in the bloodstream; have been used to treat sex offenders and certain medical conditions

4. **Depo-Provera** — a well-known antiandrogen

5. **hypogonadism** — a state of androgen deprivation that results from certain diseases of the endocrine system

6. **cerebral cortex** — the "grey matter" of the brain that is responsible for higher functions like thinking, feeling, remembering, and language abilities

7. **limbic system** — a subcortical brain system composed of several interrelated structures that influences the sexual behavior of humans and other animals

8. **primary erogenous zones** — areas of the body containing dense concentrations of nerve endings very responsive to tactile pleasuring; e.g., genitals, buttocks, anus, breasts, mouth, armpits, neck, thighs, earlobes, navel, etc.

9. **secondary erogenous zones** — areas of the body other than primary erogenous zones that have become erotically sensitive through learning and experience

10. **pheromones** — substances secreted by the body, related to reproductive functions, that produce certain odors

11. **vomeronasal system** — a channel of sensory input whose exclusive task is to detect pheromones

12. **copulins** — pheromones from the vaginal secretions of rhesus monkeys

13. **alpha androstenal** — pheromones secreted by pigs; it has also been found in the perspiration of humans

14. **aphrodisiac** — a substance that allegedly arouses sexual desire and increases the capacity for sexual activity

15. **yohimbine hydrochloride** — a crystalline alkaloid derived from the sap of the tropical evergreen yohimbe tree in West Africa that appears to be an aphrodisiac for rats and perhaps for humans

16. **anaphrodisiacs** — substances that are known to inhibit sexual behavior — such as tranquilizers, opiates, antihypertensives, and nicotine

17. **Kaplan's model of sexual response** — three stages of sexual response that include desire, excitement, and orgasm

18. **Masters and Johnson's sexual response cycle** — four phases in sexual response for men and women that include excitement, plateau, orgasm, and resolution

19. **vasocongestion** — the engorgement of blood vessels in particular body parts in response to sexual arousal

20. **myotonia** — increased muscle tension that occurs throughout the body in response to sexual arousal

21. **sex flush** — a pink or red rash that appears in the chest or breasts during sexual arousal

22. **orgasmic platform** — the increased engorgement of the outer third of the vagina during the plateau phase of the sexual response cycle

23. **vulval orgasm** — a type of orgasm described by Singer and Singer that may be induced by coital or manual stimulation

24. **uterine orgasm** — a type of orgasm described by Singer and Singer that occurs only as a result of vaginal penetration and is characterized by specific breathing patterns

25. **blended orgasm** — a type of orgasm described by Singer and Singer that is a combination of vulval and uterine orgasms

26. **multiple orgasm** — more than one orgasm experienced within a short time period

27. **refractory period** — in the male resolution phase of Masters and Johnson's sexual response cycle, a recovery stage in which there is a temporary inability to reach orgasm

Chapter Overview With Fill-Ins

After reading each of the major sections in the chapter, check your retention by filling in each of the blanks in the corresponding sections below. The answers are provided at the end of the chapter.

Sexual Arousal

1. About 95 percent of the androgens produced by the male are secreted by the testes in the form of _____.

2. The remaining 5 percent are produced by the _____ glands.

3. In medical terms, castration is called _____.

4. Castration is sometimes performed to treat genital tuberculosis and _____ cancer.

5. A class of drugs called _____ drastically reduces the amount of testosterone circulating in the bloodstream.

6. These drugs have been used to treat _____ _____ and certain medical conditions such as advanced prostate cancer.

7. _____ is a state of androgen deprivation that occurs when hormone production in the testes is impaired.

8. The hormone _____ helps maintain vaginal elasticity and contributes to the production of vaginal lubrication.

9. The role of estrogens in female sexual motivation is _____.

10. _____ plays an important role as the major libido hormone in females.

11. Total testosterone is made up of _____ and bound testosterone, the former of which is most influential regarding sexual motivation.

12. The fact that sexual arousal can occur without any sensory stimulation at all — that arousal and even orgasm may be produced by fantasy alone — demonstrates the important role of the _____ in our sexuality.

13. Of the major senses, _____ tends to predominate during sexual sharing.

14. _____ erogenous zones contain dense concentrations of nerve endings and include the genitals, buttocks, anus, perineum, breasts, inner thighs, armpits, navel, neck, ears and mouth.

15. _____ erogenous zones include all other areas of the body that become endowed with erotic significance through sexual conditioning.

16. Next to touch, _____ is second in the hierarchy of stimuli that people view as sexually arousing.

17. Current research has demonstrated strong _____ in the responses of males and females to visual erotica when measured physiologically.

18. However, when sexual arousal is measured by self-reports rather than physiological devices, _____ are less inclined than _____ to report being sexually aroused by visual erotica.

19. In regard to the sense of smell, the females of many species secrete certain substances called _____ during their fertile periods that appear to play a role in sexual arousal.

20. _____ seems to play a relatively minor role in human sexual arousal.

21. An _____ is a substance that supposedly arouses sexual desire or increases a person's capacity for sexual activities.

22. A variety of foods, especially those resembling male external _____, have been ascribed various aphrodisiac qualities, but aside from a person's subjective assessment, there have been no objective data to substantiate these claims.

23. _____ has been viewed as a sexual stimulant, although it actually has a depressing effect on higher brain centers.

24. Research has demonstrated that with _____ levels of alcohol intake, both men and women experience _____ sexual arousal (as measured physiologically), decreased pleasure and intensity of orgasm, and increased difficulty in attaining orgasm.

25. A crystalline alkaloid derived from the sap of a tree that grows in West Africa, _____ hydrochloride, apparently induces intense sexual arousal and performance in _____, although recent research regarding similar effects on _____ has been inconclusive.

26. Substances that inhibit sexual behavior are called _____.

27. Anaphrodisiacs include: opiates, tranquilizers, antihypertensives, antidepressants and _____, one of the most widely used and least recognized anaphrodisiacs.

Sexual Response

28. Kaplan's model of sexual response contains three stages: _____, excitement and orgasm.

29. Masters and Johnson outline four phases in the sexual response cycle: excitement, _____, orgasm and resolution.

30. Masters and Johnson's also include a _____ period — a recovery stage in which there is a temporary inability to reach orgasm — in the male resolution phase.

31. Two fundamental physiological responses to effective sexual stimulation occur in both men and women: _____, or the blood engorgement that occurs; and _____, the increased muscle tension that occurs throughout the body.

32. Women tend to have more _____ in their sexual response patterns than men.

33. The presence of a _____ period in men represents another major difference.

34. Finally, women have the capacity to achieve _____ orgasms to a far greater degree than men, although recent research suggests that men may be capable of training themselves to experience a series of orgasms as well.

Matching

Match the phases below with the appropriate descriptions of various changes that occur in the sexual response cycle. Note that each phase may be used more than once, and there may be more than one answer for each description.

a. female excitement
b. male excitement
c. female plateau
d. male plateau
e. female orgasm

f. male emission phase of orgasm
g. male expulsion phase of orgasm
h. female resolution
i. male resolution
j. male refractory

_____1. formation of orgasmic platform

_____2. testicles return to unstimulated size

_____3. onset of "sex flush"

_____4. labia minora increase in size and begin to deepen in color

_____5. breast size increases

_____6. penis becomes erect, but the erection is not necessarily stable

_____7. contraction of orgasmic platform

_____8. testicles begin to swell and elevate

_____9. Cowper's glands become active

_____10. prostate gland and seminal vesicles contract

_____11. uterus is fully elevated

_____12. onset of vaginal lubrication

_____13. clitoris slowly descends from beneath hood

_____14. vestibular bulbs increase in size

_____15. nipples become erect

_____16. clitoral glans is retracted under hood

_____17. areola increases in size, causing nipple to appear less erect

_____18. penile urethra and rectal sphincter contract

_____19. stable erection

_____20. temporary inability to reach orgasm

_____21. labia majora separate away from vaginal opening

_____22. uterus contracts

_____23. Bartholin's glands may secrete fluid

Sample Short Answer Test Questions

1. Name two sources of androgens in men.

2. Name two sources of androgens in women.

3. What is the dominant androgen in both men and women?

4. Describe how testosterone influences male sexuality.

5. Define orchidectomy and describe its effects on sexual interest and activity.

6. List two ways in which antiandrogens have been used.

7. Describe the effects of hypogonadism in preadolescent males as well as in adult males.

8.   Name two functions that estrogens serve in women.

9.   What hormones appear to play the strongest role in female sexuality? Briefly summarize research to support this.

10. What two types of testosterone make up total testosterone? Which type is more influential in sexual desire?

11. List four symptoms of testosterone deficiency.

12. What parts of the brain are associated with sexual motivation and activity?

13. Distinguish between primary and secondary erogenous zones.

14. How do men and women respond to visual erotica when measured by self-reports? When measured physiologically?

15. List two pheromones and describe their sources.

16. What is the function of the vomeronasal system?

17. In one research study, what effect did the silence of their male partners have on women's sexual arousal?

18. Describe the effects of alcohol consumption on sexual arousal and orgasm from both a subjective and objective (physiological) point of view.

19. Briefly assess the **objective** aphrodisiac properties of the following drugs or chemicals:

    a.   cantharides (Spanish fly)

    b.   marijuana

    c.   amphetamines

    d.   cocaine

    e.   amyl nitrate

f. L-dopa

g. barbiturates

h. yohimbine hydrochloride

i. psychedelic drugs

j. alcohol

k. antidepressants

l. Libido

20. List six types of drugs that are anaphrodisiacs.

21. Name two ways in which nicotine retards sexual motivation.

22. What distinguishes Kaplan's model of sexual response from Masters and Johnson's?

23. Define vasocongestion and myotonia.

24. For the excitement phase in Masters and Johnson's sexual response cycle, briefly summarize the physiological changes that take place in both sexes, in women, and in men.

both sexes:

female responses:

male responses:

25. For the plateau phase in Masters and Johnson's sexual response cycle, briefly summarize the physiological changes that take place in both sexes, in women, and in men.

both sexes:

female responses:

male responses:

26. For the orgasm phase in Masters and Johnson's sexual response cycle, briefly summarize the physiological changes that take place in both sexes, in women, and in men.

both sexes:

female responses:

male responses:

27. For the resolution phase in Masters and Johnson's sexual response cycle, briefly summarize the physiological changes that take place in both sexes, in women, and in men.

    both sexes:

    female responses:

    male responses:

28. How have each of the following individuals described female orgasm?

    a. Freud

    b. Masters and Johnson

    c. Singer and Singer

29. Where is the Grafenberg spot located? How may it be stimulated?

30. What is the source of the female ejaculate? Of what is this fluid composed?

31. Briefly describe the differences in sexual response patterns between men and women.

32. Briefly outline three possible explanations for the existence of a refractory period in men.

33. Even though most women have the capacity for multiple orgasm, why is it that such a small percentage of women report having them?

34. It appears that some men may be capable of experiencing a series of orgasms within a short time. How do they do this?

Sample Multiple Choice Test Questions

Select the best alternative. Check your answers with the answer key at the end of the chapter.

1. Which of the following statements concerning androgens is **true**?
   a. Most of the androgens produced by men are secreted by the adrenal glands.
   b. Estrogen is a type of androgen.
   c. Androgens are present in both men and women.
   d. Orchidectomy would eliminate about half of the androgens that men produce.

2. Research indicates that testosterone generally has a greater impact on
   a. male genital sensitivity.
   b. male orgasmic intensity.
   c. male sexual functioning.
   d. male sexual desire.

3. Depo-Provera is a type of
   a. androgen.
   b. antiandrogen.
   c. estrogen.
   d. chemical aphrodisiac.

4. Hypogonadism is
   a. the surgical removal of the testes.
   b. treated with Depo-Provera.
   c. when the testicles become infected and swollen.
   d. a state of androgen deprivation.

5. Which of the following statements regarding hypogonadism is **true**?
    a. If it occurs in adulthood, sexual desire and function is always impaired.
    b. If it occurs before puberty, the effects are highly variable depending upon the individual.
    c. Androgen insensitivity is one of the effects of this condition.
    d. This condition results from certain diseases of the endocrine system.

6. At the present time, the evidence linking _____ with female sexuality is more substantial than that which supports _____.
    a. androgens; estrogens
    b. estrogens; androgens
    c. progesterones; androgens
    d. estrogens; progesterones

7. Researchers have reported increased sexual activity in rats when the anterior and posterior regions of the _____ are stimulated.
    a. gonads
    b. adrenal glands
    c. hypothalamus
    d. cerebellum

8. Which of the following statements concerning the cerebral cortex is **most accurate**?
    a. Key structures include the septal area, amygdala and parts of the adrenals.
    b. When certain parts of it are surgically destroyed, there may be a significant reduction in sexual behavior of males and females.
    c. This is referred to as the "pleasure center" of the brain.
    d. Strictly mental events like fantasies are produced here.

9. Amyl nitrate
    a. is used in the treatment of a variety of mental and physical conditions; can heighten arousal and orgasm.
    b. has frequently been used to treat Parkinson's disease; can heighten arousal and orgasm.
    c. is used to sexually rejuvenate older males; can cause priapism.
    d. is used to treat heart pain; can intensify arousal and orgasm.

10. Which of the following statements concerning priapism is **true**?
    a. It is associated with frequent use of amyl nitrate.
    b. It is a painful condition independent of sexual arousal.
    c. It occurs during the orgasm phase of the sexual response cycle.
    d. It is brought about by the use of testosterone replacement therapy.

11. Which of the following terms does **not** belong with the others?
    a. pheromones
    b. potassium nitrate
    c. copulins
    d. alpha androstenal

12. This substance may be a true aphrodisiac, at least for rats.
    a. LSD
    b. Benzedrine
    c. yohimbine
    d. L-dopa

13. Drugs used for treating high blood pressure as well as drugs used to treat a variety of emotional disorders may
    a. inhibit sexual behavior.
    b. induce priapism.
    c. be linked with the development of prostate cancer.
    d. increase sexual desire.

14. How does nicotine affect sexual arousal and function?
    a. It promotes relaxation and loosens inhibitions.
    b. It increases testosterone levels in the blood.
    c. It expands the blood vessels thereby enhancing vasocongestive response.
    d. It delays and decreases sexual arousal.

15. The desire stage is one of the significant features of whose sexual response model?
    a. Singer and Singer's
    b. Masters and Johnson's
    c. Kaplan's
    d. Freud's

16. Which of the following is the **best** example of myotonia?
    a. vaginal lubrication
    b. erection of the penis
    c. muscular spasms during orgasm
    d. the formation of the orgasmic platform

17. All of the following are examples of vasocongestion **except**
    a. erection of the penis.
    b. vaginal lubrication.
    c. engorgement of the clitoris.
    d. uterine contractions during orgasm.

18. The labia majora flatten and move away from the vaginal opening during the _____ phase of sexual response.
    a. excitement
    b. plateau
    c. orgasm
    d. resolution

19. If the Cowper's glands produce secretions, this will typically occur in the _____ or _____ stage of sexual response.
    a. desire; plateau
    b. orgasm; plateau
    c. desire; excitement
    d. excitement; plateau

20. Which of the following statements concerning the orgasmic platform is true?
    a. It develops during the plateau phase.
    b. It refers to the vaginal expansion that occurs in the inner two-thirds of the vagina.
    c. It is an example of myotonia.
    d. It ceases to develop after menopause.

21. Which of the following types of orgasm described by the Singers most closely corresponds to the type of orgasmic response described by Masters and Johnson?
    a. vulval
    b. uterine
    c. blended
    d. clitoral

22. The Grafenberg spot may be stimulated by
    a. applying pressure to the mons veneris.
    b. vigorous palpation of the anterior wall of the vagina.
    c. applying pressure to the urethral opening.
    d. gently stroking the clitoris.

23. A recent study of U.S. and Canadian women disclosed that _____ percent of the respondents had experienced fluid release and ejaculation at the point of orgasm.
    a. 20
    b. 40
    c. 60
    d. 80

24. The fluid that some women ejaculate following Grafenberg spot stimulation is chemically similar to
    a. urine.
    b. menstrual fluid.
    c. seminal fluid.
    d. Bartholin's glands secretions.

25. The _____ is when all of the sexual systems return to their nonaroused state.
    a. refractory period
    b. resolution phase
    c. denouement
    d. plateau phase

26. The clitoris is retracted under the hood during the _____ and _____ phases of sexual response.
    a. desire; excitement
    b. excitement; plateau
    c. plateau; orgasm
    d. orgasm; resolution

27. That ejaculation triggers a short-term neurological inhibitory mechanism is **one** explanation for
    a. the male resolution phase.
    b. the male "monthly cycle."
    c. multiple orgasms in men.
    d. the male refractory period.

28. The _____ refers to the period of time immediately after male orgasm when no amount of additional stimulation will result in orgasm.
    a. resolution phase
    b. charge phase
    c. postejaculatory remission period
    d. refractory period

29. In comparing Kinsey's survey to more contemporary surveys, the number of women who experience multiple orgasms
    a. has decreased significantly.
    b. has increased significantly.
    c. has stayed about the same.
    d. Kinsey's survey did not include this information.

30. One explanation for the difference in the number of women who are capable of having multiple orgasms and the number of women who actually experience them is
    a. the source of sexual stimulation.
    b. whether or not the women own vibrators.
    c. variations in penis size.
    d. whether or not the G-spot was stimulated.

31. Vasocongestion is to blood vessels as myotonia is to
    a. muscles.
    b. respiration.
    c. heart rate.
    d. excitement.

Critical Thinking/Personal Reflection

1. Thinking in terms of the five senses listed below, give examples of what you find sexually arousing as well as sexually inhibiting or irritating. You may think in terms of a partner or potential partner (specific visual, olfactory, auditory stimuli related to that person) or in more general terms, or both.

	Sexually Arousing Stimuli	Sexually Irritating Stimuli
Touch		
Vision		
Smell		
Taste		
Hearing		

2. Take some time to think about what your conditions are for good sex—alone or with a partner—from physical, psychological and emotional perspectives. Examples of these might include the environment in which you would most enjoy sex, being free of fears of unwanted pregnancy or of contracting a sexually transmitted disease, specific sexual behaviors or positions you most enjoy, degree of privacy you would like, if you are well-rested or freshly showered, how you feel about your body, the kind of thoughts or fantasies you enjoy prior to sexual interaction, how you are feeling about yourself in general, yourself in relationship to your partner (if you have one), and the degree of love, trust, affection and commitment in the relationship, etc. Write down your conditions for good sex. How aware have you been of your conditions for good sex in seeking sexual gratification for yourself or with a partner? If you are in a relationship (or reflecting back on past relationships), have you been willing to make your conditions for good sex known to your partner? Have you been willing to discover theirs? If not, why not? Is that something you would like to change?

3. In reflecting on (1) and (2) above, do you think there would be overall sex differences in what men and women find arousing or what their conditions are for good sex? If so, to what might this be attributed?

Chapter Overview With Fill-In Answers

1. testosterone
2. adrenal
3. orchidectomy
4. prostate
5. antiandrogens
6. sexual offenders
7. Hypogonadism
8. estrogen
9. unclear
10. Testosterone
11. free
12. brain
13. touch
14. Primary
15. Secondary
16. vision
17. similarities
18. women; men
19. pheromones
20. Taste
21. aphrodisiac
22. genitals
23. Alcohol
24. increased; reduced
25a. yohimbine
25b. rats
25c. humans
26. anaphrodisiacs
27. nicotine
28. desire
29. plateau
30. refractory
31. vasocongestion; myotonia
32. variation
33. refractory
34. multiple

Matching Answers

1. c	2. i	3. a–d	4. a	5. a	6. b	7. e	8. b
9. b, d	10. f	11. c	12. a	13. h	14. a	15. a, b	16. c, e
17. c, e	18. g	19. d, f, g	20. j	21. a	22. e	23. c	

Sample Multiple Choice Answers

1. c	2. d	3. b	4. d	5. d	6. a	7. c	8. d
9. d	10. b	11. b	12. c	13. a	14. d	15. c	16. c
17. d	18. a	19. d	20. a	21. a	22. b	23. b	24. c
25. b	26. c	27. d	28. d	29. c	30. a	31. a	

7

Love and the Development of Relationships

Introduction

Until recently, attempts to define, measure, explain or control the concept of love have remained elusive. However, this chapter presents current information from a variety of psychological, sociobiological, philosophical, cross-cultural and clinical perspectives that enable us to better understand this mysterious and intriguing part of our lives. Specific sections in the text deal with the relationship between love and sex, how to deal with jealousy, the development of intimacy, and maintaining relationship satisfaction over time.

Review of Key Terms and Concepts

Key terms and concepts are listed and defined below. Refer to the subject index in the back of your textbook for additional information.

1. **Rubin's love scale** — a 13-item measurement device designed by Zick Rubin that attempted to measure a couple's level of attachment, caring and intimacy

2. **attachment** — a component of Rubin's love scale that refers to a person's desire for the physical presence and emotional support of the other person

3. **caring** — a component of Rubin's love scale that refers to an individual's concern for the other's well-being

4. **intimacy** — a component of Rubin's love scale that refers to the desire for close, confidential communication with the other

5. **philia** — love between friends, known to the ancient Greeks as philia, involves concern for the other's well-being

6. **passionate love** — romantic love or infatuation, characterized by intense feelings of tenderness, elation, anxiety, sexual desire, and ecstasy

7. **companionate love** — characterized by a friendly affection and a deep attachment that is based on extensive familiarity with the loved one

8. **Sternberg's triangular theory of love** — a theoretical framework for conceptualizing what people experience when they report being in love; includes the components of passion, intimacy, and commitment

9. **nonlove** — the absence of Sternberg's three components of love; what we feel in casual relationships

10. **friendship** — what we experience when just the intimacy component of Sternberg's theory of love is present

11. **infatuation** — what we experience when just the passion component of Sternberg's theory of love is present

12. **empty love** — the presence of Sternberg's love component of commitment without passion and intimacy; often characteristic of a long-term, static relationship

13. **companionate love** — the presence of Sternberg's love components of intimacy and commitment but without passion; often characteristic of happy couples who have been together for a long time

14. **fatuous love** — the presence of Sternberg's love components of passion and commitment but without intimacy; often characteristic of whirlwind courtships

15. **romantic love** — the presence of Sternberg's love components of passion and intimacy but without commitment

16. **consummate love** — when all three components of Sternberg's theory of love are present: passion, intimacy, and commitment

17. **Lee's styles of loving** — a theory that describes six different styles of loving that include romantic, game-playing, possessive, companionate, altruistic and pragmatic love styles

18. **phenylethylamine (PEA)** — a neurotransmitter chemically similar to amphetamines that produces feelings of euphoria and giddiness

19. **endorphins** — neurotransmitters chemically similar to morphine that produce feelings of tranquillity and security

20. **mere exposure effect** — phenomena by which repeated exposure to novel stimuli tends to increase an individual's liking for such stimuli

21. **reciprocity** — the notion that when we receive expressions of liking and loving we tend to respond in similar ways

22. **self-love** — genuine interest, concern, and respect for ourselves

23. **inclusion** — the first step a person takes in meeting another; e.g., eye contact, a smile, or a greeting

24. **response** — how a person responds to a gesture of inclusion, the nature of which will determine future contact

25. **care** — a genuine concern for another's welfare

26. **trust** — a belief that each partner in a relationship will act consistently in ways that promote the relationship's growth and stability, and that affirm each partner

27. **affection** — characterized by feelings of warmth and attachment, it elicits a desire to be physically close to another; usually expressed by holding hands, sitting close, hugs and caresses

28. **playfulness** — a phase in the development of intimacy where each person exhibits delight, exhilaration, and laughter in the presence of the other

29. **genitality** — sexual feelings in an intimate relationship that culminate in genital sex

30. **jealousy** — an aversive emotional reaction evoked by a real or imagined relationship involving one's partner and a third person

Chapter Overview With Fill-Ins

After reading each of the major sections in the chapter, check your retention by filling in each of the blanks in the corresponding sections below. The answers are provided at the end of the chapter.

What is Love?

1. One of the more ambitious attempts to measure love was undertaken by psychologist
_____ _____, who developed a 13-item measurement device that he
called a _____ _____.

2. As measured by the scale above, love has three components: _____, caring and
    _____.

Types of Love

3. Love between friends, known to the Ancient Greeks as _____, involves concern for
    the other's well-being.

4. _____ love (also known as romantic love or infatuation) is characterized by
    intense emotional and sexual desire.

5. _____ love is characterized by affection and deep attachment.

6. Robert Sternberg has proposed a _____ theory of love that has three
    components: passion, intimacy and _____.

7. Various combinations of these components create _____ different types of love.

8. John Lee's theory suggests six different styles of loving: romantic, game-playing,
    possessive, companionate, altruistic and _____.

Falling in Love: Why and With Whom?

9. The natural high experienced in intense passion may be partially attributed to brain
    chemistry, especially the neurotransmitter _____ (PEA).

10. Another factor that affects why people fall in love with whom they do is _____,
    or physical nearness of that individual.

11. Another factor is _____ in social class, religious orientation, educational
    background, etc.

12. The principle of _____ explains why we tend to like or love people who like us.

13. _____ _____ also plays a dominant role in drawing lovers together,
    especially in the early stages of a relationship.

The Development of Intimacy

14. Satisfying intimacy within a relationship begins with _____-_____,
    which has been defined as a genuine interest, concern and respect for ourselves.

15. The different phases of a relationship are: (a) _____, when one person extends
    the invitation to relate to another; (b) _____, the nature of which will determine
    whether a relationship begins; c) _____, or the genuine concern for another's
    welfare; (d) _____, a feeling that is essential to the ongoing development of a
    relationship; (e) _____, or feelings of warmth and attachment; (f) _____,
    which is characterized by delight, exhilaration, and expansive laughter that is expressed
    in the relationship; and (g) _____, when the couple agrees to express feelings
    through genital sex.

Issues in Loving Relationships

16. A number of surveys indicate that _____ link love and sex to a greater extent
    than _____ do.

17. Recent studies reveal a _____ of male and female attitudes about the
    relationship between love and sex.

18. The first step in integrating sex into your life in a meaningful way is to consider what you _____ in life and relationships before initiating a sexual involvement with another.

19. You can also ask yourself if your decision to engage in a sexual relationship will _____ your positive feelings about your-self and the other person.

20. Jealous feelings may be increased by _____ of characteristics of the rival.

21. In general, women were more envious of _____ and _____.

22. Men were more envious of _____ and _____.

23. In another study, it was found that women are more likely to _____ jealous feelings and men are more likely to _____ them.

Maintaining Relationship Satisfaction

24. A study of 300 happily married couples revealed that the most frequently named reason for an enduring and happy marriage was seeing one's partner as one's _____ _____.

25. Maintaining frequent positive _____ and response experiences contributes to the continued satisfaction of committed couples.

26. For some people, maintaining _____ excitement in their relationship is a high priority.

27. However, some people find sexual _____ a comfort and a source of security.

Matching

Match the theorists below with the appropriate descriptions or quotations. Note that each theorist may be used once, more than once, or not at all, but choose only **one** answer for each blank.

a. Zick Rubin
b. Erich Fromm
c. Robert Sternberg
d. John Allen Lee
e. Liebowitz and Walsh

f. John Money
g. Helen Fisher
h. Jankowiak and Fischer
i. Erik Erikson
j. David Buss

_____1.   three components of love include intimacy, passion and commitment

_____2.   the game-playing love style is described as one that is characteristic of people who like to "play the field"

_____3.   the natural high characteristic of passionate love is the result of surging levels of neurotransmitters

_____4.   documented the existence of romantic love in 147 out of 166 societies

_____5.   "romantic love is a delicious art form but not a durable one"

_____6.   conducted research to determine to what extent romantic love is a human universal

_____7.   eminent sexologist who maintains that loving someone of the same sex, as opposed to having sex itself, is the key ingredient that distinguishes being homosexual from heterosexual

_____8.   attempted to measure love by developing a device called a love scale

_____9.   defines fatuous love as typical of the whirlwind courtship

_____10. a human development scholar; believed that positive self-feelings are a basis for a satisfying relationship.

_____11. three components of love include attachment, caring and intimacy

_____12. anthropologist and author of *Anatomy of Love* who believes that love is a basic primitive human emotion

_____13. suggested that union with another person is the deepest human need

_____14. conducted a cross-cultural study on sex differences in homosexual mate preferences

Sample Short Answer Test Questions

1. List and describe the three components of Rubin's love scale.

2. According to research, what behavior was observed in "strong lovers" as opposed to "weak lovers?"

3. List the three components of Sternberg's theory of love.

4. List and briefly describe the eight love patterns that are the result of various combinations of the three components of Sternberg's theory of love.

5. List and briefly describe Lee's six different styles of loving.

6. According to Liebowitz and Walsh, which three neurotransmitters are responsible for the 'natural high' characteristic of passionate love? Of these three, which is most important?

7. Which neurotransmitters may be associated with the feelings of peace and tranquillity that characterize long-term relationships?

8. Explain how the mere exposure effect partially accounts for the people to whom we become attracted.

9. According to research, is it true that opposites attract? Explain.

10. Briefly discuss the concept of self-love and the role it plays in the development of intimacy.

11. What did Erik Erikson believe regarding self-love in a relationship?

12. List and briefly describe the seven phases of a relationship.

13. Briefly summarize the results of research studies on how men and women view the relationship between love and sex, and how that has changed over time.

14. Describe how heterosexual men and women's views of love and sex compare with those of gay men and lesbians.

15. What questions might you ask yourself in order to clarify your values in relation to a specific decision regarding sexual activity?

16. Describe three steps you can take to let a person know that you are not ready for sex yet.

17. Describe three characteristics of people who are most likely to experience jealousy.

18. In what ways do men and women tend to respond to jealousy differently?

19. List five conditions that would most likely result in motivating a jealous person to deal with the problem.

20. List four suggestions for the person whose partner is being unreasonably jealous.

21. What does the research say regarding the reasons why happily-married couples are able to remain that way over time?

22. List at least six suggestions that the authors offer for couples who wish to maintain sexual excitement in their relationships.

23. Jankowiak and Fischer documented the existence of romantic love in 147 out of 166 societies. How did they explain its absence in the other 19 societies?

24. What did David Buss' cross-cultural study on mate preferences reveal?

Sample Multiple Choice Test Questions

Select the best alternative. Check your answers with the answer key at the end of the chapter.

1. All of the following are components of Rubin's love scale **except**
    a. attachment
    b. inclusion
    c. intimacy
    d. caring

2. Love that involves concern for the other's well-being is
    a. ludus.
    b. eros.
    c. philia.
    d. mania.

3. Generalized physiological arousal is one characteristic of
    a. philia.
    b. companionate love.
    c. storge.
    d. passionate love.

4. Another word for companionate love is
    a. agape.
    b. storge.
    c. ludus.
    d. mania.

5. According to authors Liebowitz and Walsh, the "high" or euphoria characteristic of passionate love is **best** explained by
    a. recognizing qualities in our lovers that we experienced with our parents when we were children.
    b. pheromones.
    c. the cognition that our feelings of attraction to someone are being reciprocated.
    d. surging levels of brain chemicals.

6. Passion, commitment and intimacy are all components of _____
    a. Sternberg's triangular theory of love.
    b. Rubin's theory of attachment.
    c. Lee's styles of loving
    d. Erikson's relationship stages.

7. Ted and Tamara have been married for a long time and are committed to staying together to raise their two children, despite the lack of passion and intimacy they experience together. Sternberg would characterize this type of love experience as
    a. companionate love.
    b. nonlove.
    c. consummate love.
    d. empty love.

8. The tendency to fall in love with people who live nearby and are seen frequently is said to be the factor of
    a. familiarity.
    b. similarity.
    c. proximity.
    d. habituation.

9. Self-love refers to
    a. selfishness.
    b. lack of consideration for others.
    c. the first component of Rubin's love scale.
    d. respect for ourselves.

10. According to the authors, the first phase of an intimate relationship is
    a. inclusion.
    b. trust.
    c. symbiosis.
    d. caring.

11. The **best** example of the response phase of a relationship is
    a. saying "hello" to someone.
    b. asking someone to dance.
    c. riding on the swings in the playground with your partner.
    d. trying to understand your partner's point of view.

12. Which of the following is an example of inclusion-response?
    a. having sex at least three times a week
    b. demonstrating caring behaviors for your partner that make him/her feel loved
    c. riding a roller coaster together
    d. avoiding routine sex

13. _____ is the phase of a relationship in which there is genuine concern for the other person's welfare.
    a. Inclusion
    b. Care
    c. Affection
    d. Response

14. The affection phase of a relationship is characterized by
    a. feelings of warmth and attachment.
    b. feelings of exhilaration and passion.
    c. genital contact.
    d. a gesture of inclusion.

15. Which of the following statements concerning love and sex is **true**?
    a. Survey results have revealed that men and women's attitudes regarding the relationship between love and sex are becoming increasingly similar.
    b. According to student surveys in the authors' classes, roughly an equal number of men and women indicated that love is a necessary component of sexual relationships.
    c. A recent study found that the majority of men and women had their first intercourse experience with someone with whom they were in love.
    d. all of the above

16. If you would like to better understand the role that sex and relationships play in your life, you should ask yourself which of the following questions?
    a. "When do I want to get married?"
    b. "Should I have sex on the first date or wait for a while?"
    c. "Where do my sexual values come from — family, friends, etc.?"
    d. "Is my partner more sexually experienced than I am?"

17. One survey indicated that, in general, women were most envious of _____ in other individuals.
    a. attractiveness and popularity.
    b. wealth and fame.
    c. social position and emotional security.
    d. attractiveness and wealth.

18. One of the traits possessed by people prone to jealousy is
    a. being distrustful of others.
    b. having low self-esteem.
    c. the tendency to repress feelings.
    d. a pessimistic outlook on life in general.

19. In general, women are more likely than men to _____ jealous feelings.
    a. project
    b. deny
    c. rationalize
    d. acknowledge

20. Which of the following would a man be **most** likely to do in response to jealous feelings?
    a. secretly search through his lover's belongings
    b. question his lover about a past romance
    c. blame himself for not being as attractive or successful as the other guy
    d. get angry at his girlfriend for wearing sexually provocative clothing

21. In the survey of 300 happily married couples, which reason was cited **most** frequently for the success of their marriages?
    a. I want the relationship to succeed.
    b. Our sexual intimacy is the best it has ever been.
    c. My partner is my best friend.
    d. We agree on aims and goals.

22. Which of the following is the **best** suggestion for maintaining sexual excitement in a relationship?
    a. flirting with someone at a party to make your partner just a little jealous
    b. having sex on a regular basis (2–3 times a week)
    c. making "dates" with each other
    d. being naked together more often

23. Two anthropologists, Jankowiak and Fischer, found that romantic love existed in 147 out of the 166 societies they studied. They speculated that the reason it was absent in the other 19 societies was because
    a. these societies were generally less culturally sophisticated than the majority.
    b. these societies had little leisure time compared to the majority.
    c. the pragmatic values of these societies didn't allow for something as indulgent as romantic love.
    d. their research methods were flawed.

24. The explanation that Buss provides regarding why men and women select the mates they do is best described as _____ in nature.
    a. psychological
    b. sociobiological
    c. psychological
    d. biological

Critical Thinking/Personal Reflection

Styles of Loving

Recent research indicates that there are six main styles of loving. The following material combines the work of three sociologists — John Alan Lee, Tom Lasswell, and Marcia Lasswell, with the research of psychologist Martin Rosenman, and explores the implications of these styles of loving. The six basic lovestyles are: Friendship, Giving, Possessive, Practical, Game-Playing, and Erotic.

You can determine your own concept of love by taking the fifty-item test below. Scoring the test shows you your position on each of the six lovestyles. After you take the test, read the description for each style of loving, bearing in mind that a person can score high in more than one lovestyle.

The Styles of Loving Test

In responding to the items below, when it is appropriate think of your most significant peer love relationships. If you cannot decide which has been the most significant, think of your most recent significant love relationship. If you wish you may think of your ideal love relationship whether you have actually experienced it or not. Answer *all* of the following items either true or false.

1. I believe that "love at first sight" is possible.

2. I did not realize that I was in love until I actually had been for some time.

3. When things aren't going right with us, my stomach gets upset.

4. From a practical point of view, I must consider what a person is going to become in life before I commit myself to loving him/her.

5. You cannot have love unless you have first had *caring* for a while.

6. It's always a good idea to keep your lover a little uncertain about how committed you are to him/her.

7. The first time we kissed or rubbed cheeks, I felt a definite genital response (lubrication, erection).

8. I still have good friendships with almost everyone with whom I have ever been involved in a love relationship.

9. It makes good sense to plan your life carefully before you choose a lover.

10. When my love affairs break up, I get so depressed that I have even thought of suicide.

11. Sometimes I get so excited about being in love that I can't sleep.

12. I try to use my own strength to help my lover through difficult times, even when he/she is behaving foolishly.

13. I would rather suffer myself than let my lover suffer.

14. Part of the fun of being in love is testing one's skill at keeping it going and getting what one wants from it at the same time.

15. As far as my lovers go, what they don't know about me doesn't hurt them.

16. It is best to love someone with a similar background.

17. We kissed each other soon after we met because we both wanted to.

18. When my lover doesn't pay attention to me, I feel sick all over.

19. I cannot be happy unless I place my lover's happiness before my own.

20. Usually the first thing that attracts my attention to a person is his/her pleasing physical appearance.

21. The best kind of love grows out of a long friendship.

22. When I am in love, I have trouble concentrating on anything else.

23. At the first touch of his/her hand, I knew that love was a real possibility.

24. When I break up with someone, I go out of my way to see that he/she is O.K.

25. I cannot relax if I suspect that he/she is with someone else.

26. I have at least once had to plan carefully to keep two of my lovers from finding out about each other.

27. I can get over love affairs pretty easily and quickly.

28. A main consideration in choosing a lover is how he/she reflects on my family.

29. The best part of love is living together, building a home together, and rearing children together.

30. I am usually willing to sacrifice my own wishes to let my lover achieve his/hers.

31. A main consideration in choosing a partner is whether or not he/she will be a good parent.

32. Kissing, cuddling, and sex shouldn't be rushed into; they will happen naturally when one's intimacy has grown enough.

33. I enjoy flirting with attractive people.

34. My lover would get upset if she/he knew some of the things I've done with other people.

35. Before I ever fell in love, I had a pretty clear physical picture of what my true love would be like.

36. If my lover had a baby by someone else, I would want to raise it, love it and care for it as if it were my own.

37. It is hard to say exactly when we fell in love.

38. I couldn't truly love anyone I would not be willing to marry.

39. Even though I don't want to be jealous, I can't help it when he/she pays attention to someone else.

40. I would rather break up with my lover than to stand in his/her way.

41. I like the idea of me and my lover having the same kinds of clothes, hats, bicycles, cars, etc.

42. I wouldn't date anyone that I wouldn't want to fall in love with.

43. At least once when I thought a love affair was all over, I saw him/her again and knew I couldn't realistically see him/her without loving him/her.

44. Whatever I own is my lover's to use as he/she chooses.

45. If my lover ignores me for a while, I sometimes do really stupid things to try to get his/her attention back.

46. It's fun to see whether I can get someone to go out with me even if I don't want to get involved with that person.

47. A main consideration in choosing a mate is how he/she will reflect on one's career.

48. When my lover doesn't see me or call for a while, I assume he/she has a good reason.

49. Before getting very involved with anyone, I try to figure out how compatible his/her hereditary background is with mine in case we ever have children.

50. The best love relationships are the ones that last the longest.

Scoring

- Score only "True" answers.
- Your friendship love score is the number of "True" answers to questions 2, 5, 8, 21, 29, 32, 37, 50.
- Your giving love score is the number of "True" answers to questions 12, 13, 19, 24, 30, 36, 40, 44, 48.
- Your possessive love score is the number of "True" answers to questions 3, 10, 11, 18, 22, 25, 39, 43, 45.
- Your practical love score is the number of "True" answers to questions 4, 9, 16, 28, 31, 38, 42, 47, 49.
- Your game-playing love score is the number of "True" answers to questions 6, 14, 15, 26, 27, 33, 34, 46.
- Your erotic love score is the number of "True" answers to questions 1, 7, 17, 20, 23, 35, 41.

	Love Score	Percentile
Friendship	_____	_____
Giving	_____	_____
Possessive	_____	_____
Practical	_____	_____
Game-Playing	_____	_____
Erotic	_____	_____

To get the correct percentile, use the following table for each love score:

Percentiles for Each of the Styles of Loving

		Friendship	Giving	Possessive	Practical	Game-Playing	Erotic
	0	1	1	3	4	1	1
	1	5	2	11	12	6	2
	2	16	8	28	26	14	29
	3	33	25	38	48	26	52
LOVE	4	56	47	53	70	34	74
SCORE	5	78	56	64	83	59	91
	6	88	71	80	91	80	98
	7	95	91	91	97	95	99
	8	99	97	96	99	99	
	9		99	99			

Interpreting the Test

Your percentile score for each style of loving tells you how you compare with other people who have taken the test. In other words, a percentile score of 78 on a lovestyle would indicate that your were higher on that lovestyle than 78 percent of the people. A percentile score of 50 on another scale would place you in the middle. A percentile score of 5 would indicate that 95 percent of the people were higher than you on that scale

Different relationships bring out different lovestyles. You might be interested in retaking the test using a different relationship as the basis.

(Thomas E. Lasswell and Marcia E Lasswell, "I Love You But I'm Not In Love With You", *Journal of Marital and Family Therapy, 2*, No. 3 (1976), pp. 222–24. Reprinted by permission.)

STYLES OF LOVING

Friendship Love

Sharing, mutual understanding, respect, compassion, and concern characterize friendship lovers. As good friends, they feel comfortable with each other and assume that their relationship will be permanent. They enjoy the security, the naturalness, the comfortableness of their love.

Friendship love usually develops gradually. Sexual intimacy often comes late in the relationship, emerging from the already existing verbal intimacy. And many friendship lovers do not realize they are in love until they have been for some time.

This lovestyle shows less preoccupation with the beloved than do the other lovestyles. Mostly absent are intense emotions, either painful or ecstatic. Taking a less romantic attitude, the intimates may forget or minimize the importance of birthdays, anniversaries, and other significant occasions.

Stability, rather than impulsiveness, permeates the relationship — the comfort of the home environment, the power of patience and loyalty, the endurance of brother-sister type love. Even if these lovers break up or move on, they try to maintain contact, and they usually have good friendships with their former intimates. This lovestyle is supportive and undemanding, allowing each partner time to pursue hobbies, platonic friendships, and professional interests. With the passage of time, shared and discussed activities enhance mutual understanding and the friendship grows.

Pitfalls. Some observers would find the predictability, security stability, and quiet homelife of this type of love to be lacking in excitement. Compared to the possessive, game-playing, and erotic types of love, friendship love is uneventful.

Giving Love

As the name implies, giving lovers are giving and forgiving.

Placing the happiness and best interests of their intimates ahead of their own, they are patient, understanding, and supportive. They have a sense of duty and obligation not only to the beloved but also to other people and to society in general. They are dependable and will come through in a crisis. Giving lovers are compassionate, altruistic, committed, loyal, and patient.

Giving lovers gradually develop, rather than fall into, love. They seek an ideal love relationship rather than an ideal type of person. Giving lovers try to perceive and accept the needs of the intimate and derive more pleasure from giving than from receiving. They have the ability to allow the partner to do what he/she needs to do and will go so far as to tolerate the partner's participation in activities that are incompatible with their own values. The giving lover will even consider giving up the intimate if that will be to the intimate's benefit, even though there will be personal pain felt as a result of the loss. The giving lover does not want to stand in the intimate's way and understands the old saying that "it is better to have loved and lost than never to have loved at all."

Pitfalls. Too much giving of any kind can become irritating rather than special. A relationship is likely to become boring if one partner excessively puts the needs and wants of the other ahead of his/her own. This is especially true in the sexual area, where at least some self-interest is needed. If one partner is so concerned with giving that she/he becomes a spectator rather than a true participant, sex can lose its excitement.

Possessive Love

Possessive lovers view jealousy as an integral part of being in love, and make statements such as "I am jealous because I love you so much" or "If you loved me, you would be more jealous." Obsessed with love, they require attention and affection and togetherness.

The possessive lover requires much time with his intimate and cannot tolerate times apart. Even brief separations elicit frequent phone calls.

Preoccupied with thoughts of the intimate, the possessive lover showers him/her with attention. Operating on the assumption that true love is not easy, he is upset over little slights, is elated by dramatic moments of coming together, and has a need to create problems when none exist. The possessive lover feels that this important love must be constantly tested, and emotional agitation is a small price to pay when experiencing deep love.

Pitfalls. Although many people like to possess an intimate completely, or feel security in being possessed, the jealousy, clinging, and forced togetherness of possessive love inevitably create problems. A possessive lover will eventually become burdensome to a more self-sufficient partner.

Practical Love

Practical lovers plan their lives, relying more on logical thoughts than on feelings. They realistically evaluate their own assets, appraise their "market value," and try to obtain the best possible deal in a partner. The practical lover, when involved with the right person, will be dependable and loving and will be committed to the mutual solution of any problems that might arise.

In a sense, this is shopping-list love; the person decides what particular assets he or she wants and then attempts to find a suitable partner. Practical lovers choose a partner for their planned lifestyle, commit themselves to finding a commonsense, practical solution to everyday problems, and accept a less idealistic view of love with fewer unrealistic expectations. Not surprisingly, they usually have stable relationships.

A practical lover will not select a mate who deviates too far from the ideal pattern.

Pitfalls. Problems will occur if one of the partners can no longer meet the needs of the other, or if one partner decides to pursue different life objectives which are unacceptable to the other. Practical lovers will at first attempt to find a rational solution to the incompatibility and will often consider professional help. If they cannot come up with an acceptable solution, they may plan a separation or a divorce based upon practical considerations — such as when the partner completes college or when a certain goal is reached or when the children grow older.

Game-Playing Love

Game-playing lovers try to minimize dependency and commitment. The game, when properly played, controls involvement and prevents the participants from being hurt. Partners best suited for this lovestyle are undemanding and self-sufficient.

By having two or more partners at the same time, the game-playing lover can lessen commitment, increase excitement, and have someone in reserve so that he or she can quickly move on if problems arise. Variety and good times are the goal, and as much emphasis is placed on playing the game as on winning the prize.

Placing emphasis on quantity, game-players are good at meeting people and are not too selective in their choice of partners. The philosophy is that if you're not with the one you love, then love the one you're with. Love is a game with much fun while it lasts. Game-players thrive on excitement and challenge.

Pitfalls. Although game-playing lovers try to avoid involvement and commitment, one partner may lose the feeling of detachment and fall into the well. Becoming overly involved is likely to result in problems. The game is no longer fun, and unless both participants are willing to modify the rules, the game is abruptly terminated. A particularly awkward, though not infrequent, situation occurs when one partner is a possessive lover.

Game-players, at times, feel guilty about their lovestyle. Many of them view game-playing as a fun stage to pass through, rather than as a permanent lifestyle.

Erotic Love

Erotic lovers search for their preconceived physical ideal. They emphasize quality rather than quantity, believe in the possibility of love at first sight, and become excited and energized when they finally find love. The closer the partner comes to the ideal — body build, face hair, height, skin, fragrance, voice, intellect, personality — the more the enchantment.

Sex and deep personal sharing usually come early because once the potential ideal person appears, the erotic lover wants to plunge into the relationship.

Commitment at first is intense, with a desire to discuss experiences ranging from day-to-day activities to past lovers to childhood memories. Erotic lovers enter into a monogamous relationship, experiment with sexual techniques, and search for new ways to please each other. Erotic love, like a fire on which most of the available logs have been piled, burns at first with great intensity — but like the fire, the intensity is destined to diminish.

Pitfalls. Erotic love, with its intensity of emotions, has many peaks and valleys. The powerful attraction of the first several weeks provides the exhilaration of being on a high mountain, but coming down is inevitable. Successful erotic lovers appreciate what they have and are willing to settle for less than the highest peak. Other erotic lovers, unable to sustain the initial excitement and unwilling to tolerate lower levels of passion, move on and often enter into a series of intense monogamous relationships.

COMPATIBLE COMBINATIONS

In general, intimates with the same style of loving are compatible. An exception might be possessive lovers who, propelled by jealousy and restrained by holding on too tightly, have a roller-coaster type of relationship. The most stable and enduring relationships occur between friendship lovers, between giving lovers, and between practical lovers, in the above order. Game-players get along best with other game-players, but the emphasis is on fun together while it lasts, rather than on making future plans. Erotics, despite the ecstasy of the first few months, will fare best if they accept the inevitable lessening of the romance and if they supplement their erotic style with an additional lovestyle.

Intimates with different lovestyles can also form compatible combinations. The possibilities are listed below:

- Friendship — with Giving or Practical

- Giving — with all types except Game-Playing

- Possessive — with Giving, and under the right circumstances with Practical or Erotic, or to a lesser extent with Friendship

- Practical — with Giving or Friendship and, under the right circumstances, with all the other types

- Game-Playing — best with Game-Playing, but under the right circumstances, with Practical

- Erotic — under the right circumstances with Friendship, Giving, Practical, or Possessive, if that person meets erotic ideals

When analyzing compatibilities, remember that a person's pattern in all six of the lovestyles has great importance. To look only at the highest score would be oversimplifying the complicated way in which a person loves.

(Martin Rosenman, *Loving Styles: A Guide for Increasing Intimacy* (NY: Prentice-Hall, 1979), pp. 6–24. Adapted with permission of the author.)

Critical Thinking/Personal Reflection

1. Based on your knowledge, experience, and what you have observed and read, how would you define love? If you wanted to measure love, what behaviors, in addition to the ones discussed in the text, do you think would be important to observe?

2. If you have been in love, **why** do you think you were? Think in terms of specific attitudes, feelings and behaviors. What led you to fall in love with the particular person(s) you did? How do your answers compare to what is in the text?

3. Have you even been jealous? **Why** do you think you were? Have you ever been involved with a partner who was extremely jealous? In each or both of the previous situations described, how did you deal with it? How do your answers compare to the discussion in the text?

4. What is the connection between love and sex for you? What knowledge and/or experiences have contributed to shaping your values on this subject?

5. In light of the discussion in the text, do you have sex and/or relationships on **your** terms? How, if at all, could you improve in this area?

6. What kinds of thoughts do you say to yourself regarding the possibility or the reality of being rejected? How do your fears of rejection restrict or inhibit the number and quality of relationships you have, if at all? How might you alter your perception of rejection in order to allow yourself to comfortably take more risks in this area?

7. If self-love is the foundation for a satisfying intimate relationship, how do you assess the degree and quality of your own self-love? Give specific examples of how you demonstrate interest, concern, and respect for yourself. How might you improve in this area, if at all?

Chapter Overview With Fill-In Answers

1. Zick Rubin; love scale
2. attachment; intimacy
3. philia
4. Passionate
5. Companionate
6. triangular; commitment
7. eight
8. pragmatic
9. phenylethylamine (PEA)
10. proximity
11. similarity
12. reciprocity
13. Physical attractiveness
14. self-love
15a. inclusion
15b. response
15c. care

15d. trust
15e. affection
15f. playfulness
15g. genitality
16. women; men
17. convergence
18. value
19. enhance
20. envy
21. attractiveness; popularity
22. wealth; fame
23. acknowledge; deny
24. best friend
25. inclusion
26. sexual
27. routine

Matching Answers

1. c   2. d   3. e   4. h   5. b   6. h   7. f   8. a
9. c   10. i   11. a   12. g   13. b   14. j

Multiple Choice Answers

1. b   2. c   3. d   4. b   5. d   6. a   7. d   8. c
9. d   10. a   11. d   12. b   13. b   14. a   15. a   16. c
17. a   18. b   19. d   20. d   21. c   22. c   23. d   24. b

8

Communication in Sexual Behavior

Introduction

Being able to talk easily and comfortably about our bodies and our sexuality is an important aspect of developing sexual intimacy with a partner. This chapter opens with a discussion on why sexual communication is difficult and goes on to elaborate on strategies used to initiate sexual interaction with a partner. The heart of the chapter focuses on specific communication techniques that couples can use, and a number of examples are provided in order to illustrate the application of these techniques.

Review of Key Terms and Concepts

Key terms and concepts are listed and defined below. Refer to the subject index in the back of your textbook for additional information.

1. **mutual empathy** — the underlying knowledge that each partner in a relationship cares for the other and knows that the care is reciprocated

2. **passive listening** — staring blankly into space, perhaps mumbling an "uh-huh" now and then while another person is talking

3. **active listening** — being actively involved in what another person is saying by attentive body language and facial expressions, asking questions, paraphrasing and reciprocating

4. **unconditional positive regard** — conveying to other people that you will continue to value and care about them no matter what they do or say

5. **paraphrasing** — summarizing, in your own words, the content or the feelings of another person's message

6. **yes or no questions** — a question that requires only a yes or no answer

7. **open-ended questions** — questions that allow the respondent to elaborate on his or her answer, as opposed to replying either "yes" or "no."

8. **either/or questions** — in asking a person a question, offering two alternative responses in the form of an either/or question, e.g. "do you like making love with the lights on or off?"

9. **I language** — sharing some personal information about yourself in hopes that the person with whom you are speaking will do the same

10. **validating** — encouraging and reassuring another person that it is okay to talk about specific feelings or wants

11. **self-disclosure** — taking responsibility by speaking in the first person when expressing feelings and wants as opposed to using "you" statements which tend to be more accusatory and judgmental

12. **giving permission** — acknowledging another person's point of view, even if you do not agree with it or have no intention of giving up your own position

13. **alexithymia** — the inability to put one's feelings or emotions into words

14. **normative male alexithymia** — a relatively common condition among men in which they are unaware of their feelings and/or unable to express them

15. **individualism** — a cultural ideology that places greater emphasis on the individual than on the couple or group

16. **collectivism** — a cultural ideology that focuses on the couple or group rather than on the individual

Chapter Overview With Fill-Ins

After reading each of the major sections in the chapter, check your retention by filling in each of the blanks in the corresponding sections below. The answers are provided at the end of the chapter.

The Importance of Communication

1. The basis for effective sexual communication is _____ _____ — the underlying knowledge that each partner in the relationship cares for the other and knows the care is reciprocated.

2. One reason why sexual communication is difficult has to do with the way we were _____ as children, which often contributes to negative attitudes, shame, or embarrassment about sexual matters.

3. A second reason relates to the lack of a suitable _____ of sex.

4. Another factor that can hinder communication between heterosexual partners is _____-_____ communication styles.

5. Finally, _____ about sexual communication may also be a problem.

Talking: Getting Started

6. The authors suggest three ways to "break the ice:" (a) _____ _____ _____; reading and (b) _____ a variety of books and articles on sexual topics that may provide the stimulus for personal conversations; and sharing sexual (c) _____.

Listening and Feedback

7. One listening skill involves being an active vs. a _____ listener.

8. Another skill, maintaining _____ _____, is one of the most vital aspects of good verbal communication.

9. Providing _____ is another listening skill that helps to clarify how you have perceived your partner's comments and also indicates that you are actively listening.

10. Because communicating about sexual matters can make a person feel quite vulnerable, _____ our partner's communication efforts when they do talk can help foster mutual _____ as well as encourage them to continue to communicate openly and candidly with us.

11. The concept of _____ _____ _____ means conveying to our partners the sense that we will continue to value and care for them regardless of what they do or say.

12. A final listening skill, _____, prevents miscommunication from occurring as it clarifies discrepancies between the communicator's intent and the listener's interpretation.

Discovering Your Partner's Needs

13. One of the most obvious ways to learn about our partner's needs is to simply ask _____.

14. You may ask yes or no, either/or, or _____-_____ questions, depending on the effect you are trying to achieve.

15. In addition to asking questions, the technique of _____-_____, or sharing your feelings regarding a particular topic, may often encourage your partner to reciprocate.

16. _____ _____ is a very natural way to discover our partner's preferences in food, music, entertainment, etc.; it can also be a way to discover our partner's sexual preferences as well.

17. Finally, a technique called _____ _____ is a way of encouraging and reassuring our partners to talk about specific feelings or needs.

Learning to Make Requests

18. Learning to ask for what you want is an integral part of sexual communication, and to begin with, it is important to take _____ for your own pleasure.

19. In asking for what you want, it is important to make your requests _____, which will maximize the possibility of your partner understanding and following through on your request.

20. In addition, using "_____" language brings the desired response more often than a general statement does.

Giving and Receiving Criticism

21. In order to give criticism effectively, be aware of your _____ in criticizing your partner.

22. A second consideration in delivering criticism is to choose the right time and _____.

23. It is also a good idea to temper the criticism with _____, or to focus on some positive aspect of your partner or the relationship in expressing your concerns.

24. Keep in mind that _____, or reverting back to old patterns and behaviors, is natural and predictable, and people typically don't alter these patterns overnight.

25. It is important to nurture _____ steps toward changes in hopes of ultimately getting what you want instead of criticizing what has not changed.

26. Avoid asking "_____" questions; these are usually thinly veiled attempts to criticize or attack our partners instead of taking responsibility for how we are feeling and what we want.

27. Express anger appropriately by focusing on the _____ as opposed to the _____ of your partner.

28. Use "_____" statements as opposed to _____ statements.

29. Finally, limit your criticism to _____ complaint per discussion.

30. In order to respond effectively to criticism, you can begin by _____ with your partner and _____ the criticism to make certain you understand exactly what your partner's concerns are.

31. Secondly, you can, if appropriate, _____ the criticism and find something with which you can agree.

32. Asking _____ questions is also helpful, especially if your partner's criticism is a bit vague.

33. You can also express your _____ in regard to the criticism rather than letting these emotions dictate your response.

34. Finally, an excellent closure to receiving criticism is to focus on future _____ that the two of you can make in order to improve the situation.

Saying No

35. One approach for saying no to invitations for intimate involvements includes three distinct phases: Step 1: express (a) _____ for the invitation, and if you want, (b) _____ the value of the other person; Step 2: say no in a clear, unequivocal fashion; and Step 3: offer an (c) _____, if appropriate.

36. Another aspect to consider in saying no is to avoid inconsistencies between _____ messages and subsequent actions either in your behavior or in that of your partner's.

Nonverbal Sexual Communication

37. Components of nonverbal communication that we should be aware of in communicating sexually with our partner are: _____ expression, _____ distance, touching, and making and hearing sounds.

Impasses

38. If your discussion with your partner results in an impasse, there are several options that might be helpful: try to see things from your partner's perspective; (a) _____ your partner's position; take a (b) _____ from each other for a while; schedule another time to talk; grant your partner the right not to (c) _____; or seek professional (d) _____.

Matching

Match each term below with the appropriate communication. Each letter is used only once.

a. mutual empathy
b. unconditional positive regard
c. "why" question
d. paraphrase
e. either/or question
f. yes/no question
g. open-ended question
h. self-disclosure
i. comparing notes
j. giving permission
k. specific request

_____1. Your partner says "I love how you talk to me when we make love" and you respond: "So you like that sweet talk, huh?"

_____2. "Do you like it when I kiss the back of your arm?"

_____3. "It's a good feeling to trust you and care about you so much, and to know you feel that way about me too."

_____4. "Do you like it when I undress you, or do you prefer to do it yourself?"

_____5. "You know how much I love you, but when you avoid being affectionate or intimate I feel very frustrated."

_____6. "Tell me where you like to be touched."

_____7. "It is difficult for me to talk about my abuse because it is still so painful for me, but each time I do I feel so much better because I feel you really care and understand."

_____8. "I would really like you to be on top this time. I love being able to watch you, and I like how you take control when you're on top."

_____9. "Why don't you ever want to go down on me?"

_____10. "I love it when you touch me very lightly with your nails or fingertips, but it seems like when I do that for you it tickles. Is that right?"

_____11. "Since you've been taking that belly-dancing class, I know you've been shy about practicing in front of me. But I just want you to know that I would **love** it; you're so sensual when you dance like that: I just love watching you."

Sample Short Answer Test Questions

1. Define mutual empathy.

2. List four reasons why sexual communication may be difficult.

3. According to Deborah Tannen, how do men and women use language differently?

4. List and describe three strategies for initiating sexual communication.

5. Define unconditional positive regard.

6. Paraphrase the following comment: "It seems like I'm the only one who ever wants to have sex around here."

7. What are the **advantages** and **disadvantages** of the following types of questions:
    a. yes or no

    b. open-ended

    c. either/or

8. Assume that you are interested in talking to your partner about the possibility of acting out some sexual fantasies together. Provide an example for each of the following types of questions in this situation.

   a. yes or no

   b. open-ended

   c. either/or

9. Describe some of the factors that may contribute to normative male alexithymia.

10. Briefly describe four phases of Levant's treatment strategy for normative male alexithymia.

11. What communication strategy eliminates the problem of your partner having to use his or her intuition to figure out what you want?

12. Rewrite the following statement using "I" language: "You are always in such a rush to have intercourse."

13. At what times or in what situations is delivering criticism inappropriate?

14. Rewrite the following complaint tempering the criticism with praise: "Whenever we have sex, it's because I initiate it."

15. What is the underlying motive behind a "why" question?

16. Distinguish between "I" and "you" statements. **Give an example of each**.

17. Empathize with and/or paraphrase the following criticism: "You never want to experiment with anything new."

18. Use the strategy of acknowledgment in response to the following criticism: "You expect me to have sex with you after you have just finished working out?"

19. Write a comment that would express your feeling in response to the following criticism: "You never seem to enjoy it very much when we have sex."

20. List the three steps that are suggested for saying no to a sexual invitation.

21. If your partner is sending you mixed messages, how do the authors suggest that you respond?

22. Name four important components of nonverbal sexual communication.

23. List six ways that a couple might respond to a communication impasse.

24. Distinguish among white Americans, African-Americans, Hispanic Americans and Asian-Americans in regard to the following:

   a. verbal and nonverbal communication

   b. individualism vs. collectivism

   c. how conflict is perceived and dealt with

Sample Multiple Choice Test Questions

1. Mutual empathy is
   a. caring for someone regardless of what they do or say.
   b. the basis for effective sexual communication.
   c. a suggested technique for "breaking the ice" in sexual conversations.
   d. a communication technique whereby both partners use "you" statements.

2. A suggested technique for getting started talking about sex is
    a. asking which method of birth control your partner prefers.
    b. seeing an erotic film together.
    c. self-disclosing the nature of any sexually transmitted diseases you have had and asking the other person to do the same.
    d. sharing sexual histories.

3. _____ is when a listener summarizes, in his or her own words, the speaker's message.
    a. Paraphrasing
    b. Validating
    c. Using "I" language
    d. Passive listening.

4. Unconditional positive regard is best described as
    a. positively acknowledging any type of criticism being received.
    b. a feeling of being spiritually connected to your partner.
    c. caring for your partner as a person regardless of what he or she says or does.
    d. the knowledge that each partner in a relationship cares for the other and knows the care is reciprocated.

5. A (an) _____ question would allow your partner the freedom to share any relevant information or feelings.
    a. yes or no
    b. either/or
    c. open-ended
    d. structured

6. Which of the following types of questions does **not** belong with the others?
    a. "What are your feelings about having sex during my menstrual period?"
    b. "What do you enjoy most about our lovemaking?"
    c. "Do you think the kids should see us naked?"
    d. "How do you feel about having sex in the morning?"

7. Sharing fantasies is suggested as one way to
    a. self-disclose.
    b. give permission.
    c. express unconditional positive regard.
    d. deliver criticism.

8. Which of the following is an example of giving permission?
    a. "I had a very traumatic sexual experience about a year ago. Since then I've had a difficult time relaxing and enjoying sex."
    b. "I realize that you're not real comfortable with nudity, but I love to look at your naked body, so anytime you want to practice feeling more comfortable, let me know."
    c. "Do you like making love in unusual places?"
    d. "I have had this fantasy about having sex with you in the bathroom while we're at a party together."

9. Which of the following does **not** belong with the others?
    a. self-disclosure
    b. comparing notes
    c. giving permission
    d. taking responsibility for your own pleasure

10. When you don't expect your partner to read your mind and you are willing to ask for what you want, you are
    a. comparing notes.
    b. taking responsibility for your own pleasure.
    c. giving permission.
    d. expressing unconditional positive regard.

11. Which of the following is a strategy for discovering your partner's needs?
    a. maintaining eye contact
    b. paraphrasing
    c. expressing unconditional positive regard
    d. self-disclosure

12. Requests are **most** likely to be understood and heeded if they
    a. are specific.
    b. are vague, so your partner doesn't feel threatened.
    c. are general, so your conversation remains open-ended.
    d. are made on a regular basis.

13. Which of the following is **not** a suggested technique for learning to make requests?
    a. taking responsibility for your own pleasure
    b. giving permission
    c. using "I" language
    d. making requests specific

14. Delivering criticism will be **most** effective if the motive behind the criticism is to
    a. let your partner know that you have been hurt and are not willing to take it anymore.
    b. bring about a change that will enhance the relationship.
    c. put your partner on the defensive, thereby making him/her more willing to listen to you.
    d. get even with your partner for not paying enough attention to you.

15. Before verbalizing a complaint to your partner, it is a good idea to
    a. rehearse what you want to say, using "you" statements.
    b. frame your complaints in general terms; specific statements will put your partner on the defensive.
    c. list all of your complaints so you do not forget to mention all of them.
    d. be aware of your motivation behind offering the criticism.

16. All of the following are suggestions for receiving criticism **except**
    a. ask clarifying questions
    b. focus on future changes you can make
    c. empathize with your partner
    d. express unconditional positive regard

17. Which of the following is **not** one of the suggested steps for saying no?
    a. Say no in a clear, straightforward manner.
    b. State specific consequences in the event that the person doesn't accept no for an answer.
    c. Express appreciation for the invitation.
    d. Offer an alternative, if appropriate.

18. Which of the following is the **best** example of a mixed message?
    a. Your partner says, "I know it's cold, but I want to make love outside anyway."
    b. Your partner says, "I know I said we could make love tonight, but I'm really tired. How about in the morning?"
    c. Your partner says, "Let's go park somewhere on the way home," and then falls asleep in the car.
    d. None of the above are examples of mixed messages.

19. When we speak of facial expression, touching and sounds, we are referring to the _____ aspects of sexual communication.
    a. nonverbal
    b. verbal
    c. intuitive
    d. interpersonal

20. Tom and Sherry have become frustrated in their communication with one another and have decided to take a break from discussion for a while. They are even considering seeking some counseling. According to the text, they are facing _____ in their communication.
    a. "the wall"
    b. an impasse
    c. a point of no return
    d. a crisis point

Critical Thinking/Personal Reflection

1. Spend some time thinking about your communication skills — with your partner or past partners, friends and family members. How would **you** assess your communication skills — and how do you think the significant other people in your life would assess them? In the space below, list some of the specific models in your life for interpersonal communication — parents or other primary caretakers, teachers, other adults or family members, friends, counselors, clergy, etc. What did you learn from each of these people — both positive and negative — about how to express your thoughts and feelings, deal with conflict, listen and show respect for another person's point of view, give and receive criticism, acknowledge and support someone, etc.?

2. Based on your assessment above, identify and list below some **specific** communication skills you would like to improve — regarding your sexual relationship or just social/emotional relationships in general (all of the skills discussed in this chapter are applicable in nonsexual situations as well).

3.   List past, current or future situations in which you would like to implement better communication skills. Based on information in the text, attempt to mentally rehearse these situations using better or different skills than you have used in the past. Then practice aloud, if possible, the way in which you might express yourself in a different way. Finally, role play this scenario with a partner or close friend — allow yourself some "simulated real life" practice. Get feedback from the other person. Offer to role play a situation of theirs if you would like. It will be awkward at first, but you will begin to become conscious of specific behaviors you would like to change, and over time, with practice, you will notice significant improvement.

4.   Finally, if you are really serious about improving your skills in this area, take a class or workshop, read a book, see a counselor that specializes in communication skills development. Learning good communication — both verbal and nonverbal — is much like learning a new language, but the benefits will pay off for you many times over in improved relationships in your personal and professional life.

Chapter Overview With Fill-In Answers

1. mutual empathy
2. socialized
3. language
4. gender-based
5. anxieties
6a. talking about talking
6b. discussing
6c. histories
7. passive
8. eye contact
9. feedback
10. supporting; empathy
11. unconditional positive regard
12. paraphrasing
13. questions
14. open-ended
15. self-disclosure
16. Comparing notes
17. giving permission
18. responsibility
19. specific
20. I
21. motivation

22. place
23. praise
24. backsliding
25. small
26. why
27. behavior; character
28. I; you
29. one
30. empathizing; paraphrasing
31. acknowledge
32. clarifying
33. feelings
34. changes
35a. appreciation
35b. validate
35c. alternative
36. verbal
37. facial; interpersonal
38a. validate
38b. break
38c. change
38d. counseling

Matching Answers

1. d	2. f	3. a	4. e	5. b	6. g	7. h	8. k
9. c	10. f, i	11. j					

Sample Multiple Choice Answers

1. b	2. d	3. a	4. c	5. c	6. c	7. a	8. b
9. d	10. b	11. d	12. a	13. b	14. b	15. d	16. d
17. b	18. c	19. a	20. b				

9

Sexual Behaviors

Introduction

Sexuality may be expressed in many ways, including decisions to practice celibacy, to engage in erotic dreams and fantasy, masturbation, oral-genital sex, tribadism, anal stimulation, and coitus. Making references to a variety of research studies as well as personal anecdotes selected from their files, the authors explore the range of options for sexual behavior in both heterosexual and homosexual relationships.

Review of Key Terms and Concepts

Key terms and concepts are listed and defined below. Refer to the subject index in the back of your textbook for additional information.

1. **complete celibacy** — a physically mature person who does not masturbate or have sexual contact with another person

2. **partial celibacy** — a physically mature person who engages in masturbation but does not have interpersonal sexual contact with another person

3. **nocturnal orgasm** — orgasm that occurs during sleep; it is experienced by both men and women

4. **masturbation (autoeroticism)** — self-stimulation of one's genitals for sexual pleasure

5. **cunnilingus** — oral stimulation of the vulva

6. **fellatio** — oral stimulation of the penis and scrotum

7. **sodomy** — an ill-defined legal category for noncoital genital contacts such as oral-genital and anal intercourse

8. **intromission** — entry of the penis into the vagina

9. **coitus** — penile-vaginal intercourse

10. **tribadism** — rubbing genitals against someone's body or genital area

11. **analingus** — oral stimulation of the anus

Chapter Overview With Fill-Ins

After reading each of the major sections in the chapter, check your retention by filling in each of the blanks in the corresponding sections below. The answers are provided at the end of the chapter.

Celibacy

1. A physically mature person who does not engage in sexual behavior is said to be
    _____.

2. There are two types of celibacy: _____ celibacy, in which a person neither masturbates nor has sexual contact with another person; and _____ celibacy, in which a person engages in masturbation but does not have sexual contact with anyone else.

Erotic Dreams and Fantasy

3. Erotic dreams and occasionally _____ may occur during sleep without a person's conscious direction.

4. _____ orgasm occurs during sleep in men and women, commonly referred to as "_____ _____" in men.

5. Erotic fantasies commonly occur during daydreams, _____, or sexual encounters with a partner.

6. Fantasies serve a variety of functions during intercourse, the most common of which is to facilitate _____ _____.

7. Similar percentages of men and women fantasize while masturbating about having _____ with a loved one.

8. Erotic fantasies are generally considered a healthy and helpful aspect of sexuality, although sometimes they have also been considered symptomatic of poor _____ relations or other problems.

Masturbation

9. Masturbation is used to describe _____-_____ of one's genitals for sexual pleasure.

10. Many of the negative attitudes toward masturbation are rooted in the early Judeo-Christian view that _____ was the only legitimate purpose of sexual behavior.

11. The most commonly reported reason for masturbating is to relieve _____ _____.

12. In adulthood, the _____ of men and women, both married and unmarried, masturbate on occasion.

13. The _____ hierarchy of sexual interactions is a model that describes _____ levels of constructive or _____ sexual expression.

Kissing and Touching

14. A classic study demonstrated that when baby monkeys' and other primates' physical needs were met but they were denied their mothers' touch, they grew up to be extremely _____.

15. The entire body responds to touching, but some specific areas are more receptive to _____ _____ than others.

16. In touching the vulva, a lubricant such as K-Y jelly, a lotion without _____, or saliva can be used.

17. In touching male genitals, gentle or firm stroking of the penile shaft and _____, and light touches or tugging on the scrotum may be desired.

18. Some men find that lubrication with lotion or _____ increases pleasure.

19. Some men enjoy manual stimulation or penetration of the _____.

Oral-Genital Stimulation

20. _____ is oral stimulation of the vulva and _____ is oral stimulation of the penis and scrotum.

21. Both of Kinsey's studies found that, in heterosexual couples, _____ were much less likely to stimulate partners orally than the reverse.

22. Experience with oral-genital sex may be affected by race, religion, educational levels and _____ status.

Anal Stimulation

23. Like oral-genital stimulation, anal stimulation may be thought by some to be a _____ act.

24. However, penile penetration of the anus is practiced regularly by about _____ percent of heterosexual couples.

25. Some women report _____ response from anal intercourse.

26. Heterosexual and homosexual men often experience _____ from stimulation during penetration.

27. Heterosexual couples should never have _____ intercourse directly following anal intercourse because bacteria that are normal in the anus often cause _____.

Gay and Lesbian Sexual Expression

28. There are several differences between sexual expression in lesbians and heterosexual women, such as the fact that lesbians tend to have _____ in a greater percentage of sexual encounters than do heterosexual married women.

29. A mistaken belief is that _____ are used extensively among lesbians.

30. The most common mode of sexual expression among gay men is _____.

31. _____ is the next most common form of sexual expression among gay men, followed by _____.

Coitus and Coital Positions

32. There are a wide range of positions a couple may choose for penile-vaginal intercourse, or _____.

33. Some couples may find mutual cooperation during _____ (entry of the penis into the vagina) helpful.

34. _____ can be a good intercourse position to use during pregnancy.

Sample Short Answer Test Questions

1. List at least five advantages of celibacy.

2. List three disadvantages of celibacy.

3. How common is sexual fantasy among men and women? Cite specific statistics.

4. What may contribute to increased sexual fantasizing?

5. According to Maltz and Boss study, what were the six common categories of roles women played in their fantasies?

6. List four functions that fantasies may serve.

7. A certain percentage of both men and women fantasize about being forced to have sex. How do their reasons for doing this differ?

8. Summarize how the content of men's and women's fantasies differ.

9. List the two most common sexual fantasies **during masturbation** for women. Then, list two for men. (refer to table 9.2)

10. List the two most common sexual fantasies **during intercourse** for men. Then, list two for women. (refer to table 9.3)

11. Under what circumstances can sexual fantasizing be problematic?

12. From an historical perspective, why has masturbation been perceived as evil and unhealthy?

13. What was Freud's perception regarding masturbation?

14. How does the Vatican describe masturbation?

15. List eight benefits of masturbation.

16. List several factors that are characteristic of adults who masturbate regularly.

17. Compare the incidence of masturbation among whites, African-Americans and Hispanics. How does educational level relate to incidence of masturbation?

18. What is the most common self-stimulation technique for women? The least common?

19. List and briefly describe the six levels of sexual interaction according to Maltz.

20. According to Masters and Johnson, what purposes does touching serve?

21. Describe how breast size is related to breast sensitivity.

22. List three types of lubrication that can be used during manual stimulation.

23. According to Kinsey's research, which was more common — fellatio or cunnilingus?

24. How do race, education, religion, and socioeconomic status affect experience with oral sex?

25. To what sexual behavior(s) does sodomy refer?

26. What percentage of heterosexual couples practice anal intercourse regularly?

27. What percentage of adults have experienced anal intercourse at least once?

28. Can women experience orgasm during anal intercourse?

29. How can the health risks associated with anal intercourse be reduced?

30. Summarize research findings that compare lesbian and heterosexual women's last sexual experience. (refer to table 9.5)

31. How often do lesbians use dildos?

32. Name three sexual behaviors common among lesbians.

33. In one survey, what percentage of gay men liked hugging, kissing and cuddling more than any other sexual behavior?

34. List in order of frequency the types of sexual behavior common to gay men.

35. What is a good intercourse position during pregnancy?

Sample Multiple Choice Test Questions

Select the best alternative. Check your answers with the answer key at the end of the chapter.

1. John and Rita have just begun a sexual relationship. They both enjoy how creative and uninhibited they are sexually, and their comfort with role flexibility allows them to communicate with each other more freely and to enjoy greater intimacy. According to the Maltz hierarchy of sexual interaction, this couple would probably be at _____ level.
    a. −1; irresponsible interaction
    b. +1; positive role fulfillment
    c. +2; making love
    d. +3; authentic sexual intimacy

2. In partial celibacy, a person
    a. neither masturbates nor has sexual contact with another person.
    b. engages in masturbation but does not have sexual contact with another person.
    c. engages in masturbation and oral sex but not sexual intercourse.
    d. does not masturbate or have sexual contact with another person for at least six months.

3. According to the text, for which of the following reasons would a person be **most likely** to say that he or she was celibate?
    a. The person has sexual problems and does not want to acknowledge them.
    b. The person is not sexually interested in the other party, so this is a way of extricating himself or herself from the situation.
    c. The person is newly recovering from drug dependency.
    d. The person wants to see how the other person will react.

4. The most common fantasy that men have during masturbation is
    a. sex with more than one person of the other sex.
    b. oral sex with stranger.
    c. intercourse with a loved one.
    d. being forced to have sex.

5. According to one study, the highest percentage of men reported which of the following as their fantasy content during intercourse?
    a. oral-genital sex
    b. having others give in to you after resisting
    c. group sex
    d. sex with a former lover

6. A review of the research found that about _____% of men and women reported having had sexual fantasies.
    a. 40
    b. 65
    c. 80
    d. 95

7. Which of the following statements concerning sexual fantasy is **true**?
    a. Twice as many women as men fantasize about being forced to have sex.
    b. Many sex therapists encourage their clients to use fantasy as a source of stimulation.
    c. One purpose of fantasy is to relieve boredom.
    d. All of the above are true statements.

8. Which of the following is **not** a word for masturbation?
   a. autoeroticism
   b. fellatio
   c. self-stimulation
   d. "jerking off"

9. Which of the following **best** describes Reverend Sylvester Graham's view of masturbation?
   a. It does not result in procreation, therefore it is sinful.
   b. Since ejaculation reduces precious vital fluids, masturbation, as well as intercourse, should be avoided.
   c. Masturbation is normal during childhood but could result in "immature" sexual development in adulthood.
   d. Masturbation is how we discover eroticism, so it should be learned and practiced.

10. Which of the following statements is **true**?
    a. Women appear to use a greater variety of masturbatory techniques than men.
    b. Some men, and to a greater degree women, enjoy using vibrators for added sexual pleasure.
    c. According to one study, females wanted to spend more time in foreplay and afterplay than men.
    d. All of the above are true statements.

11. A way to tell if you are "masturbating to excess" is when
    a. it interferes significantly with any aspect of your life.
    b. your hand develops calluses.
    c. you begin to lose your eyesight.
    d. you sleep frequently due to your constant state of relaxation.

12. Which of the following individuals would be **least likely** to masturbate?
    a. a single, college educated African-American man
    b. a married, high school educated white woman
    c. a single, high school educated Hispanic woman
    d. a married, college educated African-American man

13. In regard to breast stimulation, which of the following statements is **most** accurate?
    a. Men do not enjoy having their nipples stimulated.
    b. The size of the breasts is not related to how erotically sensitive they are.
    c. Women can become highly aroused by breast stimulation but are unable to achieve orgasm this way without additional clitoral stimulation.
    d. A woman's breasts are usually tender immediately following her menstrual period.

14. _____ is oral stimulation of the penis and scrotum.
    a. Oralingus
    b. Analingus
    c. Fellatio
    d. Cunnilingus

15. Which of the following statements concerning oral-genital sex is **true**?
    a. The risk of contracting HIV while practicing this behavior is high.
    b. "69" is another term for cunnilingus.
    c. Career women are more likely than homemakers to consider oral sex a normal act.
    d. The incidence of oral sex has decreased over the last forty years

16. Sodomy refers to
    a. rear-entry coitus.
    b. oral-genital stimulation.
    c. anal intercourse.
    d. oral-genital stimulation and anal intercourse.

17. Which of the following statements concerning anal intercourse is **true**?
    a. Oral-genital sex is more risky than anal intercourse in terms of HIV transmission.
    b. Due to the scarcity of nerve endings surrounding the anus, most of the pleasure comes from depth of penetration.
    c. It is practiced regularly by about 20 percent of heterosexual couples.
    d. If vaginal intercourse is also practiced during the sexual encounter, it should precede anal intercourse.

18. An encyclopedia of health published in 1918 describes the effects of masturbation as
    a. extremely debilitating, resulting in the hopeless ruin of mind and body.
    b. a potential health hazard if not monitored closely.
    c. inconsequential in terms of physical or mental health.
    d. extremely positive, in that it increases self-awareness and reduces tension.

Critical Thinking/Personal Reflection

1a. If you began dating someone to whom you were very attracted who announced that he or she was celibate, how would you respond? Think in terms of your verbal response as well as what you would say to yourself.

1b. Do you think your reaction to a person's choice to be celibate would vary depending upon the person's gender? If so, why?

2. Do you engage in sexual fantasy alone and/or with a partner? If so, what functions do your fantasies serve? What is the content of your fantasies during masturbation and/or intercourse? How does this compare to the information presented in the text?

3. What are your feelings regarding masturbation? Is it something you do and enjoy, do and feel somewhat guilty and ashamed of, or choose to not do at all? If you do engage in masturbation, is it something you would acknowledge with your partner or avoid discussing? How does it affect your feelings about yourself and/or your relationship with your partner? What are the reasons you choose to masturbate? Is this something you would do in your partner's presence (while your partner held or caressed you) or have your partner do for you? Why or why not? How would you feel if you knew your partner masturbated in addition to being sexually active with you?

4. What are your personal feelings regarding fellatio and cunnilingus? Would you/do you feel comfortable discussing various aspects of these behaviors with your partner (for example: how you feel about genital odors and secretions; your willingness to comfortably give and receive; whether or not you prefer to do this simultaneously, if at all; will the activity culminate in ejaculation for the male partner and if so, is that comfortable/acceptable for the other partner? Will the ejaculate be swallowed or not?) In receiving oral-genital stimulation are you capable of asking specifically for what you want as well as receiving feedback from your partner?

5. Where would you place yourself on the Maltz hierarchy of sexual interactions? Where would you place your partner, if you have one? Is that where you are comfortable being? If not, how might you move to another level?

6. One study of college students indicated that men prefer coitus and women prefer foreplay and afterplay. Based on your knowledge and experience, would you agree with this? If so, why do you think this is the case?

7. Although penile-vaginal intercourse is the "main event" of sexual sharing for many heterosexual couples, that is certainly not the case for everyone. For many individuals, while intercourse may be pleasurable for them, it is not as pleasurable as other activities or it may be difficult to achieve orgasm that way. In addition, individuals with a homosexual orientation, individuals who are physically disabled in some way, or individuals with chronic illnesses or other medical conditions may be unable or unwilling to have intercourse. If you have experienced intercourse, what are your feelings about it? Are you easily aroused and/or orgasmic with intercourse? Is it ever awkward/uncomfortable/painful for you? If so, why? Which coital positions do you prefer? Why? Have you been able to communicate your preferences to your partner? If not, what gets in the way?

8. If you are gay, lesbian or bisexual, how do your experiences compare with what is described in the text? If you could rewrite/edit/add to this chapter, what would you say?

Chapter Overview With Fill-In Answers

1. celibate
2. complete; partial
3. orgasm
4. Nocturnal; wet dreams
5. masturbation
6. sexual arousal
7. intercourse
8. sexual
9. self-stimulation
10. procreation
11. sexual tension
12. majority
13. Maltz; six; destructive
14. maladjusted
15. sexual feelings
16. alcohol
17. glans
18. saliva
19. anus
20. Cunnilingus; fellatio
21. women
22. socioeconomic
23. homosexual
24. 10
25. orgasmic
26. orgasm
27. vaginal; infections
28. orgasms
29. dildos
30. fellatio
31. mutual masturbation; anal intercourse
32. coitus
33. intromission
34. Rear entry

Sample Multiple Choice Answers

1. c
2. b
3. c
4. c
5. a
6. d
7. d
8. b
9. b
10. d
11. a
12. c
13. b
14. c
15. c
16. d
17. d
18. a

10

Sexual Orientations

Introduction

The chapter begins by introducing Kinsey's continuum of sexual orientation. Several types of bisexuality are discussed, followed by various psychosocial and biological theories that have attempted to clarify what determines sexual orientation. Societal attitudes toward homosexuality over time are explored, and the range of homosexual lifestyles is also examined. The chapter concludes with a discussion of some of the social and political issues facing the homosexual population today.

Review of Key Terms and Concepts

Key terms and concepts are listed and defined below. Refer to the subject index in the back of your textbook for additional information.

1. **homosexual** — an individual whose primary erotic, psychological, emotional and social interest is in a member of the same sex, even though those interests may not be overtly expressed

2. **gay** — a common synonym for homosexual

3. **lesbian** — a common term for homosexual women

4. **bisexuality** — attraction to both same-sex and other-sex sex partners

5. **Kinsey's continuum of sexual orientation** — Alfred Kinsey's seven-point scale analyzing sexual orientation, ranging from 0 (exclusive heterosexual contact) to 6 (exclusive homosexual contact)

6. **rejecting-punitive orientation** — a current theological position which unconditionally rejects homosexuality and bears a punitive attitude toward gay people

7. **rejecting-nonpunitive orientation** — a current theological position that maintains that homosexuality is unnatural, but because of God's grace, supports the civil liberties of gay people

8. **qualified acceptance orientation** — a current theological position maintaining that homosexuality is a sin but can't be changed so that gay people who can't refrain from sexual interaction should maintain fully committed relationships

9. **full acceptance** — a current theological position that views sexuality as intrinsic to the capacity for human love, and therefore supports loving relationships regardless of the sexual orientation of the partner

10. **homophobia** — irrational fears of homosexuality in others or within oneself, or self-loathing because of one's homosexuality

11. **gender nonconformity** — the extent to which individuals conform to stereotypic characteristics of masculinity or femininity during childhood

12. **tribadism** — rubbing genitals against someone's body or genital area

13. **coming out** — acknowledging, accepting and openly expressing one's homosexuality; there are several steps involved in this process

14. **passing** — a term that is sometimes used to describe maintaining the false image of heterosexuality

Chapter Overview With Fill-Ins

After reading each of the major sections in the chapter, check your retention by filling in each of the blanks in the corresponding sections below. The answers are provided at the end of the chapter.

A Continuum of Sexual Orientations

1. _____ refers to attraction to both same and other-sex partners.

2. Alfred Kinsey devised a _____-point continuum in his analysis of sexual orientations in American society.

3. The continuum ranges from 0 (exclusive contact with and erotic attraction to the _____ sex) to 6 (exclusive contact with and attraction to the _____ sex).

4. Category 3 represents _____ homosexual and heterosexual attraction and experience.

5. There are several different types of bisexuality: bisexuality as a real _____, as a transitory orientation, as a _____ orientation, or as homosexual _____.

What Determines Sexual Orientation?

6. The "_____" theory explains a homosexual orientation as the result of unhappy heterosexual experiences or the inability to attract partners of the opposite sex.

7. The research of _____ and his colleagues has found no data to support this view.

8. Another myth that research has shown to be false is that young men and women become homosexual because they have been seduced by _____ homosexuals.

9. Some people believe that homosexuality can be "_____" from someone else, i.e., a homosexual teacher, etc.

10. In fact, a homosexual orientation appears to be established before _____ _____, and modeling is not a relevant factor.

11. Freud's theory regarding the development of homosexuality has to do with certain patterns in a person's _____ background.

12. However, it has not been clearly established that _____ factors are the critical determinants in the development of a homosexual orientation.

13. Bem's theory of the development of sexual orientation is based on the premise that the "_____ becomes _____."

14. In addition to psychosocial causes, researchers have looked into a number of areas in an effort to establish _____ causes for sexual orientation.

15. Some researchers have speculated that _____ levels in adults may contribute to homosexuality.

16. Even if consistent differences were found in the hormonal patterns of homosexual and heterosexual adults, it would remain unknown whether the differences were a _____ or a _____ of sexual orientation.

17. Some researchers speculate that _____ hormone imbalances can alter the masculine and feminine development of the fetal _____ and that this may contribute to a homosexual orientation.

18. Simon LeVay reported structural differences in the _____ of homosexual and heterosexual men, supporting a biological explanation for sexual orientation.

19. Other research has confirmed the possibility that _____ factors may contribute to the development of male homosexuality.

20. Bell and his colleagues believe that evidence for a biological predisposition for homosexuality is the strong link between adult homosexuality and _____ _____ as a child.

21. Gender nonconformity is a variable the researchers used that measured the extent to which the research subjects conformed to _____ characteristics of masculinity or femininity during childhood.

22. In conclusion, research is suggesting that there is a _____ predisposition to exclusive homosexuality, but the causes of sexual orientation in general, and homosexuality specifically, remain speculative at this point.

Societal Attitudes

23. Within the Judeo-Christian tradition, homosexuality has been viewed _____.

24. The pursuit of sexual pleasure outside of the purpose of _____ was viewed as immoral.

25. One survey of 190 societies found that _____ of them considered homosexuality socially acceptable for certain individuals or on specific occasions.

26. The Sambia society of New Guinea _____ men to engage in homosexual activities until they marry.

27. One theologian has described four current positions toward homosexuality: 1) a _____-_____ orientation; 2) the rejecting-nonpunitive position; 3) the qualified acceptance position; and finally, 4) the _____ _____ position.

28. The belief that homosexual people are sinners has been replaced to some degree by a belief that they are "_____", and that they can be cured by means of a variety of medical and psychological treatments.

29. However, current research _____ this notion, and in 1973, the American _____ Association removed homosexuality per se from the category of a _____ disorder.

30. _____ is defined as irrational fear of homosexuality in others, the fear of homosexual feelings within _____, or self-loathing because of one's homosexuality.

Lifestyles

31. There are several steps in the process of _____ _____: self-acknowledgment, self-acceptance, disclosure, telling the family, and involvement in the _____ _____.

32. One study reported that heterosexual couples were likely to adhere more closely to traditional _____-_____ expectations than were _____ couples.

33. Lesbians are likely to have had _____ sexual partners, and _____ couples are more likely than male couples to have monogamous relationships.

34. Several studies have found that lesbians differ from homosexual men in the extent to which they associate _____ _____ with sex.

35. Although _____ between two people of the same sex is not legally recognized by any state, many homosexual couples share significant one-to-one relationships.

36. Some homosexual individuals or couples become _____ with adopted or foster children, or they have children who were born in previous _____ marriages.

37. Lesbian mothers have been found to be similar to heterosexual mothers in lifestyle, maternal interest, and _____ behavior.

38. Children may also be adopted or conceived by lesbians through _____ _____.

39. A homosexual man who wants to be a father may make a personal agreement with a woman who agrees to _____ his child.

The Gay Rights Movement

40. The symbolic birth of gay activism occurred in 1969 in _____ _____ _____ when police raided a gay bar, the _____.

41. The Stonewall incident acted as a catalyst for the formation of _____ _____ groups and other activities such as Gay Pride Week.

42. Since the early 1970s, groups have worked to end various kinds of _____ against gay people.

43. The gay rights movement has been primarily concerned with legislation related to _____ _____ and civil rights.

44. A major legislative goal of gay rights advocates is an amendment to the 1964 _____ _____ _____ that would broaden it to include "affectional or sexual preference" along with race, creed, color, and sex.

Matching

Match the people below with their ideas or contributions. Note that each person may be used once, more than once, or not at all, but choose only **one** answer for each blank.

a. Alfred Kinsey   d. Alan Bell
b. James B. Nelson   e. Sigmund Freud
c. Martin Weinberg   f. Simon LeVay

_____1. used the term "homophobia" to describe anti-homosexual attitudes

_____2. has conducted the most comprehensive study to date regarding the development of sexual orientation

_____3. his data have been criticized for producing an inflated estimate of the number of homosexual people in our society

_____4. a theologian who has described four positions on homosexuality that are represented in contemporary Christianity

_____5. believed that men and women passed through a "homoerotic" phase in the process of establishing a heterosexual orientation

_____6. devised a seven-point continuum of sexual orientation

_____7. found structural differences in the brains of homosexual and heterosexual men

_____8. his subjects were asked in-depth questions regarding childhood, adolescence and sexual practices during four-hour, face-to-face interviews

Sample Short Answer Test Questions

1. Define "homosexual".

2. Describe Kinsey's continuum scale of sexual orientation. On what grounds has it been criticized?

3. According to the National Health and Social Life Survey, what percentage of men and women identify themselves as homosexual?

4.   Comment on the degree of erotic interest that bisexual individuals appear to demonstrate compared to heterosexual or homosexual individuals.

5.   List and briefly describe the four types of bisexuality.

6.   Briefly describe each of the following theories of the development of a homosexual orientation and then comment on the extent to which the theory is substantiated by research to respond

    a. "by default" theory

    b. seduction theory

    c. Freudian theory

    d. "exotic becomes erotic" theory

7.   What is the current focus of therapy for homosexual clients?

8.   Compare hormone levels in adult heterosexual and homosexual men.

9. Briefly summarize the research on the influence of prenatal hormone levels on sexual orientation.

10. What did LeVay find in his study of brain differences in homosexual and heterosexual men?

11. Explain how genetic factors may contribute to the development of male homosexuals.

12. What is known concerning the relationship between sexual orientation and gender nonconformity?

13. Briefly summarize research conclusions regarding the cause of a homosexual orientation.

14. In a cross-cultural survey of 190 societies, what percent found homosexuality acceptable for some people or in some situations?

15. Briefly explain how negative attitudes toward homosexuality have evolved, beginning
    with the reformation movement that began in the seventh century B.C.

16. Cite two cross-cultural examples in which homosexuality was/is considered acceptable.

17. List and briefly describe four current theological positions on homosexuality.

18. What are some of the treatments people have been subjected to in an attempt to "cure"
    their homosexuality?

19. In 1973, what action did the American Psychiatric Association take regarding the
    treatment of homosexuality as a mental illness?

20. List at least three examples of homophobia.

21. Can homophobic attitudes be changed? If so, how?

22. Summarize ways in which homosexuality has been portrayed in the media over the past ten years.

23. List and briefly describe the five steps in the process of "coming out".

    a.

    b.

    c.

    d.

    e.

24. Briefly describe the general attitudes that each of the following have toward homosexuality:

    a. Native Americans

    b. Hispanic Americans

    c. Asian Americans

    d. African Americans

25. Describe the similarities or differences between homosexual men and women in the following areas:

   a. number of sexual partners

   b. tendency to associate emotional closeness with sex

   c. likelihood of sharing a household

26. What did one study find was most important in a love relationship, regardless of the couples' sexual orientation?

27. Summarize the research that compares the children of lesbian and heterosexual mothers, as well as the parenting behavior of the two groups of women.

28. What is considered to be the symbolic birth of gay activism?

29. List some of the current goals of the gay rights movement.

Sample Multiple Choice Test Questions

Select the best alternative. Check your answers with the answer key at the end of the chapter.

1. A homosexual person is best defined as an individual
   a. who has sexual contact with a person of the same sex.
   b. whose gender identity is inconsistent with his or her biological sex.
   c. who is sexually and emotionally attracted to a person of the same sex.
   d. whose primary erotic, psychological and emotional interest is in a person of the same sex.

2. In Kinsey's scale of sexual orientation, the number "3" represents
   a. exclusive homosexual contact and attraction.
   b. exclusive heterosexual contact and attraction.
   c. equal homosexual and heterosexual contact and attraction.
   d. a person who is asexual.

3. The recent *National Health and Social Science Life Survey* found that _____ percent of women and _____ percent of men identified themselves as homosexual.
   a. 1.5; 3
   b. 3; 5.5
   c. 4.5; 7
   d. 6; 8.5

4. Bisexual behavior can be a _____, in which a person is changing from one exclusive orientation to another.
   a. transitory orientation
   b. transitional orientation
   c. denial of one's homosexuality
   d. real orientation

5. A woman who earns a living having sex with men for money has fantasized about women since she can remember and has lived with her female lover for the past five years. According to information presented in the text, this woman's sexual orientation would **best** be described as
   a. bisexual as the result of homosexual denial.
   b. transitory bisexual.
   c. transitional bisexual.
   d. true bisexual.

6. Current theological positions toward homosexuality
   a. unconditionally reject homosexuality.
   b. maintain that while homosexuality is a sin, people are unable to change their orientation, so committed homosexual relationships should be accepted.
   c. are fully accepting of homosexuality.
   d. demonstrate a great range of convictions.

7. Influenced by Judeo-Christian tradition, our society has for centuries believed that homosexuality was _____. This view was replaced to a large extent with the belief that homosexuality was _____.
   a. an illness; immoral
   b. immoral; an illness
   c. conditionally acceptable; an illness
   d. an illness; conditionally acceptable

8. All of the following are expressions of homophobia **except**
   a. You find out a friend of yours is gay, and so you invest less time in the relationship.
   b. You do not go to a gay bar for fear that someone you know might see you.
   c. You laugh at a "queer" joke.
   d. You prefer to wear clothing that is clearly congruent with your gender identity (i.e., either very masculine or very feminine).

9. Which of the following would be **least** indicative of homophobia?
   a. being outspoken about lesbian and gay rights but making sure everyone knows that you are straight
   b. thinking that if a gay or lesbian person touches you that they are making sexual advances
   c. feeling that a lesbian is just a woman who can't find a man
   d. firing your gardener, who is gay, because you have not been pleased with the quality of his work

10. The cause of lesbianism is
    a. a history of poor sexual relationships with men.
    b. related to an abnormal hormonal imbalance.
    c. the result of faulty parenting.
    d. unknown.

11. Which of the following statements is **true**?
    a. In general, lesbians are less attractive than heterosexual women.
    b. Young men and women often become homosexual because they have been seduced by older homosexuals.
    c. Sexual orientation is not fully established until the onset of puberty, so care should be taken prior to that time to provide children with appropriate heterosexual role models.
    d. Lesbian mothers are similar to heterosexual mothers in parenting behavior.

12. Research comparing levels of sex hormones in adult heterosexual and homosexual males has indicated that
    a. the heterosexual group has consistently higher levels of sex hormones than the homosexual group.
    b. the homosexual group has consistently higher levels of sex hormones than the heterosexual group.
    c. there are no differences between the two groups.
    d. The data have been contradictory.

13. Gender nonconformity rates in childhood are
    a. higher for female homosexuals than heterosexuals.
    b. higher for male homosexuals than heterosexuals.
    c. higher for both male and female homosexuals than heterosexuals.
    d. approximately the same for both homosexuals and heterosexuals.

14. Which of the following statements about the relationship between hormones and the development of homosexuality **best** reflects the current state of knowledge?
    a. Treating male homosexuals with estrogen increases the degree to which they experience gender nonconformity.
    b. Treating male homosexuals with testosterone reduces their sexual desire.
    c. A homosexual orientation causes the fluctuations of hormone levels.
    d. Homosexuality could cause differences in hormone levels and differences in hormone levels could cause homosexuality.

15. Which of the following statements is **false**?
    a. In Bell and Weinberg's study, three-fourths of lesbians and one-half of gay men were in primary relationships.
    b. Heterosexual couples were likely to adhere more closely to traditional gender-role expectations than were homosexual couples.
    c. Lesbian couples are more likely than male couples to have monogamous relationships.
    d. As of June 1988, marriage between two people of the same sex is not legally recognized by any state.

16. Simon LeVay of the Salk Institute found differences in the _____ of the homosexual and heterosexual men he studied.
    a. brains
    b. gonads
    c. hormone levels
    d. childhood sexual and family history

17. In one study, _____ was most important in homosexual male love relationships, and _____ was most important in heterosexual love relationships.
    a. "having a satisfying sexual relationship"; "being able to talk about my most intimate feelings"
    b. "being able to talk about my most intimate feelings"; "being able to talk about my most intimate feelings"
    c. "being able to talk about my most intimate feelings"; "having a satisfying sexual relationship"
    d. "having a satisfying sexual relationship"; "having a satisfying sexual relationship"

18. According to research, the parenting behavior of lesbians
    a. is generally more consistent than that of heterosexual mothers.
    b. is generally less consistent than that of heterosexual mothers.
    c. is similar to that of heterosexual mothers.
    d. The data are inconsistent.

19. Which of the following statements about men in the Sambia society of New Guinea is **true**?
    a. They experience fellatio with other men but not with their wives.
    b. Once married, heterosexual contact is primary, but homosexual contact continues on an occasional basis.
    c. They believe that drinking the semen of post pubertal boys makes them become better warriors.
    d. With the exception of ceremonial heterosexual contacts, homosexuality is the primary form of sexual expression throughout the life cycle.

Critical Thinking/Personal Reflection

1.   In terms of behavior, attraction, fantasy, and self-identity, how would you describe your sexual orientation? Have you ever had difficulty understanding or accepting people with a sexual orientation that differs from your own? If so, why? If, over time, you have noticed a difference in your ability to understand and accept people with different orientations, what factors have contributed to that change?

2.   In what ways have you observed homophobia expressed? Give specific examples.

3.   If a close friend or family member of yours were to tell "queer" jokes, make homophobic comments, or demonstrate other homophobic behavior, how would you respond, if at all? Be specific.

4.   From what you have observed, how do you think the AIDS epidemic has affected attitudes toward homosexuality? From a personal standpoint, how has it affected your attitudes and behavior, if at all?

5. If available in your community, rent any of the following films that deal with sexual orientation and/or gender identity in thoughtful, provocative ways: *Celluloid Closet; French Twist; Priscilla, Queen of the Desert; Carrington; Priest; Strawberry and Chocolate; My Life in Pink; The Crying Game; Orlando.*

Add others to the list that you think would be appropriate. View the film(s) and answer the following questions:

a. How does this film further your understanding of sexual orientation and/or gender identity? Make specific reference to the film to illustrate your points.

b. What perspectives or insights are offered that are not typically represented in mainstream films? Cite specific examples.

c. Discuss at least one character to whom you were particularly sympathetic or with whom you could identify or a character whom you had difficulty liking or understanding. Discuss reasons for your choices, making reference to the film and/or your own life experiences to support your view.

Chapter Overview With Fill-In Answers

1. Bisexuality
2. seven
3. other; same
4. equal
5a. orientation
5b. transitional
5c. denial
6. by default
7. Bell
8. older
9. caught
10. school age
11. family
12. childhood
13. exotic; erotic
14. biological
15. hormone
16. cause; result
17. prenatal; brain
18. brains
19. genetic
20. gender nonconformity
21. stereotypic
22. biological
23. negatively
24. procreation
25. 2/3
26. require
27. rejecting-punitive; full acceptance
28. sick
29. Psychiatric; mental
30. Homophobia; oneself
31. coming out; gay community
32. gender-role; homosexual
33. fewer; lesbian
34. emotional closeness
35. marriage
36. parents; heterosexual
37. parenting
38. artificial; insemination
39. carry
40. New York City; Stonewall
41. gay rights
42. discrimination
43. consensual sex
44. Civil Rights Act

Matching Answers

1. c   2. d   3. a   4. b   5. e   6. a   7. f   8. d

Sample Multiple Choice Answers

1. d   2. c   3. a   4. b   5. b   6. d   7. b   8. d
9. d   10. d   11. d   12. c   13. c   14. d   15. a   16. a
17. b   18. c   19. c

11

Contraception

Introduction

The chapter begins by presenting the historical and social perspectives on contraception. With an emphasis on shared contraceptive responsibility on the part of both men and women, currently available contraceptive methods are discussed, examining the advantages, disadvantages, effectiveness, and safety of each. Finally, new directions in contraception are explored.

Review of Key Terms and Concepts

Key terms and concepts are listed and defined below. Refer to the subject index in the back of your textbook for additional information.

1. **Comstock laws** — laws that Anthony Comstock succeeded in enacting that prohibited the dissemination of contraceptive information by mail on the grounds that this information was obscene

2. **Griswold v. Connecticut** — a 1965 Supreme Court ruling mandating that states could not prohibit the use of contraceptives by married people

3. **Eisenstadt v. Baird** — a 1972 Supreme Court ruling that extended the right to privacy to unmarried individuals by decriminalizing the use of contraception by single people

4. **"outercourse"** — noncoital forms of sexual intimacy such as kissing, touching, petting, mutual masturbation, oral and anal sex

5. **constant-dose combination pill** — the most commonly used oral contraceptive in the U.S.; contains synthetic estrogen and progestin which are released at constant levels throughout the menstrual cycle

6. **multiphasic pill** — an oral contraceptive designed to reduce total hormone dosage and side effects by providing fluctuations of estrogen and progesterone levels throughout the menstrual cycle

7. **progestin-only pill** — an oral contraceptive that contains no estrogen and only 0.35 mg of progestin — one third the amount of an average combination pill

8. **ACHES** — an acronym that summarizes serious problems associated with oral contraceptives: abdominal pain; chest pain; headaches; eye problems; severe leg pain

9. **Norplant** — a contraceptive method in which six thin capsules of synthetic progestin are implanted in a woman's upper arm; provides effective contraception for five years

10. **diaphragm** — a contraceptive device consisting of a latex dome on a flexible spring rim. The diaphragm is inserted into the vagina with contraceptive cream or jelly and covers the cervix.

11. **cervical cap** — a plastic or rubber thimble-shaped cup that covers the cervix in order to provide a contraceptive barrier to sperm

12. **vaginal spermicides** — chemical substances used in foam, suppositories, the contraceptive sponge, creams and jellies and contraceptive film that are inserted in the vagina prior to intercourse in order to kill sperm

13. **condom** — a latex or membrane sheath that fits over the penis and is used for protection against unwanted pregnancy and sexually transmitted diseases

14. **intrauterine devices** — a small, plastic device that is inserted into the uterus for contraception

15. **PAINS** — an acronym that summarizes problems associated with the IUD: period late or no period; abdominal pain; increased temperature, fever, chills; nasty discharge; spotting, bleeding, heavy periods

16. **mucus method** — a birth control method that is based on determining the time of ovulation by means of the cyclical changes of the cervical mucus

17. **calendar method** — a method of birth control based on abstinence from intercourse during the estimated calendar time of her menstrual cycle when she is ovulating and fertile

18. **basal body-temperature method (BBT)** — a method of birth control based on temperature changes before and after ovulation

19. **female sterilization** — the leading method of birth control in the U.S. whereby the fallopian tubes are tied off or clipped by any one of the following methods: minilaparotomy; laparoscopy; or culpotomy

20. **vasectomy** — a male sterilization procedure that involves removing a section from each vas deferens

21. **vasovasostomy** — surgical reconstruction of the vas deferens after vasectomy

22. **Depo-Provera** — an injectable contraceptive that contains progestin and is effective for twelve weeks

23. **RU-486** — an anti-progesterone substance that has the potential to be used as contraception and emergency contraception, as well as in several other ways

Chapter Overview With Fill-Ins

After reading each of the major sections in the chapter, check your retention by filling in each of the blanks in the corresponding sections below. The answers are provided at the end of the chapter.

Historical and Social Perspectives

1. _____ _____ was the person most instrumental in promoting changes in birth control legislation and availability in the United States.

2. The first birth control pills came on the U.S. market in the year _____.

3. In _____ v. _____, the Supreme Court ruled that states could not prohibit use of contraceptives by married people.

4. In 1992, in _____ v. _____, the Supreme Court ruled that unmarried individuals had the legal right to contraception.

Sharing Responsibility and Choosing a Birth Control Method

5. Sharing the responsibility of contraception can _____ a relationship.

6. Ways in which contraceptive responsibility might be shared include: a) for either partner to initiate a discussion of birth control before having _____ the first time; b) reading about and _____ various alternatives; c) for a man to _____ his partner to a medical exam if appropriate; and d) to share the _____ for the exam and birth control.

7. Some of the most important considerations to be aware of in choosing a birth control method are convenience, safety, expense and _____.

8. Noncoital forms of sexual intimacy are called "_____."

9. "Outercourse" includes _____, touching, petting, mutual _____, and oral and anal sex.

10. The voluntary avoidance of coitus offers effective protection from _____, is free from side effects, but does not eliminate the risk of spreading _____ _____ _____.

Hormone-Based Contraceptives

11. There are three basic types of oral contraceptives currently on the market: the _____-_____ combination pill, the multiphasic pill and the _____-only pill.

12. Advantages of oral contraceptives include: convenience; high rate of _____; elimination of _____ (pain at ovulation); reduction of menstrual cramps and premenstrual tension symptoms; treatment of a wide variety of medical problems; reduction of the incidence of rheumatoid arthritis, and of _____ and endometrial cancers; enlargement of the breasts; and improvement of acne.

13. Disadvantages of oral contraceptives can be summarized by the acronym ACHES, which stands for: Abdominal pain; _____ pain; Headaches; _____ problems; or Severe leg pain.

14. _____ consists of six, thin capsules filled with _____ that are implanted under the skin of a woman's upper arm.

15. These capsules prevent conception for _____ years.

16. Depo-Provera is an _____ contraceptive that needs to be given once every _____ weeks.

Barrier Methods

17. _____ are currently the only temporary method of birth control available for men.

18. Condoms can be made of natural skin (sheep membrane), latex or _____ .

19. _____ condoms, which were approved for sale in the United States in 1988, resemble regular condoms but are worn _____ by women.

20. The _____, a round, soft latex dome with a thin, flexible spring around the rim, is inserted into the vagina with a contraceptive cream or jelly, and fits around the back of the _____ and underneath and behind the pubic bone.

21. The diaphragm provides a chemical as well as a mechanical _____ to prevent _____ from entering the cervix and uterus.

22. The _____ _____ is a thimble-shaped cup made of rubber or plastic that fits over the cervix and can be left in place longer than a diaphragm.

23. It is usually recommended that _____ be used with the cap.

24. There are several types of vaginal spermicides: foam, suppositories, creams, jellies and vaginal contraceptive _____ (VCF).

Intrauterine Devices

25. Intrauterine devices, or IUDs, are small plastic objects that are inserted into the _____ through the vaginal canal and cervical _____.

26. Two types of IUDs are currently available: the _____, called the ParaGard, and the Progestasert T.

27. Both the copper and the progesterone in IUDs prevent _____.

28. Serious problems associated with the IUD can be summarized by the acronym PAINS, which stands for: Period late, no period; _____ pain; _____ temperature, fever, chills; Nasty or foul discharge; and Spotting, bleeding, and clots.

Emergency Contraception

29. The most common methods of emergency contraception are birth control pills or insertion of _____ _____.

Methods Based on the Menstrual Cycle

30. There are three methods of birth control that are based on the menstrual cycle: the mucus method, also called the _____ method, which is based on the cyclic changes of cervical mucus; the calendar method, also called the _____ method, in which a woman estimates the calendar time during her cycle when she is ovulating and fertile; and the _____-_____ _____ method, in which a woman takes her temperature on a regular basis and is able to determine when she is ovulating because the BBT, immediately prior to ovulation, _____ slightly.

Sterilization

31. _____ is the most effective method of birth control except abstinence from coitus, and it is the leading method of birth control in the United States.

32. One method of female sterilization is _____ sterilization, which can be accomplished by a variety of techniques including minilaparotomy, laparoscopy, and _____.

33. In general, male sterilization is _____, considerably less expensive, and as _____ as female sterilization.

34. _____ is a minor surgical procedure that involves cutting and tying the _____ _____, the two sperm carrying ducts.

35. Some men request a _____, a reversal of a vasectomy.

Less Than Effective Methods

36. _____ a baby delays the return to fertility after childbirth; however, it is not a reliable method because there is no way of knowing when _____ will resume.

37. The practice of _____ is not very effective as a birth control method for several reasons.

38. _____ is another ineffective method as it may actually help sperm reach the opening of the cervix.

New Directions in Contraception

39. Research efforts with respect to male contraception concentrate on inhibiting sperm production, _____, or maturation.

40. A range of techniques are currently under experimentation for women, including hormone injections; a _____ _____, and variations on diaphragms, cervical caps and _____ .

41. An antiprogesterone substance, _____ has been approved in the United States but anti-abortion groups have prevented it from being distributed as of this time.

Matching

Match the birth control methods below with the correct descriptions. Note that each method may be used more than once and there may be more than one answer for each blank.

a. combination pill
b. IUD
c. Norplant
d. diaphragm
e. condom
f. cervical cap

g. ovulation method
h. rhythm method
i. BBT method
j. sterilization
k. progestin-only pill

_____1. should be inserted no longer than six hours prior to intercourse

_____2. available without prescription

_____3. contains synthetic progestin that is released over 5-year period

_____4. may damage cervix

_____5. inhibits ovulation

_____6. should not be used by women with history of PID (pelvic inflammatory disease)

_____7. women learn to monitor changes in vaginal secretions

_____8. reduces the risk of endometrial cancer

_____9. some contain nonoxynol-9

_____10. after removal, fertility resumes within 24 hours

_____11. increased risk of blood clots, heart attacks and liver tumors

_____12. next to the pill, the contraceptive most commonly used by college-age adults

_____13. alters cervical mucus to block sperm

_____14. can be used for postcoital contraception

_____15. should not be left in for longer than 24 hours

_____16. both men and women can use this method

_____17. most commonly used reversible method of birth control used by women in U.S. today

_____18. the copper and progesterone in them prevent fertilization

_____19. a woman keeps a chart of the length of her monthly cycles

_____20. cases of toxic shock syndrome have been associated with using it

_____21. when a yellow or white sticky discharge begins, should use back-up method of birth control

_____22. ovulation is determined by measuring body temperature

_____23. the leading method of birth control around the world today

Sample Short Answer Test Questions

1. When did efforts to control conception begin? List four methods of birth control used prior to this century.

2. What were the Comstock laws?

3. What was the purpose of the clinic that Margaret Sanger opened?

4. When did birth control pills first come on the market?

5. Briefly discuss the difference between Griswold v. Connecticut and Eisenstadt v. Baird.

6. According to research, when condoms are available at no cost at school, how does it affect the rate of sexual activity?

7. According to one study, how did contraceptive use among Catholic and non-Catholic women compare?

8. Identify five ways in which couples can practice shared responsibility concerning birth control.

9. What characteristics do men and women who do not use birth control have in common?

10. List the five most reliable birth control methods.

11. Name six behaviors that constitute "outercourse."

12. List three types of oral contraceptives and briefly explain the differences among them.

13. List four advantages of oral contraceptives.

14. Explain the potential side effects associated with the pill using the acronym ACHES.

15. List three serious health problems associated with oral contraceptive use.

16. What is Norplant and for how long is it effective?

17. What is Depo-Provera and for how long is it effective?

18. List three different materials from which condoms are made and describe how effective they are in preventing the transmission of sexually transmitted diseases.

19. List five considerations to be aware of in using condoms.

20. How does the female condom compare to the male condom in terms of protection against sexually transmitted diseases?

21. How far in advance of intercourse can a diaphragm be inserted? How long should it remain in afterwards?

22. What medical problem has been associated with diaphragms?

23. List the advantages and disadvantages of the cervical cap.

24. What is the most common type of vaginal spermicide?

25. How does the IUD prevent pregnancy?

26. List two types of IUDs currently available.

27. List the disadvantages of using an IUD.

28. List symptoms of potential problems associated with the IUD using the acronym PAINS.

29. List two main types of emergency contraception.

30. Briefly describe how the following methods based on the menstrual cycle work:
   a. mucus method

   b. calendar method

   c. basal body-temperature method

31. In using the ovulation method, at what point should unprotected intercourse be avoided?

32. What does the BBT do immediately prior to ovulation?

33. List and briefly describe three types of tubal sterilization.

34. What happens to a woman's egg production after tubal sterilization? Does she continue to menstruate?

35. What problems may be associated with vasectomy?

36. Define recanalization.

37. Define vasovasostomy. What factor influences its success?

38. Explain why nursing, withdrawal and douching are not reliable methods of birth control.

39. What is NoFertil and how does it work?

40. What is RU-486 and how is it used?

Sample Multiple Choice Test Questions

Select the best alternative. Check your answers with the answer key at the end of the chapter.

1. In 1965, the Supreme Court ruled in _____ that states could not prohibit the use of contraceptives by married people.
   a. Griswold v. Connecticut
   b. Eisenstadt v. Baird
   c. Sanger v. McCormack
   d. Roe v. Wade

2. _____ was the person most instrumental in promoting the changes in birth control legislation and availability in the United States.
   a. William Masters
   b. Alfred Kinsey
   c. Katherine Dexter McCormack
   d. Margaret Sanger

3. Women who are uncomfortable with their sexuality are likely to
   a. insist that their partners wear condoms.
   b. use birth control pills.
   c. take a passive role in contraceptive decision-making.
   d. seek sterilization earlier than other women.

4. "Outercourse" includes all off the following **except**
   a. kissing.
   b. mutual masturbation.
   c. oral sex.
   d. coitus.

5. Which of the following is the **most effective** birth control method if used correctly and consistently?
   a. diaphragm and spermicide
   b. progestin-only birth control pills
   c. Norplant
   d. estrogen-progestin pills

6. The combination pill works by
   a. releasing a constant dose of estrogen and progestin.
   b. releasing a variable dose of estrogen and progestin.
   c. releasing a constant dose of pituitary hormones LH and FSH.
   d. altering the cervical mucus to a thick and tacky consistency.

7. If a woman forgets to take one of her birth control pills, she should
   a. take two pills immediately.
   b. take the missed pill as soon as she remembers it and her next pill at the regular time.
   c. consult her health practitioner.
   d. consider IUD insertion to terminate a possible pregnancy.

8. Birth control pills may do all of the following **except**
   a. reduce menstrual cramps.
   b. decrease acne.
   c. enlarge breasts.
   d. minimize yeast infections

9. All of the following are potential risks associated with oral contraceptives **except**?
   a. increased incidence of liver tumors
   b. increased risk of ovarian cancer
   c. increased possibility of heart attacks
   d. increased risk of blood clots

10. ACHES, which is an acronym that is associated with danger signs for birth control users, stands for
    a. abdominal pain, chest pain, heart palpitations, eye problems, and stomach ache.
    b. abdominal pain, chest pain, headaches, eye problems, and severe leg pain.
    c. abdominal pain, chest pain, hypoglycemia, eye problems, and side aches.
    d. abdominal pain, chest pain, high blood pressure, ear ache, and slight cramping.

11. Which of the following statements regarding Norplant is **false**?
    a. The capsules are implanted in a woman's upper arm.
    b. The capsules are filled with synthetic progestin.
    c. A woman's ability to become pregnant returns within one month after removal of the capsules.
    d. The most common side effect is menstrual irregularity.

12. There is **less** chance of a condom breaking if
    a. it is kept in a warm, dry place prior to use.
    b. it does not have a reservoir tip.
    c. it is lubricated.
    d. all of the above

13. Sexually transmitted diseases can pass through _____ condoms but not _____ condoms.
    a. latex; natural-skin and polyurethane
    b. natural-skin; latex and polyurethane
    c. natural-skin and polyurethane; latex
    d. polyurethane; natural-skin and latex

14. To date, the most effective method of emergency contraception is
    a. the copper IUD.
    b. RU-486.
    c. NoFertil.
    d. LHRH agonist.

15. A diaphragm should remain in the vagina at least _____ hour(s) following intercourse.
    a. one
    b. two
    c. four
    d. six

16. A woman may need a different diaphragm after
    a. a pregnancy.
    b. one year of regular use.
    c. after using a water-based lubricant.
    d. being diagnosed for a sexually transmitted disease.

17. All of the following may be disadvantages associated with diaphragm use **except**
    a. increased incidence of pelvic inflammatory disease
    b. possible interference with oral sex
    c. poor diaphragm fit
    d. bladder discomfort

18. A _____ is usually recommended when using the cervical cap.
    a. spermicide
    b. lubricating jelly
    c. vaginal douche
    d. condom

19. Which of the following statements concerning the cervical cap is **true**?
    a. It is available at local pharmacies.
    b. It is used in conjunction with spermicide.
    c. It can be left in place indefinitely.
    d. It comes in one size that can accommodate most women.

20. Spermicides containing _____ may help protect against HIV transmission and other sexually transmitted diseases.
    a. VCF
    b. nonoxynol-9
    c. K-Y jelly
    d. progestin

21. The _____ may work by slightly irritating and inflaming the uterine lining, thereby resulting in the fertilized ovum not attaching.
    a. cervical cap
    b. diaphragm
    c. IUD
    d. birth control pill

22. The most serious complication related to the IUD is that it increases a woman's chance of
    a. liver tumors.
    b. pelvic inflammatory disease.
    c. hypertension.
    d. ovarian cancer.

23. The calendar method is also called the _____ method.
    a. body-temperature
    b. mucus
    c. rhythm
    d. ovulation

24. Present research indicates that methods based on the menstrual cycle
    a. are more effective than most other methods.
    b. are less effective than most other methods.
    c. are more convenient than most other methods.
    d. have more side effects than most other methods.

25. Female sterilization can be done in several ways. The procedure called _____ involves one or two incisions at the navel and below the public hair line. A lighted instrument is inserted to locate the fallopian tubes.
    a. minilaparotomy
    b. laparoscopy
    c. culpotomy
    d. vasectomy

26. Which of the following statements regarding vasectomy is **false**?
    a. It is not as safe as female sterilization.
    b. It is less expensive than female sterilization.
    c. It is a minor surgical procedure.
    d. It may be associated with an increase in prostate cancer.

27. The success rate of vasovasostomy is dependent upon
    a. the sperm count prior to vasectomy.
    b. how recently the vasectomy was performed.
    c. the thickness of the vas deferens.
    d. the age of the man

28. Which of the following statements regarding RU-486 is **false**?
    a. It may promote growth of breast tumors.
    b. It prevents implantation of the zygote from occurring.
    c. It appears to be helpful in treating endometriosis.
    d. It is an antiprogesterone substance.

Critical Thinking/Personal Reflection

1. If you are sexually active, how have you assumed total responsibility or shared responsibility for birth control? Give specific examples. What are your thoughts about shared responsibility? How do you think our society reinforces or discourages shared responsibility with respect to birth control issues? Give specific examples.

2. What are your thoughts about presenting contraceptive information to adolescents and children? Is there a particular age or grade that would be most appropriate to address this information? How many times and in what context should it be discussed? How thoroughly should the information be presented? Should it be presented in conjunction with other kinds of information on human sexuality? If so, what other topics might be included? What type of format, in your opinion, would be appropriate?

3. Do you think men and women should be able to choose sterilization at any age? For example, should a 22-year-old woman be able to have a tubal sterilization? If so, what types of screening procedures, if any, should be implemented for young adults who seek this type of birth control option?

4. How would you describe your personal comfort level in discussing contraception with a partner or potential partner? When and how do you do this? Is there anything you would like to change? If so, what is it?

Chapter Overview With Fill-In Answers

1. Margaret Sanger
2. 1960
3. Griswold v. Connecticut
4. Eisenstadt v. Baird
5. enhance
6a. intercourse
6b. discussing
6c. accompany
6d. expenses
7. effectiveness
8. outercourse
9. kissing; masturbation
10. pregnancy; sexually transmitted diseases
11a. constant-dose
11b. progestin
12a. effectiveness
12b. mittelschmerz
12c. ovarian
13a. Chest
13a. Eye
14. Norplant; progestin
15. five
16. injectable; twelve
17. Condoms
18. polyurethane
19. Female; internally
20. diaphragm; cervix
21. barrier; sperm
22. cervical cap
23. spermicides
24. film
25. uterus; os
26. Copper T
27. fertilization
28. Abdominal; Increased
29. copper IUDs
30a. ovulation
30b. rhythm
30c. basal body-temperature
30d. drops
31. Sterilization
32a. tubal
32b. culpotomy
33a. safer
33b. effective
34. Vasectomy; vas deferens
35. vasovasostomy
36. Nursing; ovulation
37. withdrawal
38. Douching
39. motility
40. vaginal ring; IUDs
41. RU-486

Matching Answers

1. d, f   2. e   3. c   4. f   5. a   6. b   7. g   8. a, k
9. e   10. c   11. a   12. e   13. a, c, k   14. a, b   15. d, f
16. e, j   17. a, k   18. b   19. h   20. d, f   21. g   22. i   23. j

Sample Multiple Choice Answers

1. a   2. d   3. c   4. d   5. c   6. a   7. b   8. d
9. b   10. b   11. c   12. c   13. b   14. a   15. d   16. a
17. a   18. a   19. b   20. b   21. c   22. b   23. c   24. b
25. b   26. a   27. b   28. a

Conceiving Children: Process and Choice

Introduction

Choosing whether or not to have a child is a major life decision. This chapter explores some of the factors that may affect that decision, and outlines some of the various options available for becoming a parent when infertility is a problem. How a woman's health care affects the developing fetus and the processes of pregnancy, birth, and postpartum adjustment are also discussed. The controversial topic of abortion is also explored from historical, social and political perspectives.

Review of Key Terms and Concepts

Key terms and concepts are listed and defined below. Refer to the subject index in the back of your textbook for additional information.

1. **endometriosis** — growths of uterine-like tissue that develop in the pelvic cavity

2. **varicocele** — a damaged or enlarged vein in the testes or vas deferens which can be a major cause of infertility in men

3. **artificial insemination** — a procedure in which semen from a woman's partner is mechanically introduced by a health care practitioner into the woman's vagina, cervix, or uterus

4. **in vitro fertilization (IVF)** — a procedure in which the eggs are removed from the ovary and are fertilized in a laboratory dish by her partner's sperm, and later introduced into the woman's uterus.

5. **zygote intrafallopian transfer (ZIFT)** — the same procedure as in vitro fertilization except that the fertilized egg is placed in the fallopian tube instead of the uterus

6. **gamete intrafallopian transfer (GIFT)** — similar to in vitro fertilization except that the sperm and ova are placed directly into the fallopian tube

7. **human chorionic gonadotropin (HCG)** — a hormone that is detectable in the urine of a pregnant woman about a month after conception

8. **trophoblast cells** — cells of the placenta that secrete human chorionic gonadotropin (HCG)

9. **spontaneous abortion (miscarriage)** — the spontaneous expulsion of the fetus from the uterus in early pregnancy, before it can survive on its own

10. **elective abortion** — a decision to terminate a pregnancy by medical procedures

11. **suction curettage** — a medical procedure for abortion that is used in the early stages of pregnancy (7–13 weeks after the last menstrual period)

12. **dilation and evacuation**— a medical procedure for pregnancy termination between 13 and 21 weeks

13. **prostaglandin induction** — a medical procedure for pregnancy termination during the second trimester

14. **medical abortions** — when medications are used to induce abortions in early pregnancy

15. **Hyde Amendment** — legislation passed in 1977 that prohibited federal Medicaid funds for abortions; in 1993 it was modified to fund abortions for rape and incest victims

16. **Roe v. Wade** — a 1973 Supreme Court ruling that legalized a woman's right to terminate her pregnancy before the fetus has reached the age of viability

17. **Rust v. Sullivan** — a 1991 Supreme Court ruling that upheld legislation barring federally funded clinics from discussing abortion with patients

18. **viability** — the fetus' ability to survive independently of the woman's body

19. **methotrexate** — an anti-cancer drug also used to induce medical abortions

20. **misoprostol** — an ulcer drug also used to induce medical abortions

21. **RU-486** — a drug used to induce medical abortions

22. **zygote** — the single cell resulting from the union of sperm and egg cells

23. **blastocyst** — a multicellular descendant of the united sperm and ovum that implants on the wall of the uterus

24. **vernix caseosa** — a waxy, protective substance on the fetus' skin

25. **thalidomide** — a drug prescribed for pregnant women in the 1960s that caused severe fetal deformities to the extremities

26. **placenta** — a disk-shaped organ attached to the uterine wall and connected to the fetus by the umbilical cord. Nutrients, oxygen and waste products pass between mother and fetus through its cell walls

27. **fetal alcohol syndrome (FAS)** — the leading cause of developmental disabilities and birth defects in the United States

28. **amniocentesis** — a procedure in which amniotic fluid is removed from the uterus and tested to determine if certain fetal birth defects exist

29. **amniotic fluid** — the fluid inside the amniotic sac surrounding the fetus during pregnancy

30. **chorionic villus sampling (CVS)** — a prenatal test that detects some birth defects, such as Down syndrome

31. **Down syndrome** — a chromosomal abnormality that results in impaired intellectual function and physical defects

32. **colostrum** — a thin, yellowish fluid secreted by the breasts during late pregnancy and the first few days following delivery

33. **effacement** — flattening and thinning of the cervix that occurs before and during childbirth

34. **first-stage labor** — the initial stage of childbirth in which regular contractions begin and the cervix dilates

35. **second-stage labor** — the middle stage of labor, in which the infant descends through the vaginal canal

36. **third-stage labor** — the last stage of childbirth, in which the placenta separates from the uterine wall and comes out of the vagina

37. **afterbirth** — the placenta and amniotic sac following their expulsion through the vagina after childbirth

38. **prepared childbirth** — birth following an education process that can involve information, exercises, breathing, and working with a labor coach

39. **toxemia** — a dangerous condition during pregnancy, an early symptom of which is high blood pressure

40. **placenta previa** — a birth complication in which the placenta is between the cervical opening and the infant

41. **episiotomy** — an incision in the perineum that is sometimes made during childbirth

42. **cesarean section** — a childbirth procedure in which the infant is removed through an incision in the abdomen and uterus

43. **postpartum period** — the first several weeks following childbirth

44. **lochia** — a reddish, uterine discharge that occurs following childbirth

45. **intracytoplasmic sperm injection (ICSI)** — procedure in which a sperm is injected into an egg

46. **Lamaze** — a method of childbirth preparation using breathing and relaxation

Chapter Overview With Fill-Ins

After reading each of the major sections in the chapter, check your retention by filling in each of the blanks in the corresponding sections below. The answers are provided at the end of the chapter.

Parenthood as an Option

1. Some of the potential advantages of not having children are: more time for a) _____; no b) _____ about providing for children's needs; more spontaneous recreational, social, and work patterns; more financial resources; increased ability to pursue c)_____; more time and energy for adult d)_____.

2. Childless marriages are less _____ than marriages with children.

3. Many potential advantages of having children which parents cite include: the satisfaction of giving and receiving _____; a positive sense of self-esteem and sense of accomplishment; and the opportunity to discover unknown areas of the self and experience greater meaning and satisfaction in life.

Becoming Pregnant

4. Predicting the time of ovulation can be done by using the _____ method, or the body-temperature and calendar methods.

5. If attempts at impregnation are not successful after _____, both partners should be medically evaluated for fertility problems.

6. Female infertility may be attributed to failure to _____.

7. If ovulation and semen quality is satisfactory, tests may be performed on the _____ mucus to see if antibodies are being produced against the partner's sperm.

8. Infections, abnormalities of the reproductive system, scar tissue, and _____ may also contribute to female fertility problems.

9. Another major cause of infertility is tubal scarring from _____ _____ _____.

10. Most causes of male infertility are related to abnormalities in sperm number and/or _____.

11. Infectious diseases of the male _____ tract, genital tract infections, STD-caused infections, environmental toxins, smoking, alcohol and drug abuse, the presence of a _____ (a damaged or enlarged vein in the testes or vas deferens), hormone deficiencies, and undescended testes may cause male sterility.

12. _____ _____ is a procedure to help couples overcome the problems of infertility, whereby semen is mechanically introduced into the woman's vagina or cervix.

13. Various procedures have been developed for a woman or couple who cannot conceive through intercourse or artificial insemination: in vitro fertilization (IVF); the _____ _____ _____ (ZIFT); and the gamete intrafallopian transfer (GIFT).

14. Donated _____ may be used in IVF-GIFT procedures, and in some cases, both donated sperm and ova.

15. Women who are willing to be artificially inseminated by the male partner of a childless couple, carry the pregnancy, deliver the child, and give the child to the couple for adoption are called _____ _____.

16. Usually the first indication of pregnancy is the absence of the _____ _____ at the expected time.

17. The blood, and therefore the urine, of a pregnant woman contains the hormone _____ _____ _____ (HCG), secreted by the _____ cells of the placenta.

Spontaneous and Elective Abortion

18. Various genetic, medical, or hormonal problems may cause _____ _____, or miscarriage, to occur, terminating the pregnancy.

19. _____ abortion involves a decision to terminate a pregnancy by medical procedures.

20. _____ _____ is an abortion procedure that is used in the early stages of pregnancy (up to 13 weeks).

21. About _____ percent of abortions are done at or before 12 weeks.

22. D and E, or _____ and evacuation, is currently the safest and most widely used technique for pregnancy termination between 13 and 21 weeks.

23. _____ (a type of human hormone) are one of the compounds used to induce termination of second trimester pregnancies.

24. Drugs used to induce medical abortions include RU-486; _____, an anti-cancer drug; and _____, an ulcer drug.

25. Late abortions are rare; about _____% occur after 20 weeks.

26. Research indicates that legal abortion does not cause lasting emotional _____.

27. However, women who have _____ abortions experience higher emotional distress in interpersonal relationships than do women having a first abortion.

28. In 1973 in the _____ v. _____ ruling, the United States Supreme Court legalized a woman's right to decide to terminate her pregnancy before the fetus has reached the age of viability.

29. Four years later, the _____ _____ was passed which prohibited federal Medicaid funds for abortion.

30. In 1991, the Supreme Court, in its _____ decision, upheld the legislation barring federally funded clinics from discussing abortion with patients.

31. A 1992 survey found that ____ percent believe that abortion should remain legal.

The Experience of Pregnancy

32. Pregnancy, once seen as predominantly the woman's domain, is now commonly viewed as a _____ experience.

33. Most research shows a progressive _____ in sexual interest and activity over the nine months of pregnancy.

34. However, it is now generally accepted that in pregnancies where there are no risk factors, sexual activity and orgasm may be _____ until the onset of labor.

A Healthy Pregnancy

35. The nine-month span of pregnancy is customarily divided into three thirteen-week segments called _____.

36. The fertilized ova, called a _____, develops into the multicelled blastocyst that implants on the wall of the uterus about one week after fertilization.

37. By the fourth month, the _____ of the fetus can often be distinguished.

38. Components of optimal _____ _____ include good nutrition, general good health, adequate rest, routine health care, exercise, and childbirth education.

39. Although the _____ (a disk-shaped organ attached to the wall of the uterus) prevents some kinds of bacteria and viruses from passing into the fetal blood system, many can penetrate it, including the AIDS virus.

40. _____ _____ _____ (FAS) is the leading cause of developmental disabilities and birth defects in the United States.

41. If fetal abnormalities are suspected for some reason, a test called _____ can be performed during the fourteenth to sixteenth week of pregnancy.

42. Another procedure for detecting birth defects is called _____ _____ sampling (CVS).

43. The rate of fetal defects due to chromosomal abnormalities rises with maternal _____.

44. _____ _____, the most common condition caused by chromosomal abnormality, results in impaired intellectual functioning and various physical defects.

Childbirth

45. The initial indication of first-stage labor may be regular _____ of the uterus, a "bloody show" (discharge from the mucus plug from the cervix), and rupturing of the amniotic sac ("breaking the bag of waters").

46. Prior to the first stage of labor, the cervix has _____ (flattened and thinned) and dilated slightly.

47. It is the extent of cervical _____ that defines the phases of first-stage labor.

48. When the _____ is fully dilated, second-stage labor begins and the infant descends farther into the birth canal.

49. The second stage ends when the infant is _____.

50. Third-stage labor lasts from the time of birth until the delivery of the _____ (afterbirth).

51. Although they are sometimes referred to as "natural" childbirth methods, _____ _____ is a more appropriate label for the Dick-Read, Lamaze and other childbirth approaches.

52. There are several options regarding where childbirth occurs: in hospitals, birth centers, or at _____.

53. Possible complications during childbirth can include premature labor, the infant in other than the head-first position, blood incompatibility between mother and fetus, _____ (water retention and high blood pressure are early symptoms), _____ _____ (the placenta positioned over the cervical opening) and multiple births, etc.

Postpartum

54. The first several weeks following birth are referred to as the _____ period.

55. Many mothers experience _____ _____, which may be due to the sudden emotional, physical, and hormonal changes following delivery.

56. Production of breast milk begins about one to three days after delivery, following production of _____ (a yellowish liquid which contains antibodies and protein).

57. Numerous advantages have been cited with respect to breast-feeding: breast milk is a digestible food filled with _____, nursing induces uterine contractions, and nursing provides close physical contact.

58. However, some women report oversensitive _____ and breasts, less vaginal lubrication, and reduced energy.

59. Couples are commonly advised that intercourse can resume after the flow of reddish uterine discharge, called _____, has stopped and after the episiotomy incision or vaginal tears have healed.

Matching

Match the terms or phrases below with the appropriate descriptions. Some terms may be used more than once and there may be more than one answer for each item.

a. endometriosis
b. ZIFT
c. Hyde Amendment
d. third trimester
e. CVS
f. below-normal percentage of body fat
g. IVF
h. first-stage labor
i. varicocele
j. first trimester

k. mumps during adulthood
l. suction curettage
m. prostaglandins
n. GIFT
o. undescended testes
p. Rust v. Sullivan
q. second trimester
r. dilation and evacuation
s. Roe v. Wade
t. FAS

_____1. fertilized egg is placed in the fallopian tube

_____2. most widely used abortion procedure between 13 and 21 weeks

_____3. ruling to make abortion a personal decision

_____4. can cause infertility in women

_____5. fertilized eggs are placed in the uterus

_____6. internal organs of the infant begin functioning

_____7. causes of infertility in men

_____8. ruling that prohibited federally funded clinics from discussing abortion with patients

_____9. most common type of abortion procedure

_____10. a rare cause of male sterility

_____11. sex of fetus can first be distinguished

_____12. skin is protected by vernix caseosa

_____13. sperm and egg are placed in the fallopian tube

_____14. ruling to prohibit federal Medicaid funds for abortion

_____15. used to induce termination of second trimester pregnancies

_____16. leading cause of developmental disabilities and birth defects in U.S.

_____17. can help detect Down syndrome

_____18. nausea and fatigue may occur

_____19. breasts may begin to secrete colostrum

_____20. fetal movements can be seen and felt from outside the abdomen

_____21. "bloody show"

Sample Short Answer Test Questions

1. What does research reveal regarding marital satisfaction of couples who do not have children?

2. Has adoption of older or disabled children increased or decreased?

3. List four methods for determining when ovulation occurs.

4. What do ovulation prediction/tests measure?

5. What is the success rate for treating couples with infertility?

6. List ten causes of female infertility.

7. List eight major causes of male infertility.

8. What is a rare cause of male sterility?

9. Explain how problems with fertility may affect a couple's sexual relationship.

10. Briefly describe the following procedures that have been used to help infertile couples:
    a. artificial insemination

    b. in vitro fertilization (IVF)

    c. zygote intrafallopian transfer (ZIFT)

    d. gamete intrafallopian transfer (GIFT)

    e. intracytoplasmic sperm injection (ICSI)

11. What laboratory techniques are currently being used to predetermine the sex of the child?

12. Name three countries where illegal sex selection abortion of female fetuses is common.

13. What is the definition of a miscarriage? When do most occur? What are the symptoms?

14. Briefly describe the age, race and marital status of women who most commonly obtain abortions.

15. How likely are Catholic women to obtain abortions as compared to non-Catholic women?

16. Briefly describe the following abortion procedures and indicate when they are used:
    a. suction curettage

    b. D and E

    c. prostaglandins

    d. medical abortions

17. List three drugs used to induce medical abortion.

18. what are the possible consequences of having two or more abortions?

19. What percent of abortions occur after 20 weeks?

20. List six reasons why some women might not use contraception reliably.

21. Briefly describe the following:

   a. Roe v. Wade

   b. Hyde Amendment

   c. Rust v. Sullivan

22. Compare African-Americans' and Whites' attitudes toward legal abortion.

23. Contrast some of the beliefs and values of pro-choice and anti-abortion individuals, aside from their beliefs regarding abortion.

24. How do sexual interest and responsiveness change through the course of pregnancy?

25. Briefly describe physical changes of the zygote/fetus in each of the following:

    a. first trimester

    b. second trimester

    c. third trimester

26. List eight risks to healthy fetal development.

27. Pregnant mothers who drink more than one cup of coffee per day may put their children at risk for what?

28. When is CVS or amniocentesis used?

29. Briefly describe some of the problems and benefits of pregnancy with increased maternal age.

30. What reproductive technology might a postmenopausal woman use to get pregnant?

31. Briefly describe each of the following:

  a. first-stage labor

  b. second-stage labor

  c. third-stage labor

32. What were Grantly Dick-Read's and Fernand Lamaze's ideas about childbirth?

33. How common is episiotomy as a medical intervention in this country as opposed to others?

34. In what situations is a cesarean section recommended?

35. List four potential beneficial effects of breast-feeding.

36. List five potential disadvantages of breast-feeding.

37. How does cigarette smoking affect the milk of a nursing mother?

38. Summarize current recommendations regarding when intercourse can resume after childbirth.

Sample Multiple Choice Test Questions

Select the best alternative. Check your answers with the answer key at the end of the chapter.

1. Which of the following was stated in the text as an advantage to having children?
    a. Parenthood can provide a sense of accomplishment.
    b. Studies show that marriages with children are happier and more satisfying than are marriages without children.
    c. Parenthood can reduce the stress on a marriage.
    d. Parenthood can help a troubled marriage in which the partners are drifting apart.

2. Which of the following is **false**?
    a. Children who are older or disabled are being placed less frequently in adoptive homes.
    b. Adoption is often very expensive.
    c. Some people adopt because of a concern with overpopulation.
    d. A common reason for adoption is a problem with infertility.

3. Ovulation-predictor tests
    a. measure basal body temperature to indicate the onset of ovulation.
    b. measure androgen levels that determine the onset of ovulation.
    c. determine the onset of ovulation by monitoring the consistency of cervical mucus.
    d. measure the rise in LH prior to ovulation.

4. _____ percent of couples who attempt it become pregnant within three months.
    a. Twenty
    b. Forty
    c. Sixty
    d. Eighty

5. All of the following may be related to failure to ovulate **except**
    a. poor nutrition
    b. emotional stress
    c. genetic factors
    d. being overweight

6. Which of the following would be **least likely** to cause female fertility problems?
   a. a cervical mucus plug that contains antibodies against men's sperm
   b. scar tissue in the fallopian tubes
   c. toxemia
   d. endometriosis

7. Which of the following affects male fertility?
   a. nutritional habits
   b. lack of exercise
   c. environmental toxins
   d. excessive exercise

8. A major cause of infertility in men is a damaged or enlarged blood vein in the testes of the vas deferens called
   a. a varicocele.
   b. colostrum.
   c. a vernix caseosa.
   d. a sebaceous cyst.

9. In artificial insemination
   a. the eggs are removed from a woman's ovary, are fertilized in a laboratory dish by her partner's sperm, and then introduced into her uterus.
   b. the male partner of a childless couple impregnates another woman who carries the baby to term and then lets the couple adopt the baby.
   c. the semen from a woman's partner is introduced into the woman's fallopian tube.
   d. semen from a woman's partner is mechanically introduced into her vagina, cervix or uterus.

10. A method called _____ attempts to facilitate fertilization by placing the ova and sperm directly into the fallopian tube.
    a. ICSI (intracytoplasmic sperm injection)
    b. GIFT (gamete intrafallopian transfer)
    c. ZIFT (zygote intrafallopian transfer)
    d. artificial insemination

11. Which of the following statements regarding IVF is **true**?
    a. It is performed more frequently than GIFT or ZIFT.
    b. The success rate is much lower than GIFT or ZIFT.
    c. It is much more expensive than GIFT or ZIFT.
    d. Babies conceived by IVF tend to have more health-related problems than those who are conceived naturally.

12. The blood of a pregnant woman contains
    a. human chorionic gonadotropin.
    b. trophoblast cells.
    c. vernix caseosa.
    d. amniotic fluid.

13. A miscarriage
    a. is also called an induced abortion.
    b. usually occurs in the second trimester of pregnancy.
    c. is usually caused by increased levels of HCG in the blood.
    d. occurs in about 10–20% of pregnancies.

14. According to research, Catholic women
    a. are more likely to obtain abortions than other women.
    b. are less likely to obtain abortions than other women.
    c. are as likely to obtain abortions as other women.
    d. rarely seek an abortion.

15. Which of the following is **false**?
    a. Approximately one-third of abortions are performed for women who have had at least one previous abortion.
    b. Contraceptive method failure is a major reason for repeat abortions.
    c. Thalidomide is one of the compounds used to induce termination of second-trimester pregnancy.
    d. D and E is currently the safest and most widely used technique for pregnancy termination between 13 and 21 weeks.

16. Unwanted pregnancies may result from all of the following **except**
    a. a low degree of guilt about sex.
    b. the traditional role of female passivity.
    c. fear of contraceptive side effects.
    d. the high social value placed on pregnancy.

17. The Roe v. Wade ruling
    a. made abortion a personal decision on the part of the individual woman.
    b. prohibited federal Medicaid funds for abortion.
    c. decided in favor of states imposing restrictions on abortion.
    d. overturned the right to abortion.

18. _____ is associated with a pro-choice position.
    a. A college education
    b. A fundamentalist religious affiliation
    c. A disapproving attitude toward government spending
    d. A low-paying job

19. According to research, U.S. senators and representatives who are opposed to legal abortion also tend to
    a. support handgun control.
    b. oppose capital punishment.
    c. have opposed the Vietnam War.
    d. oppose legislation that promotes the health and well-being of families and children.

20. Research regarding race differences in support for legal abortion reveals that _____ have the strongest pro-choice attitudes while _____ have the weakest support for legal abortion.
    a. older White men; older African-American men
    b. older African-American men; older White men
    c. older White women; older African-American women
    d. older African-American women; older White women

21. The multicelled _____ implants in the uterus about one week after fertilization.
    a. varicocele
    b. zygote
    c. chorionic villus
    d. blastocyst

22. The protective, waxy substance that covers the fetus is called the
    a. lochia.
    b. vernix caseosa.
    c. placental encasement.
    d. amniotic lubricant.

23. How do nutrients and oxygen in the mother's bloodstream enter the bloodstream of the infant?
    a. Blood vessels of the mother and infant are directly connected to each other at the placenta.
    b. A major artery of the mother flows directly into the fetus' umbilical cord.
    c. Substances in the mother's bloodstream enter the amniotic fluid and are absorbed through the epidermis of the fetus.
    d. Although the two bloodstreams are not connected, substances pass into the fetus' bloodstream through the cell walls in the placenta.

24. Fetal alcohol syndrome
    a. is the leading cause of developmental disabilities and birth defects in the United States.
    b. is the leading cause of Down Syndrome.
    c. is related to damage to an infant's teeth.
    d. is related to a high incidence of reading disorders.

25. Regarding pregnancy after age 35, which of the following statements is **true**?
    a. Because of increased risks to the fetus and the mother, the number of women deciding to have children after age 35 is decreasing.
    b. Women over 35 experience more anxiety and depression than first-time mothers in their mid-twenties.
    c. Women over 35 may have higher rates of pregnancy and delivery complications.
    d. The ability to become pregnant increases after age 35.

26. Most research demonstrates that
    a. a man's active involvement in childbearing bears little relationship to father-newborn interaction.
    b. a man's active involvement in childbearing is positively related to father-newborn interaction.
    c. fathers are not as nurturant as mothers, in spite of training to promote this quality.
    d. none of the above

27. Which stage of labor is the longest?
    a. the first
    b. the second
    c. the third
    d. All three stages of labor are approximately equivalent in length.

28. The third stage of labor is characterized by
    a. labor lasting approximately 10–16 hours.
    b. an effaced cervix.
    c. the delivery of the placenta.
    d. the "transition" phase.

29. The Lamaze method is also referred to as
    a. the water-birthing technique.
    b. the relaxation method.
    c. prepared childbirth.
    d. the isometric method.

30. Toxemia
    a. is also called placenta previa.
    b. is characterized by water retention and high blood pressure.
    c. results in anoxia.
    d. results from Rh incompatibility.

31. An episiotomy is
    a. an incision in the abdomen to facilitate a cesarean section.
    b. an emergency procedure performed in birth complications such as breech-fetal presentation.
    c. an incision in the perineum from the vagina toward the anus.
    d. an emergency procedure performed on the umbilical cord.

32. "Postpartum blues" refers to
    a. the discoloration of the genitals after delivery.
    b. the fretful fussing of the infant upon delivery.
    c. the withdrawal and jealousy many new fathers experience.
    d. a period after birth when some mothers cry easily and feel sad.

33. All of the following are advantages of breast-feeding **except**
    a. inhibits ovulation, so it can be used as a temporary method of birth control
    b. heightens emotional experience for the mother
    c. induces uterine contractions that help return the uterus to its normal size
    d. provides digestible food source for the infant

Critical Thinking/Personal Reflection

1. Under what circumstances would you use a preconception sex selection technique, if any? Why or why not? If these techniques were readily available, accurate, and inexpensive, do you think many people would use them? If so, what might be the effects of that?

2. If you wanted to have children, but you and/or a partner were infertile, would you consider any of the conception alternatives discussed in the text? Why or why not? If so, which alternative would you consider and why?

3. Do you believe that a man should have the right to demand or deny abortion for his partner? Why or why not?

4. How would you describe your personal values or beliefs on abortion? On what knowledge and/or experience do you base your views? How have your values changed over time, if at all? To what degree are you able to empathize with or understand an opposing view? What has been your personal experience with abortion, either for yourself, your partner, or close friend or family member? How have those experiences (or lack of them) affected you, if at all?

5. Discuss the controversy surrounding assisted reproductive technology and post menopausal women.

Chapter Overview With Fill-In Answers

1a. oneself
1b. worries
1c. careers
1d. relationships
2. stressful
3. love
4. mucus
5. six months
6. ovulate
7. cervical
8. endometriosis
9. sexually transmitted diseases
10. motility
11. reproductive; varicocele
12. Artificial insemination
13. zygote intrafallopian transfer
14. ova
15. surrogate mothers
16. menstrual period
17. human chorionic gonadotropin; trophoblast
18. spontaneous abortion
19. Elective
20. Suction curettage
21. 90
22. dilation
23. Prostaglandins
24. methotrexate; misoprostol
25. 1%
26. trauma
27. repeat
28. Roe v. Wade
29. Hyde Amendment
30. Rust v. Sullivan
31. 71
32. shared
33. decline
34. continued
35. trimesters
36. zygote
37. sex
38. prenatal care
39. placenta
40. Fetal alcohol syndrome
41. amniocentesis
42. chorionic villus
43. age
44. Down syndrome
45. contractions
46. effaced
47. dilation
48. cervix
49. born
50. placenta
51. prepared childbirth
52. home
53. toxemia; placenta previa
54. postpartum
55. postpartum depression
56. colostrum
57. antibodies
58. genitals
59. lochia

Matching Answers

1. b	2. r	3. s	4. a, f	5. g	6. j	7. i, k	8. p
9. l	10. o	11. q	12. d	13. n	14. c	15. m	16. t
17. e	18. j	19. q	20. d	21. h			

Sample Multiple Choice Answers

1. a	2. a	3. d	4. c	5. d	6. c	7. c	8. a
9. d	10. b	11. a	12. a	13. d	14. c	15. c	16. a
17. a	18. a	19. d	20. c	21. d	22. b	23. d	24. a
25. c	26. b	27. a	28. c	29. c	30. b	31. c	32. d
33. a							

13

Sexuality During Childhood and Adolescence

Introduction

This chapter traces the development of sexuality from infancy through adolescence. Childhood sexual development, physical, social, and sexual changes that occur during adolescence, the double standard, incidence and frequency of various types of adolescent sexual behavior, homosexuality, teenage pregnancy, and androgynous childrearing are among the topics discussed. The authors also suggest strategies for reducing the teenage pregnancy rate, and address questions regarding the nature and timing of sex education.

Review of Key Terms and Concepts

Key terms and concepts are listed and defined below. Refer to the subject index in the back of your textbook for additional information.

1. **contact comfort** — being touched and held (in this context, during the first few months or years of life)

2. **puberty** — the stage of life between childhood and adulthood during which the reproductive organs mature

3. **gonadotropins** — pituitary hormones that stimulate activity in the gonads (ovaries and testes)

4. **secondary sexual characteristics** — the physical sexual characteristics other than genitals that indicate sexual maturity such as body hair, breasts and deepened voice

5. **menarche** — the initial onset of the first menstrual period

6. **petting** — erotic physical contact that may include kissing, holding, touching, mutual masturbation or oral-genital stimulation

7. **homosocial** — relating socially, primarily with members of the same sex

8. **androgyny** — flexibility in gender roles

Chapter Overview With Fill-Ins

After reading each of the major sections in the chapter, check your retention by filling in each of the blanks in the corresponding sections below. The answers are provided at the end of the chapter.

Sexual Behavior During Infancy and Childhood

1. In the first few years of life, many children discover the pleasures of _____ stimulation.

2. Recent surveys indicate that most children participate in some form of _____ play with friends or siblings.

3. By the time a child is age _____ or _____ there is a tendency for boys and girls to play separately and show their curiosity about sexual matters by asking questions about reproduction and sexuality.

4. During late childhood some _____ activity is not uncommon.

5. _____ is one of the most common sexual expressions during the childhood years.

The Physical Changes of Adolescence

6. In Western societies, _____ is the transition between childhood and adulthood.

7. _____ is a term frequently used to describe the period of rapid _____ changes in early adolescence.

8. Secondary sex characteristics such as breasts, deepened voice, and facial and pubic hair result from _____ in the bloodstream.

9. Under the influence of _____ stimulation, the internal organs of the male and female undergo further development and the female eventually begins _____.

10. The first menstrual period is called _____.

11. Although boys may experience orgasm throughout childhood, _____ is not possible until the prostate and seminal vesicles begin functioning under the influence of increasing _____ levels.

12. The physical changes experienced by the adolescent may be a source of pride or concern and may contribute to feelings of self-consciousness, which may result in a _____ (relating socially primarily with members of the same sex) pattern.

Sexual Behavior During Adolescence

13. In most areas of adolescent sexuality, the male-female _____ _____ prevails, although recent research suggests that this negative influence may be on the _____.

14. _____ is an increasingly frequent practice in adolescence.

15. _____ refers to erotic physical contact that may include kissing, holding, touching, manual stimulation , or oral-genital stimulation — but not _____.

16. Perhaps one of the most noteworthy recent changes in the pattern of adolescent petting behaviors involves oral sex; _____ being reported more frequently than _____ by adolescents of both sexes.

17. It appears that contemporary adolescents are most likely to be sexually intimate with someone they _____ or to whom they feel emotionally attached than in earlier decades.

18. The term _____ sex is misleading for two reasons: 1) it excludes a broad array of _____ heterosexual and homosexual activities, and 2) it implies that _____ is the ultimate goal.

19. There has been an _____ in the percentages of young men and women who have experienced adolescent intercourse over the last several decades.

20. The above trend has _____ _____ over the past decade, although that change in the trend has not occurred among the very _____ teenagers.

21. There are variations in adolescent sex among American _____ groups.

22. A number of health professionals are concerned that American teenagers are particularly at risk for becoming infected with _____.

23. High-risk adolescent behaviors may include: 1) engaging in intercourse without condoms and _____; using drugs and alcohol; _____ _____ among intravenous drug users; and exposing themselves to _____ partners.

24. Although homosexuality affects a _____ of adolescents, the homosexual experience can create serious problems for the young person.

Adolescent Pregnancy

25. Of the approximately eleven million unmarried adolescent females who are sexually active, about _____ million become pregnant every year.

26. Over half of these pregnancies result in live births, and of these, _____ percent choose to keep their babies.

27. Many adverse consequences of adolescent pregnancy have been cited, ranging from negative health consequences for the adolescent mother to the negative impact on the adolescent mother's _____ progress, and financial resources.

28. In addition, the offspring of teenage mothers are at a greater risk of having physical, _____, and emotional problems than are children of adult mothers.

29. The United States has the _____ rate of teenage pregnancy in the industrialized world.

30. Suggestions for reducing teenage pregnancy include _____ _____ available to all who want them; compulsory sex education at all _____ _____; _____ assuming more responsibility for birth control; and fewer governmental restrictions on advertising and distributing _____.

Sex Education

31. The authors suggest that we should start telling our children about sex when the child begins to _____ questions.

32. Most young people prefer that their _____ be the primary source of sex information.

33. Several studies have shown that _____ are the principal source of sex information for young people in this country.

Androgynous Child Rearing and Sexuality

34. _____ is a term used to describe flexibility in gender roles.

35. The authors emphasize that strict adherence to stereotypic gender roles has a _____ effect on sexual functioning.

Sample Short Answer Test Questions

1. At what ages do many boys and girls discover the pleasures of genital stimulation?

2. Describe the relationship between affection and physical violence as described in one cross-cultural study of 49 societies.

3. What are possible ways to interpret same sex play during the late childhood years?

4. Describe the physiological changes during puberty for:
    a. males

    b. females

5. What is the relationship of body fat to menarche? Of fertility to menarche?

6. In one study of over 17,000 girls, at what age did puberty typically begin?

7. What do the authors speculate regarding the cause for the above?

8. At what point do males begin ejaculating with orgasm?

9. Define homosocial.

10. Briefly comment on childhood and adolescent sexuality in the following cultures:

a. Mangaia

b. Marquesas Islands

c. Kwoma society of New Guinea

d. Chewa of Central Africa

e. Lepcha of the Himalayas

11. Is the double standard on the increase or decrease among adolescents?

12. How has the incidence of oral sex among adolescents changed over time? Which is more common — fellatio or cunnilingus?

13. How has sexual intimacy changed in adolescence since Kinsey's time?

14. Give two reasons why the term "premarital sex" is misleading.

15. How have rates of adolescent coitus changed over the last 5 decades?

16. Briefly compare adolescent coital rates among African-Americans, Hispanic-Americans and whites.

17. To what are the above ethnic differences most likely attributed?

18. What is the primary reason men give for wanting to have intercourse the first time? What reason do women give?

19. Describe the effect of AIDS education on nonmarital coital rates and sexual behavior among adolescents.

20. What percent of adolescent girls and boys have reported having same-sex contact during their teenage years?

21. Cite the following statistics:

    a. number of adolescent pregnancies each year

    b. percent of pregnancies that result in elective abortion

    c. percent of pregnancies that result in spontaneous abortion

    d. percent of pregnancies that result in live births

    e. percent of live births in which mothers keep their babies

22. List at least three possible negative outcomes of teenage pregnancy.

23. According to the study of adolescent pregnancy in six countries, which country had the highest adolescent pregnancy rate? The second highest rate? Which countries had the lowest rate?

24. Regarding the comparative study on adolescent pregnancy cited in the text, what are three factors which contribute to high pregnancy rates among American adolescents?

25. Briefly outline four suggestions given by the authors to help reduce the teenage pregnancy rate.

26. What do the authors suggest in terms of when to tell our children about sex? At what age do children usually begin asking about where babies come from?

27. From whom do young people prefer to acquire information about sex? How do most children actually get information about sex?

28. How does open parent-child communication about sexual activity affect teenage sexual activity? Use of contraceptives?

29. How does increased availability of condoms in schools affect rates of sexual activity?

30. Define the term androgyny and explain the benefits of this approach for human experience.

Sample Multiple Choice Test Questions

Select the best alternative. Check your answers with the answer key at the end of the chapter.

1. Which of the following statements is **false**?
   a. Orgasm has been observed in infants who are several months old.
   b. Vaginal lubrication has been observed in female infants.
   c. Penile erection has been observed in male infants.
   d. The research of Masters and Johnson has provided the foundation for our knowledge regarding childhood sexuality.

2. During puberty, the pituitary secretes _____ into the bloodstream.
   a. gonadotropins
   b. hypothalamic hormones
   c. androgen
   d. estrogen

3. Childhood masturbation
   a. is one of the early signs of deviant or dysfunctional adult sexual behavior.
   b. is a common form of sexual expression in youth.
   c. is related to a high sex drive in adulthood.
   d. decreases when the child becomes well-adjusted in school.

4. _____ is a term used to describe the period of rapid physical changes in early adolescence.
   a. Menarche
   b. Maturation
   c. Adolescent transition
   d. Puberty

5. The sequence of events in puberty is
   a. hormone production, appearance of secondary sex characteristics, growth spurt, menarche/ejaculation.
   b. menarche/ejaculation, growth spurt, hormone production, growth of axillary hair.
   c. growth of axillary hair, hormone production, secondary sex characteristics.
   d. hormone production, appearance of secondary sex characteristics, growth of axillary hair, growth spurt.

6. Which of the following statements is **true**?
   a. The onset of puberty is approximately one year earlier for girls than for boys.
   b. Many girls are fertile before experiencing menarche.
   c. Growth of pubic hair is an example of a secondary sex characteristic.
   d. During puberty, the pituitary secretes androgen into the bloodstream.

7. Homosocial behavior refers to
   a. cultivating homosexual relationships as a prelude to "coming out".
   b. social interaction with homosexuals.
   c. relating sexually to the same sex.
   d. relating socially to the same sex.

8. The double standard encourages
   a. males to focus on the sexual conquest.
   b. females to realize their full potential.
   c. females to be sexually aggressive.
   d. males to be sensitive regarding female issues.

9. Recent research suggests that the sexual double standard among American adolescents
   a. is increasing.
   b. has leveled off.
   c. is decreasing.
   d. is no longer an issue.

10. According to several studies, a recent change in adolescent sexual relationships is that
    a. the incidence of oral sex has decreased while the incidence of intercourse has increased.
    b. approximately 40% of females and almost 20% of males had their first intercourse on their wedding night.
    c. females are more likely to use condoms and spermicides as a consistent method of birth control.
    d. males are more likely to have emotional connections with their partners than in the past.

11. The term "premarital sex" is misleading for all of the following reasons **except**
    a. many sexually active people choose not to marry.
    b. it overlooks many homosexual activities.
    c. it excludes a broad array of noncoital heterosexual behaviors.
    d. it implies that there is a difference in actual sexual behavior before and after marriage.

12. With respect to HIV infection, teenagers
    a. have decreased their sexual activities in order to minimize contact with the virus.
    b. are conscientiously seeking out information about the disease.
    c. are likely to engage in safer sexual practices in order to protect themselves.
    d. have the information but have not changed their behavior.

13. Which of the following statements is **true**?
    a. Most homosexual individuals openly acknowledge their sexual orientation.
    b. It is not uncommon for heterosexuals to have early homosexual experiences.
    c. There is good social support for gays who "come out" during adolescence.
    d. The majority of homosexual contacts in adolescence are with older adults.

14. Of the approximately 1 million adolescents who become pregnant each year, _____ percent result in live births.
    a. 10
    b. 25
    c. 50
    d. 85

15. Of the adolescent girls who become pregnant, approximately _____ percent have elective abortions.
    a. 10
    b. 20
    c. 40
    d. 60

16. Teenage mothers are likely to
    a. be dependent on welfare services.
    b. continue their education after the birth of their child.
    c. be employed full-time.
    d. provide parenting of the same quality as adult mothers.

17. Offspring of teenage mothers are at a greater risk for
   a. physical problems.
   b. cognitive problems.
   c. emotional problems.
   d. all of the above

18. According to one in-depth study, which of the following countries has the second highest adolescent pregnancy rate?
   a. England
   b. the United States
   c. France
   d. Sweden

19. The extensive comparative study of six developed countries including the United States revealed that a lower incidence of adolescent pregnancy is related to all of the following **except**
   a. comprehensive sex education at all grade levels.
   b. available contraception that is low or no cost.
   c. use of birth control pills.
   d. interactive sex education programs that involve children, parents and school personnel.

20. In European countries, sex is viewed as
   a. private.
   b. natural.
   c. shameful.
   d. synonymous with procreation.

21. A mother finds her son in the bathtub, playing with his penis. According to information presented in the text, the **most** appropriate response in this situation would probably be for the mother to
   a. gently inform the boy that his behavior is inappropriate.
   b. give him a rubber ducky to play with instead.
   c. acknowledge her understanding that the child's action is pleasurable, but that it is a private behavior.
   d. tell her son she will buy him a new toy if he never does that again.

22. The authors' response to the question "When should we start telling our children about sex?" is
   a. when the child is two years old.
   b. when the child begins to ask questions.
   c. when you first notice that the child is masturbating.
   d. when the child first begins to "play doctor" with siblings or neighborhood friends.

23. The principal source of information for young people about sexual matters is
   a. parents.
   b. teachers.
   c. movies.
   d. friends.

24. Which of the following statements is **most** accurate?
    a. Open parent-child communication about sex encourages children to experiment sexually.
    b. Open parent-child communication reduces an adolescent's likelihood to engage in nonmarital sex.
    c. There is no evidence that sex education leads to sexual activity.

25. An important factor in rearing children in an androgynous fashion is
    a. encouraging play with a variety of toys.
    b. parental modeling of gender-free behaviors.
    c. reinforcing play with opposite-sex children.
    d. all of the above

26. Research has demonstrated that adhering to traditional gender-role behaviors is linked with _____ and _____.
    a. having a greater number of sexual partners; less effective contraceptive use
    b. less sexual experimentation within a relationship; more effective contraception use
    c. reluctance to participate in school sex education programs; more effective contraceptive use
    d. earlier age of sexual activity; less effective contraception

Critical Thinking/Personal Reflection

1. If you were a sexually active single parent, how would you deal with this aspect of your life with your elementary school age children? Adolescent children? Would you allow your partner to spend the night with you? Why or why not? What issues might surface regarding this? What kinds of values or information do you think it would be important to be addressed? Be specific.

2. Brainstorm a list of questions that a child might ask a parent, e.g., "Where do babies come from?" "What is a rubber?" "What is '69'?" "What does 'screwing' mean?" Role play with a friend or partner your responses to these questions. Then brainstorm a list of questions that an adolescent might ask and repeat the process. Give each other feedback on suggestions for improvement.

3. If you found your eight-year-old child with a neighborhood friend in the process of visually exploring each other's naked bodies, how would you respond? If they were touching each other's bodies, would your response be any different? How would your response vary, if at all, depending upon the sex of your child? Would the age of the other child affect your response? How? Would you tell the friend's parents about the incident? Why or why not?

4. Would you provide birth control information and devices to your teenage children? Why or why not? Would the sex of your child affect the kind of information you would discuss? If so, why?

5. Assume you have a teenage son or daughter who is dating. What would you think about allowing your child private space or time alone in your home? For example, would you let your daughter or son take a partner into his or her bedroom? With the door closed? Would you allow them to be home alone in the house while you were gone? Why or why not? How would you deal with or address your teenager's needs for privacy, if at all?

6. Complete the sentences below and then provide a specific example from your own life experiences to elaborate upon what you have written. Reflect upon your answers later. If you would like, you could also have a friend or partner complete the exercise and then discuss/compare your answers.

a. My major source of sexual information as I was growing up was _____

   Example: _____

b. As a child, how I learned about my body and my sexuality was _____

   Example: _____

c. How my family dealt with nudity at home was _____

   Example: _____

d. Physical affection in my family _____

   Example: _____

e. The way my family dealt with sexual questions or concerns was _____

   Example: _____

f. As an adolescent, I learned the most about my body and my sexuality when _____

   _____

   Example: _____

g. The way I felt about my body and/or physical appearance in general while I was growing up was _____

   Example: _____

h. One thing I liked about my body as I was growing up was _____

   Example: _____

i. How I found out about masturbation was _____

   _____

   Example: _____

j. My experience with masturbation and how it felt was _____

   Example: _____

k. What I remember regarding sex play as a child _____

   Example: _____

l. My first menstruation/ejaculation _____

   Example: _____

m. The sense I had of my parents' sexual relationship and/or activity was _____

   Example: _____

n. An embarrassing or humiliating sexual experience I had was _____

Example: _____

o. A painful or traumatic sexual experience I had was _____

Example: _____

p. My first sexual intercourse experience (if applicable) was _____

Example: _____

q. What I like about my sexuality today is _____

Example: _____

r. How I feel regarding all of the above and how it relates to who I am sexually today is

_____

Example: _____

s. What I would like to change, if anything, regarding my sexual values, attitudes, or

behavior today is _____

Example: _____

Chapter Overview With Fill-In Answers

1. genital
2. sex
3. 8; 9
4. homosexual
5. Masturbation
6. adolescence
7. Puberty; physical
8. gonadotropins
9. hormone; menstruation
10. menarche
11. ejaculation; testosterone
12. homosocial
13. double standard; decline
14. Masturbation
15. Petting; coitus
16. cunnilingus; fellatio
17. love
18. premarital; noncoital; marriage
19. increase
20. leveled off; young
21. ethnic
22. HIV
23a. spermicides
23b. needle sharing
23c. multiple
24. minority
25. one
26. 95
27. educational
28. cognitive
29. highest
30a. free contraceptives
30b. grade levels
30c. men
30d. contraceptives
31. ask
32. parents
33. friends
34. Androgyny
35. detrimental

Sample Multiple Choice Answers

1. d	2. a	3. b	4. d	5. a	6. c	7. d	8. a
9. c	10. d	11. d	12. d	13. b	14. c	15. c	16. a
17. d	18. a	19. d	20. b	21. c	22. b	23. d	24. c
25. d	26. d						

14

Sexuality and the Adult Years

Introduction

As adults, we may experience one or perhaps several different relationship styles ranging from single living, cohabitation, marriage, open marriage, and extramarital involvement to divorce and widowhood. In this chapter, the authors explore these relationship alternatives and discuss the patterns of sexual interaction in each. In addition, some of the psychological and lifestyle changes that occur in individuals as they age are discussed.

Review of Key Terms and Concepts

Key terms and concepts are listed and defined below. Refer to the subject index in the back of your textbook for additional information.

1. **cohabitation** — living together in a sexual relationship without being married

2. **serial monogamy** — a single person who has a succession of sexually exclusive relationships

3. **domestic partnership** — an unmarried couple living in the same household in a committed relationship

4. **monogamy** — marriage between one man and one woman

5. **polygyny** — marriage between one man and several women

6. **polyandry** — marriage between one woman and several men

7. **extramarital relationship** — sexual interaction experienced by a married person with someone other than her or his spouse

8. **nonconsensual extramarital sex** — engaging in an outside sexual relationship without the consent (or presumably knowledge) of his or her spouse

9. **consensual extramarital relationship** — a sexual and/or emotional relationship that occurs outside the marriage bond with the consent of one's spouse

10. **open marriage** — a marriage in which spouses, with each other's permission, have intimate relationships with other people as well as the marital partner

11. **swinging** — the exchange of marital partners for sexual interaction

12. **miscegenation** — sex between members of different races, whether or not the couple was married. This was illegal until the Supreme Court invalidated those laws.

Chapter Overview With Fill-Ins

After reading each of the major sections in the chapter, check your retention by filling in each of the blanks in the corresponding sections below. The answers are provided at the end of the chapter.

Single Living

1. Several factors contribute to increasing numbers of people in our society who live alone: people marrying at a a)_____ age; more people who never marry; more women putting b)_____ objectives ahead of marriage; an increase in the number of cohabiting couples; rising c)_____ rates; a greater emphasis on advanced education; more women who no longer depend upon marriage for economic reasons; and changes in societal d)_____ toward the single lifestyle.

2. Recent research indicates that _____ people experience higher levels of sexual activity than singles.

Cohabitation

3. Recently, there has been a dramatic increase in _____ (living together in a sexual relationship without being married).

4. There is some evidence that _____ has no demonstrable effect on subsequent marriage, positive or negative.

5. Other research has indicated that cohabitors have lower rates of marital stability, _____ satisfaction or likelihood of divorce.

Marriage

6. Although marriage is an institution that is found in virtually every society, there is diversity in its form among different cultures, ranging from a)_____ (one man and one woman) to b)_____ (one man and several women) and c)_____ (one woman and several men).

7. One study of 141 couples in satisfying marriages found that they had a high degree of a)_____ combined with a sense of individual b)_____.

8. Gottman and his colleagues have revealed that all of the following are related to a decline in mutual satisfaction: facial expressions of disgust, fear, and misery; a)_____ on the part of both partners; wife's verbal expressions of b)_____; and husband's c)"_____".

9. A premarital inventory called a)_____ has predicted, with about b)_____ percent accuracy, couples who divorced from those who were happily married.

10. Since _____ percent or more of all first marriages in the United States will end in separation or divorce, premarital counseling might be advisable.

11. Compared to the people in a)_____'s research groups, contemporary American married women and men appear to engage in sexual b)_____ more often, experience a wider repertoire of sexual behaviors, and enjoy sexual interaction more.

12. One survey of 7000 couples found that _____ of marital sexual interaction was strongly associated with sexual satisfaction.

13. In addition to the above, a)_____ in initiating sex, female orgasm, women taking an b)_____ role in sexual sharing, and good communication were positively correlated with sexual pleasure.

14. There are a number of factors which may interfere with marital sexual enjoyment: new role a)_____, reduced independence, less motivation to maintain personal b)_____, busy lifestyle, children, and boredom.

Extramarital Relationships

15. A term for sexual interaction by a married person with someone other than his or her spouse is called an _____ relationship.

16. In _____ extramarital sex, the married person does not have the consent of his or her spouse.

17. The effects of extramarital sex on a marriage may _____.

18. _____ extramarital relationships occur in marriages where both partners are informed about and are supportive of sexual involvements outside the primary marriage bond.

19. An _____ marriage maintains that couples willingly allow each other intimate emotional relationships, with or without sexual sharing, with members of either sex without compromising their primary relationship.

20. _____ refers to a form of consensual extramarital sex that a married couple shares.

Divorce

21. Current estimates suggest that _____ or more of all first marriages will end in divorce.

22. Although the proportion of marriages ending in divorce has increased steadily since the 1950s, recent statistics reveal that the divorce rate has begun to level off and even _____.

23. A recent study of divorced people cited a)_____ difficulties as the most frequent complaint, followed by unhappiness and b)_____.

24. Research has also revealed that age at marriage and level of _____ may be related to the decision to divorce.

25. Adjusting to divorce is a difficult process and is often compared to the sense of loss a person feels when a loved one _____.

26. Despite the problems newly single people encounter in establishing non marital sexual expression, a majority of divorced individuals become sexually active within the _____ year of the breakup of their marriage.

27. Approximately _____ out of five divorced persons remarry.

28. Many report that the second marriage is better than the first, but evidence suggests that a)_____ marriages are more likely to end in b)_____ than first marriages.

Sexuality and Aging

29. There are several reasons why aging in our society is often associated with sexlessness: American culture is still influenced by the philosophy that equates sex with a)_____; there is a disproportionate focus on b)_____ and the assumption that love, sex, and romance belong exclusively to young people; and there is also an unspoken assumption that it is not c)_____ for older people to have sexual needs.

30. The a)_____ _____ that affects male and female sexual expression during adolescence and adulthood continues into old age, having an especially negative effect on b)_____.

31. Despite the fact that women's erotic and orgasmic capabilities continue after _____, women are often considered to be past their "sexual prime" relatively early in their life.

32. In contrast, the physical and sexual attractiveness of _____ is often considered to be enhanced by the aging process.

33. Three factors affect sexual activity in later years: a person's a)_____ activity levels in early adulthood; b)_____ of sexual expression; and health and illness.

34. _____ _____ have been criticized for their insensitivity to the human rights of aged individuals, and in this case, especially antisexual prejudice and practices.

35. Because it is often assumed that older people are not sexual, _____ are sometimes prescribed without consideration of their effects on sexuality.

36. Concerned individuals, progressive nursing home personnel and organizations such as the _____ _____, as well as others, are beginning to have some effect on restrictive practices in nursing homes.

37. Many older adults remain interested in _____, even if partners are no longer available.

38. Research indicates that a majority of men and women ages 80 to 102 _____ about sex.

39. Another study found that more older people approved of _____ than engaged in it.

40. _____ becomes more important in later years.

41. With age, couples may increasingly emphasize a)_____ rather than b)_____ of sexual experience.

42. The limited research available suggests that gay men and lesbians may be better prepared for dealing with the adjustments of aging than _____ men and women.

43. Development toward _____ in personal, interpersonal, and sexual styles occurs for many people in later life.

Widowhood

44. Widowhood usually occurs later in life and, in most cases, it is the _____ who dies first.

45. The ratio of widows to widowers has _____ during this century.

46. The postmarital adjustment of widowhood is different in some ways from that of _____.

47. About _____ of widowed men and _____ of widowed women remarry.

Sample Short Answer Test Questions

1. List seven factors which contribute to the increasing number of single adults.

2. Compare the sexual activity of single people to that of married people.

3. What is serial monogamy?

4. List five advantages of cohabitation.

5. List three disadvantages of cohabitation.

6. What do studies indicate with respect to cohabitation and subsequent marital satisfaction and success?

7. How common is the institution of marriage from a cross-cultural perspective?

8. What functions does marriage serve?

9. Compare the practices of monogamy, polygyny, and polyandry.

10. What were the findings of one study of 141 couples in satisfying marriages?

11. List five patterns that Gottman's team identified as predictors of marital dissatisfaction.

12. List three different marriage styles that Gottman identified, and briefly describe the advantages and disadvantages of each style.

13. What is the ratio of positive to negative interactions that are predictive of marital satisfaction according to Gottman?

14. Describe two patterns of successful marital interaction that Gottman has recently identified.

15. What is PREPARE and what relationship areas does it assess?

16. How accurate is PREPARE?

17. What percent of all first marriages will end in divorce?

18. How has sexual behavior within a marriage changed since Kinsey's research? Cite specific examples.

19. According to various researchers, what factors are associated with marital sexual satisfaction?

20. What factors may interfere with marital sexual enjoyment?

21. List seven reasons why someone might engage in nonconsensual extramarital sexual activity.

22. What factor did Wegner and associates identify that adds to the appeal of an illicit relationship?

23. According to Kinsey, how common were extramarital affairs?

24. According to the NHSLS, how common are extramarital affairs now?

25. Explain George and Nena O'Neill's concept of sexually open marriage.

26. What is another term for comarital sex, and how common is it?

27. When was swinging most popular?

28. Describe the changes in the divorce rate since the 1950s and especially what is happening most recently.

29. List six reasons that have been suggested for high divorce rates.

30. What are the conditions of "covenant" marriage and which state was the first to offer this option?

31. According to one study of 600 divorced men and women, what were the three most frequently cited reasons for divorce?

32. What two variables may be associated with the decision to divorce?

33. According to Helen Fisher, when are people naturally inclined to leave a relationship? Why?

34. Compare the sexual activity and behavior of married men and women to divorced men and women.

35. What percentage of divorced persons remarry?

36. Why are second marriages more likely to end in divorce than first marriages?

37. List two reasons why aging in our society is often associated with sexlessness.

38. Describe the double standard as it affects male and female sexual expression in later years.

39. According to one research study, compare the aspects of sexuality that contribute to a general feeling of well-being among older men and women.

40. How does Susan Sontag suggest that women approach their later years?

41. List three factors that affect sexual activity in later years.

42. List at least four nursing home practices which negatively affect the sexual expression of their elderly residents.

43. What changes are beginning to take place in nursing homes as the result of efforts made by the Gray Panthers and other organizations?

44. What percentage of older men and women fantasize about sex?

45. What percentage of older people approve of masturbation?

46. Describe the incidence of masturbation among older men and women

47. According to one study, what sex activities techniques did respondents use to enhance their sexual enjoyment?

48. How do homosexual men and women cope with the adjustments of aging compared to heterosexual men and women?

49. What may contribute to men and women's tendency to be more androgynous as they age?

50. How has the incidence of widowhood changed from 1900 to 1990?

51. How does postmarital adjustment to widowhood compare to that of divorce?

52. What percentage of widowed men and women remarry?

Sample Multiple Choice Test Questions

Select the best alternative. Check your answers with the answer key at the end of the chapter.

1. Many singles report all of the following **except**
   a. practicing celibacy.
   b. practicing serial monogamy.
   c. concurrent sexual involvement with many partners.
   d. higher levels of sexual activity than married people.

2. All of the following are factors contributing to the increase in the number of single adults **except**
   a. rising divorce rates
   b. people marrying at a later age
   c. more women dropping out of college
   d. a greater number of couples cohabiting

3. Studies of cohabitation show that
   a. marriage is usually the initial goal at the time a couple enters into a cohabitation relationship.
   b. an increasing number of couples do not believe that an eventual marriage commitment is necessary to begin cohabiting.
   c. most cohabitors are college students who benefit economically from the arrangement.
   d. most cohabitors experience similar role expectations as married couples.

4. Which of the following **best** summarizes current research on the impact of cohabitation on a subsequent marriage?
   a. Couples who had lived together were just as likely to divorce as those who did not.
   b. There were no differences between cohabitors and noncohabitors regarding relationship stability and sexual satisfaction.
   c. Couples who cohabited prior to marriage were at higher risk of subsequent marital disruption.
   d. Various research studies have reported all of the above.

5. Theorists who propose that living together will have an overall negative impact on marriage suggest that
   a. the immorality of the arrangement will eventually corrode the relationship.
   b. couples who have lived together may treat a marital commitment as casually as a cohabitation arrangement and therefore may terminate a relationship more easily.
   c. our society needs more structure, higher values, and increased commitment rather than temporary, loosely defined relationships.
   d. children learn what they live.

6. Polyandry is a form of marriage between
   a. one woman and several men.
   b. one man and several women.
   c. one woman and one man.
   d. several men and several women.

7. Marriage in our society has typically served all of the following functions **except**
   a. defining inheritance rights to family property.
   b. regulating sexual behavior.
   c. providing for social and emotional support.
   d. providing for more gender role flexibility.

8. All of the following may be characteristic of domestic partnerships **except**
   a. a man and woman who practice serial monogamy
   b. a gay couple living together in a committed relationship
   c. a heterosexual couple living together in a committed relationship
   d. a lesbian couple living together in a committed relationship

9. In Gottman's study of marital interaction patterns, all of the following were cited as behaviors predictive of marital discord **except**
   a. making excuses and denying responsibility for disagreements
   b. verbal expressions of contempt
   c. "stonewalling"
   d. whining and crying

10. A premarital inventory called _____ predicted couples who would get divorced from those who were happily married with about _____ percent accuracy.
    a. PREPARE; 50
    b. Premarital Success Inventory; 65
    c. PREPARE; 80
    d. Premarital Success Inventory; 90

11. In the Blumstein and Schwartz survey, frequency of marital sexual interaction was associated with
    a. age at marriage.
    b. sexual satisfaction.
    c. socioeconomic class.
    d. prior sexual experiences.

12. Nonconsensual extramarital sex means that
    a. both partners engage in sexual relationships outside of their marriage, and they are aware of it but do not talk about it.
    b. a married person engages in an outside sexual relationship without the consent of his or her spouse.
    c. extramarital sex is an occasional, but not a habitual practice.
    d. an individual is having a long-term affair as opposed to a one-night stand.

13. Swinging appeared to be **most** popular
    a. in the 1940s and early 1950s.
    b. in the 1950s and early 1960s.
    c. in the 1960s and early 1970s.
    d. in the 1970s and early 1980s.

14. According to Gottman's research, which of the following is **most important** in terms of maintaining marital satisfaction?
    a. being sexually compatible
    b. having similar financial goals and values
    c. maintaining a five to one ratio of positive to negative interactions in the relationship
    d. being able to avoid frequent arguments and talk things out calmly and rationally

15. Research indicates that _____ may be associated with getting a divorce.
    a. having children
    b. different communication styles
    c. having a one-career family
    d. getting married at an early age

16. Which of the following is **true**?
    a. Coitus is the most common form of adult sexual activity in all societies.
    b. The aborigines of Western Australia practice serial monogamy.
    c. A minority of societies have restrictive norms pertaining to extramarital sex.
    d. With few exceptions, women around the world are allowed greater access to extramarital coitus than men are.

17. Current estimates suggest that _____ of all marriages will end in divorce.
    a. one-quarter
    b. one-half
    c. three-quarters

18. All of the following were given as reasons for the high divorce rates in the United States **except**
    a. the liberalization of the divorce laws
    b. the reduction of social stigma attached to divorce
    c. a greater abundance of wealth
    d. increasing influence of organized religion

19. Approximately _____ of divorced persons remarry.
    a. one in five
    b. two out of five
    c. three out of five
    d. four out of five

20. According to anthropologist Helen Fisher, humans are biologically programmed for serial pair bonding that is characterized by a natural inclination to leave a relationship after _____ years.
    a. two
    b. four
    c. six
    d. ten

21. Which of the following is **most important** to a woman's feeling of well-being regarding her sexuality as she ages?
    a. being on hormone replacement therapy
    b. having consistent orgasms
    c. being attractive to men
    d. sexual performance

22. Which of the following statements regarding widowhood is **false**?
    a. In most marriages, it is the man who dies first.
    b. The ratio of widows to widowers has been slowly decreasing since the early 1900s.
    c. About half of widowed men remarry.
    d. About one-quarter of widowed women remarry.

Critical Thinking/Personal Reflection

1. What is your current lifestyle and/or relationship style? How do the benefits and problems you experience with this lifestyle compare to what you have read in the text? Would you choose a different relationship style if you could? Why?

2. Assume that you and a significant other have decided to cohabit and/or get married. List at least twelve aspects of your relationship that you think would be important to discuss before you made that commitment. In addition to the topics themselves, what specific aspects or dimensions of each of those topics do you think would be important to explore?

3. From your observations and experience, what factors contribute to a successful relationship? When you see people that appear to be dissatisfied or unhappy in their relationships, what seem to be the factors associated with the distress? What might you do in the future to maximize your own relationship satisfaction? How does this compare to information presented in your text?

4. Have you ever experienced a nonconsensual extramarital relationship? What were your reasons for becoming involved with a person outside of your primary relationship? Would you do it again? What effect did that have on your primary relationship, if any? To your knowledge, has your partner ever engaged in a nonconsensual extramarital relationship? If your partner did, how would that affect you and the relationship?

5. Reflect on television programs you watch, movies you attend, books and magazines you read, and people you observe in your daily life, and cite specific examples of how the double standard of aging is reinforced and supported, as well as challenged or discouraged.

6. If you were responsible for establishing and implementing educational and/or entertainment programs on sexuality, as well as guidelines for sexual behavior in a nursing home, how would you go about it? Cite specific examples.

7. What kinds of opportunities and challenges do you expect as you grow older, especially in the area of sexual development? Think of your parents and/or grandparents, and imagine how you would like your life in general, or your sexual experiences in particular, to be different or similar to theirs.

8. List attitudes and behaviors of your own that have discriminated against older people, especially in regard to their sexuality. In studying this chapter, has your knowledge base changed in any way that would alter these assumptions or behaviors? Give specific examples.

Chapter Overview With Fill-In Answers

1a. later
1b. career
1c. divorce
1d. attitudes
2. married
3. cohabitation
4. cohabitation
5. sexual
6a. monogamy
6b. polygyny
6c. polyandry
7a. closeness
7b. independence
8a. defensiveness
8b. contempt
8c. stone-walling
9a. PREPARE
9b. 80
10. 50
11a. Kinsey
11b. intercourse
12. frequency
13a. mutuality
13b. active
14a. expectations
14b. attractiveness
15. extramarital
16. nonconsensual
17. vary
18. Consensual
19. open
20. Swinging
21. half
22. decline

23a. communication
23b. incompatibility
24. education
25. dies
26. first
27. four
28a. second
28b. divorce
29a. procreation
29b. youth
29c. acceptable
30a. double standard
30b. women
31. menopause
32. men
33a. sexual
33b. regularity
34. Nursing homes
35. medications
36. Gray Panthers
37. sexuality
38. fantasize
39. masturbation
40. Intimacy
41a. quality
41b. quantity
42. heterosexual
43. androgyny
44. man
45. increased
46. divorce
47a. half
41b. a quarter

Sample Multiple Choice Answers

1. d	2. c	3. b	4. d	5. b	6. a	7. d	8. a
9. d	10. c	11. b	12. b	13. d	14. c	15. d	16. a
17. b	18. d	19. d	20. b	21. c	22. b		

15

The Nature and Origin of Sexual Difficulties

Introduction

The authors begin with a discussion of the organic, cultural, individual and relationship influences that may negatively affect sexual expression. From that point, they go on to explore a range of desire, excitement, and orgasm phase sexual difficulties that men and women experience. Some of the factors that contribute to painful intercourse in women and men are also presented.

Review of Key Terms and Concepts

Key terms and concepts are listed and defined below. Refer to the subject index in the back of your textbook for additional information.

1. **diabetes** — an inherited disease that occurs when the pancreas fails to secrete insulin. Nerve damage or circulatory problems resulting from diabetes can cause sexual problems

2. **arthritis** — a progressive, systemic disease that results in inflammation of the joints. It does not directly impair sexual response, but body image problems may diminish interest in sex

3. **multiple sclerosis** — a neurological disease of the brain and spinal cord that affects vision, sensation and voluntary movement

4. **cerebrovascular accidents (CVA)** — commonly called strokes, often result in residual impairments of motor, sensory, emotional and cognitive functioning that can have a negative effect on sexuality

5. **spinal cord injuries (SCI)** — damage to the spinal cord that obstructs the pathway between body and brain, resulting in body paralysis that will vary according to the location of the injury

6. **paraplegic** — a person with an injury lower on the spinal cord characterized by loss of feeling and voluntary muscle function of the trunk and legs

7. **quadriplegic** — a person with an injury higher on the spinal cord characterized by loss of feeling and voluntary muscle function of the arms or hands as well as the trunk and legs

8. **sensory amplification** — the method used by some disabled men and women to achieve maximum pleasure from a sensory input

9. **cerebral palsy (CP)** — caused by damage to the brain that may occur before or during birth or during early childhood, it is characterized by mild to severe lack of muscle control

10. **hypoactive sexual desire (HSD)** — a sexual difficulty involving lack of interest in sexual fantasy and activity

11. **sexual aversion disorder** — extreme and irrational fear of sexual activity

12. **female sexual arousal disorder** — a woman's persistent inability to attain or maintain the vaginal lubrication-swelling response

13. **male erectile disorder** — a sexual difficulty whereby a man's penis does not become erect in response to sexual stimulation

14. **impotence** — the inappropriate and pejorative term often applied to male erection difficulty; literally means "without power"

15. **female orgasm disorder (anorgasmia)** — a sexual difficulty involving the absence of orgasm in women

16. **frigidity** — an imprecise and pejorative term traditionally used to describe a variety of female sexual problems

17. **male orgasmic disorder** — the inability of a man to ejaculate during sexual activity, usually intercourse

18. **premature ejaculation** — a sexual difficulty whereby a man ejaculates so rapidly as to impair his own or his partner's pleasure

19. **faking orgasms** — a sexual difficulty whereby a person pretends to experience orgasm during sexual interaction

20. **dyspareunia** — pain or discomfort during intercourse

21. **Peyronie's disease** — abnormal fibrous tissue and calcium deposits in the penis which may result in pain or discomfort during intercourse

22. **vulvar vestibulitis syndrome** — a condition that can result in severe pain at the entrance of the vagina

23. **endometriosis** — a condition in which tissue that normally grows on the walls of the uterus implants on various parts of the abdominal cavity

24. **vaginismus** — a sexual difficulty in which a woman experiences involuntary spasmodic contractions of the muscles of the outer third of the vagina

Chapter Overview With Fill-Ins

After reading each of the major sections in the chapter, check your retention by filling in each of the blanks in the corresponding sections below. The answers are provided at the end of the chapter.

Origins of Sexual Difficulties

1. Some of the general causes of sexual difficulties can be described under four different categories: organic factors, cultural influences, individual and _____ factors.

2. Diabetes is an inherited disease that occurs when the _____ fails to secrete insulin.

3. Diabetes is a disease of the endocrine system and a leading cause of _____ problems.

4. Research indicates that women who develop diabetes in _____ report few sexual difficulties.

5. However, women whose diabetes begins in adulthood are likely to have problems with sexual desire, lubrication, and _____.

6. Arthritis is a progressive, systemic disease that results in inflammation of the _____.

7. Arthritis does not directly impair _____ _____, but body image problems, depression, and chronic pain and fatigue may lessen a person's sexual interest.

8. Arthritic impairment of hands, hips, knees, and arms may make masturbation difficult or impossible, and/or may interfere with certain _____ positions.

9. Cancer and its therapies can impair hormonal, _____, and neurological function necessary for normal sexual function.

10. Although all forms of cancer can affect sexual functioning, many people are most concerned by the effects of cancers of the _____ organs.

Chronic Illnesses

11. Multiple sclerosis (MS) is a neurological disease of the a)_____ and b)_____ _____ in which damage occurs to the myelin sheath that covers nerve fibers.

12. Vision, _____, and voluntary movement are affected in people who have MS.

13. Most MS patients experience changes in their sexual functioning and at least _____ have had sexual problems.

14. Cerebrovascular accidents (CVA), commonly called _____, often result in residual impairments of motor, sensory, emotional, and cognitive functioning that can have a negative effect on sexuality.

15. Stroke survivors frequently report a decline in the frequency of interest, _____, and sexual activity.

16. People with spinal cord injuries (SCI) have reduced motor control and sensation because the damage to the spinal cord obstructs the pathway between body and _____.

17. Although the injury does not necessarily impair sexual a)_____, an SCI person may have impaired ability for arousal and b)_____.

18. _____ _____, the act of thinking about a physical stimulus, concentrating on it, and amplifying the sensation in your mind to an intense degree is one technique to increase feelings of pleasure.

19. Cerebral palsy (CP) is caused by damage to the _____ before or during birth or during childhood.

20. CP is characterized by mild to severe lack of _____ control.

21. A person's _____ may or may not be affected, although it is often mistakenly assumed that people with CP are mentally disabled because of their physical difficulty in communicating.

22. _____ sensation is unaffected by CP.

23. Spasticity or deformity of arms and hands may make a)_____ difficult, and the same problems in hips and knees may make certain b)_____ positions painful or difficult.

24. The _____ losses of blindness and deafness can affect a person's sexuality in several ways.

25. One cultural influence that may contribute to sexual problems people experience is negative _____ _____ which may result in guilt, discomfort, anxiety, or embarrassment concerning sexuality that may affect our sexual functioning as we mature.

26. Although the rigidity of the _____ _____ appears to be lessening somewhat, the notion that women should be sexually passive while men should be ultimately responsible for sexual interaction still lingers, often creating discomfort, frustration, and resentment in sexual relations between men and women.

27. The cultural notion that sex equals _____-_____ intercourse has placed a disproportionate emphasis on coitus while at the same time minimizing the enjoyment of relating sexually in a variety of other ways.

28. _____ anxiety is another cultural influence that can block natural sexual arousal and release.

29. Individual factors that may affect sexual expression include: the sexual knowledge and attitudes people acquire about sex; an individual's a)_____-_____; emotional difficulties such as anxiety or depression; childhood sexual abuse and adult sexual b)_____.

30. A variety of relationship factors can also affect sexual satisfaction, such as unresolved relationship problems, ineffective a)_____, fear of pregnancy or sexually transmitted diseases, and conflicts regarding sexual b)_____.

31. A person may experience sexual problems in all situations with all partners (_____) or only in specific situations or with specific partners (_____).

32. _____ _____ _____, or lack of "sexual appetite," is a common problem experienced by both men and women.

33. Another type of desire phase difficulty is when sexual partners may have _____ in their preferences for amount, type, and timing of sexual activities.

34. When low desire includes a fear of sex and a strong desire to avoid sexual situations, it is considered _____ _____.

Excitement Phase Difficulties

35. _____ _____ is a woman's first physiological response to sexual arousal.

36. If lack of lubrication is a persistent problem, a woman is experiencing female _____ _____ disorder.

37. Problems with male a)_____ disorder can be classified into two broad types: men with lifelong erectile disorder, who have never maintained penetration with a partner throughout their entire lives; and men with b)_____ erectile disorder, who have had erections with partners in the past but who are no longer able to do so in current situations.

Orgasm Phase Difficulties

38. The word that is commonly used now to refer to absence of orgasm in women is _____.

39. A woman who has _____, lifelong anorgasmia has never experienced orgasm by masturbation or with a partner.

40. _____ anorgasmia refers to a woman who experiences orgasm rarely, or in some situations but not in others.

41. _____ _____ disorder refers to the inability of a man to ejaculate during sexual activity.

42. A common orgasm difficulty that men experience is _____ ejaculation.

43. a)_____ orgasms is typically discussed in reference to b)_____, although a smaller percentage of c)_____ do this as well.

Dyspareunia

44. _____ is the medical term for painful intercourse, which occurs most commonly in women but which men may experience this as well.

45. Men may experience painful intercourse if they are uncircumcised and the a)_____ is too tight, if b)_____ accumulates underneath the foreskin, or if they have c)_____ disease, a condition where fibrous tissue and calcium deposits develop in the space above and between the cavernous bodies of the penis.

46. For women, discomfort at the vaginal opening or inside the vaginal walls is usually due to inadequate arousal and _____.

47. Physiological conditions such as insufficient _____ may also reduce lubrication.

48. Other causes of painful intercourse include: a)_____ infections; contraceptive foams, creams, or jellies; allergic reactions to condoms or diaphragms; an intact b)_____; or scar tissue at the vaginal opening.

49. _____ _____ syndrome results in severe pain at the entrance of the vagina.

50. Pain deep in the pelvis during coitus may be due to the jarring of the a)_____ or stretching of the b)_____ ligaments.

51. Another source of deep pelvic pain is _____, a condition in which tissue that normally grows on the walls of the uterus implants on various parts of the abdominal cavity.

52. _____ is characterized by strong involuntary muscle contractions in the outer third of the vagina.

53. The contractions may be so strong that attempts to insert a _____ into the vagina are very painful.

54. The incidence of vaginismus is believed to be very _____.

Matching

Match the terms below with the appropriate descriptions. Note that some terms may be used more than once but choose only **one** answer for each.

a. HSD
b. male erectile disorder
c. premature ejaculation
d. sexual aversion
e. anorgasmia
f. faking orgasms
g. dyspareunia

h. lubrication inhibition
i. Peyronie's disease
j. male orgasmic disorder
k. vulvar vestibulitis
l. endometriosis
m. vaginismus

_____1. Approximately 5–10 percent of women experience this problem.

_____2. the most common sexual problem men experience

_____3. One study indicated that 60 percent of heterosexual women and 17 percent of heterosexual men have had this experience.

_____4. may experience nausea, diarrhea, dizziness as a result of this

_____5. may occur as the result of low estrogen levels

_____6. Twenty-five percent of the authors' male students say this is an ongoing problem.

_____7. Eighty percent of the cases involve organic impairment.

_____8. lack of sexual appetite

_____9. This problem may be decreasing in incidence due to available self-help books.

_____10. Eight percent of men experience this problem

_____11. don't fantasize or initiate sex but may be sexually responsive

_____12. may be a result of prolonged intercourse

_____13. This problem is a conscious decision

_____14. the medical term for painful intercourse

_____15. Birth control pills are sometimes prescribed to control this condition.

_____16. can result in curvature of the penis

_____17. severe pain at vaginal entrance

_____18. Two percent of women experience this.

Sample Short Answer Test Questions

1. According to the National Health and Social Life Survey, what is the most common sexual problem that men report having? That women report having?

2. How may each of the following affect sexual functioning?

    a. alcohol

    b. marijuana

    c. tobacco

3. Define diabetes. How may it affect sexual functioning in men? In women?

4. What differences exist in women who develop diabetes in adolescence as opposed to adulthood?

5. Define arthritis and discuss how it may affect sexual expression.

6. Define multiple sclerosis and describe how common it is.

7. How may multiple sclerosis affect sexual desire and function?

8. How may CVA negatively affect sexuality?

9. Distinguish between paraplegic and quadriplegic.

10. How may SCI affect a man's sexuality?

11. How may SCI affect a woman's sexuality?

12. Cite research that indicates how many SCI men experience erections.

13. Explain the technique of sensory amplification. In what situations is it used?

14. What causes cerebral palsy?

15. What are the effects of CP and what mistaken assumptions about people with CP are often made as a result of this?

16. How does CP affect sexual functioning?

17. List four types of cultural influences that may contribute to sexual problems.

18. List four individual factors that may contribute to sexual difficulties.

19. List four relationship factors that may contribute to sexual problems.

20. What are the two terms used to describe how sexual problems may vary in duration and focus?

21. Define HSD. Can people who have HSD experience excitement and/or orgasm?

22. What common pattern emerges when sexual partners have significant differences in their preferences for amount, type, and timing of sexual activities?

23. List some of the physiological symptoms that people with sexual aversion might experience.

24. List at least five situations in which women might experience lubrication inhibition.

25. List and briefly describe two types of male erectile disorder.

26. What percentage of erectile disorder cases involve some degree of organic impairment?

27. List and describe two different types of anorgasmia.

28. What percentage of women experience generalized, lifelong anorgasmia? Why does the number of women who experience this problem seem to be decreasing?

29. Cite research to indicate how commonly women experience orgasm during coitus without additional manual-clitoral stimulation.

30. What percentage of men experience male orgasmic disorder?

31. How long does intercourse last for the average American couple? Considering this, how is premature ejaculation defined?

32. Cite evidence that indicates how common premature ejaculation is.

33. What percentage of women and what percentage of men have faked orgasm?

34. List four conditions that may cause painful intercourse in men.

35. What is Peyronie's disease?

36. List at least six factors that might account for pain at the vaginal opening or inside the vaginal walls.

37. List three possible causes of deep pelvic pain during intercourse.

38. Define vaginismus. How common is it?

Sample Multiple Choice Test Questions

Select the best alternative. Check your answers with the answer key at the end of the chapter.

1. Which of the following statements is **false**?
    a. Research indicates that many happily married couples who experience sexual problems still feel positively about their marriages.
    b. Premature ejaculation is the sexual problem most commonly reported by men.
    c. The National Health and Social Life Survey indicated that approximately twice as many women as men experienced lack of sexual desire.
    d. According to several studies, anorgasmia is the sexual problem that is most commonly reported by women.

2. Vulvar vestibulitis is
    a. a desire difficulty.
    b. an arousal difficulty.
    c. an orgasm difficulty.
    d. a type of dyspareunia.

3. All of the following are cultural factors that might contribute to sexual difficulties **except**
    a. the double standard
    b. a narrow definition of sexuality
    c. negative childhood learning
    d. emotional difficulties

4. A person who is diagnosed as having generalized, lifelong HSD
   a. did not exhibit sexual curiosity as a child and, as an adult, does not fantasize or demonstrate interest in being sexually involved.
   b. has masturbated since childhood but has no interest in being sexually involved as an adult.
   c. did not exhibit sexual curiosity as a child, but is now sexually active yet unable to experience orgasm.
   d. is sexually interested and responsive with a lover but exhibits no interest in being sexually involved with a spouse.

5. Which one of the following statements concerning HSD is **false**?
   a. Generalized, lifelong HSD is a fairly common sexual problem.
   b. Certain medications may be associated with HSD.
   c. HSD would be an adaptive response to a partner who is verbally or physically abusive.
   d. A person with HSD can experience excitement and/or orgasm.

6. _____ is a neurological disease of the brain and spinal cord.
   a. Cerebral palsy
   b. Diabetes
   c. Arthritis
   d. Multiple sclerosis

7. A man who experiences sexual aversion
   a. may exhibit physiological symptoms such as sweating and trembling.
   b. will probably desire sex more frequently than his partner.
   c. probably enjoys fantasizing about sex even though he has difficulty responding sexually when he is with a woman.
   d. usually has problems with ejaculatory inhibition.

8. A woman exhibits little interest in initiating and participating in sex with her partner, although when she does have sex, she becomes aroused and is orgasmic. Her sexual problem would **best** be described as
   a. female sexual arousal disorder.
   b. hypoactive sexual desire.
   c. situational anorgasmia.
   d. delayed sexual response.

9. Diminished lubrication is normal in all of the following situations **except**
   a. breast-feeding
   b. following menopause
   c. during prolonged intercourse
   d. during masturbation

10. Erection of the penis is equivalent to _____ in women.
    a. sex flush
    b. vaginal lubrication
    c. orgasmic response
    d. sexual desire

11. Which of the following comes from the Latin and means "without power"?
    a. frigidity
    b. impotence
    c. erectile inhibition
    d. sine pudendum

12. A man is unable to have an erection in his sexual encounters with his partner, but that does not bother him and it is acceptable to her as long as he brings her to orgasm in other ways. What the authors would have to say regarding this is that
    a. the man is impotent.
    b. the man has acquired erectile inhibition.
    c. the man suffers from hypoactive sexual desire.
    d. neither the man nor his partner have a problem, since they are satisfied with the situation.

13. Which of the following is affected in people who have MS?
    a. intellectual functioning
    b. hearing
    c. respiration
    d. voluntary movement

14. Which of the following statements concerning orgasmic disorders is **false**?
    a. Women with this problem may still maintain sexual desire.
    b. Women may feel highly disappointed or distressed by this condition.
    c. The incidence of generalized, lifelong anorgasmia among women is decreasing.
    d. Most women who experience orgasmic disorders are unable to reach orgasm through manual, oral, or intravaginal stimulation.

15. According to Hite's research, how many women have orgasms during intercourse without additional manual-clitoral stimulation?
    a. 80 percent
    b. 50 percent
    c. 30 percent
    d. 10 percent

16. Which of the following statements is **true**?
    a. Causes of anorgasmia are typically physiological in origin.
    b. Approximately 30 percent of adult women in the United States have generalized, lifelong anorgasmia.
    c. A woman with situational anorgasmia experiences orgasm in some situations but not in others.
    d. The number of women with generalized, lifelong anorgasmia is increasing slightly.

17. Men who have never been able to experience intravaginal ejaculation would be diagnosed as having
    a. generalized, lifelong male orgasmic disorder.
    b. situational, acquired male orgasmic disorder.
    c. premature ejaculation.
    d. retrograde ejaculation.

18. Based on data available regarding the general public, as well as what male student's in the authors' human sexuality classes have reported, over _____ percent of men have experienced premature ejaculation as an ongoing problem.
    a. 5–10
    b. 15–20
    c. 25–30
    d. 40–50

19. Dyspareunia is
    a. experienced by men.
    b. experienced by women.
    c. experienced equally by both women and men.
    d. experienced by both sexes but most commonly by women

20. A condition in which tissue that normally grows on the walls of the uterus implants on various parts of the abdominal cavity is called
    a. Peyronie's disease.
    b. endometriosis.
    c. vulvar vestibulitis syndrome.
    d. ectopic adhesions.

21. Which of the following statements is **true**?
    a. Jarring of the ovaries during intercourse may cause pain at the vaginal opening.
    b. Vaginismus is a fairly common problem that women experience.
    c. Vulvar vestibulitis syndrome results in deep pelvic pain.
    d. Vaginismus may be associated with a homosexual orientation.

22. Nerve damage or circulatory problems from _____ can cause sexual problems.
    a. uterine cancer
    b. diabetes
    c. heart disease
    d. testicular cancer

23. Which of the following statements concerning men and diabetes is **false**?
    a. Loss of sexual desire is the most common sexual problem they experience as a result of their illness.
    b. Some diabetic men ejaculate into their bladders.
    c. Heavy alcohol use and poor blood sugar control increase the chance of erectile problems.
    d. It is a leading organic cause of erectile disorders.

24. Cerebrovascular accidents, commonly called _____, often result in motor, sensory, and emotional impairments that may negatively affect sexuality.
    a. heart attacks
    b. aneurysms
    c. anginas
    d. strokes

25. One source of painful intercourse that can result in curvature of the penis is
    a. phimosis.
    b. priapism.
    c. Peyronie's disease.
    d. nocturnal penile tumescence.

26. _____ refers to loss of feeling and voluntary muscle function of the arms or hands, as well as the trunk and legs.
    a. Paraplegia
    b. Quadriplegia
    c. Cerebromuscular degeneration
    d. Muscular atrophy

27. In spinal cord injuries, injuries lower on the spine result in _____ while higher injuries cause _____.
    a. paraplegia; quadriplegia
    b. quadriplegia; paraplegia
    c. skeletal paralysis; skeletal deformity
    d. skeletal deformity; skeletal paralysis

28. According to various studies, what percentage of SCI men are able to experience erections?
    a. less than 10 percent
    b. approximately 25 percent
    c. over 50 percent
    d. over 90 percent

29. Which of the following is the **best** example of sensory amplification?
    a. A woman who has lost all genital sensation is able to think about the inside of her arm, which is extremely sensitive, and transpose previously experienced genital sensations to this area, which can result in arousal and/or orgasm.
    b. Despite loss of all genital sensation as the result of a spinal cord injury, a man uses a vibrator on his penis to enhance sexual pleasure.
    c. A woman with CP focuses on pleasurable genital sensations to distract her from knee and hip pain.
    d. You are listening to music you enjoy and you turn up the volume, but it is too loud and your eardrums rupture.

Critical Thinking/Personal Reflection

1. Have you, a partner, or someone close to you ever experienced a sexual problem? If so, what values and information contributed to your understanding of the problem at the time? Based on what you know now, how would you have perceived or dealt with the problem differently?

2. Think in terms of your own childhood learning, the double standard, the cultural notion that "real sex" equals intercourse, and the goal-oriented nature of sexual expression in our society today. To what extent have these cultural influences affected your sexuality? Give specific examples. Are there any aspects of this with which you are dissatisfied? If so, how might you change them?

3. How would you assess your sexual knowledge and attitudes, as well as your self-concept in terms of how it affects your sexual expression? Are there areas that you would like to change or improve? If so, how might you go about doing that?

4. Describe your worst sexual experience — alone or with someone. "Worst" could be painful, traumatic, embarrassing, humiliating. Knowing what you know now — about sexual problems, sexual functioning, sexual communication, etc. — how could the trauma of that experience be minimized if you could do it over? Give specific details and examples.

5.   Think about specific individuals whom you have encountered in your life that have had various illnesses and disabilities. What incorrect assumptions, if any, did you make about the sexual nature and expression of these people, as well as other people with whom you have had more casual contact? How has your perspective changed, if at all, as a result of what you have read as well as your own life experiences?

6.   What do you think about institutions such as nursing homes or hospitals providing for the sexual needs of the residents? If you support this idea, what are some specific provisions regarding available facilities, staff training and development, etc. that would be important to establish?

Chapter Overview With Fill-In Answers

1. relationship
2. pancreas
3. erectile
4. adolescence
5. orgasm
6. joints
7. sexual response
8. intercourse
9. vascular
10. reproductive
11a. brain
11b. spinal cord
12. sensation
13. half
14. strokes
15. arousal
16. brain
17a. desire
17b. orgasm
18. Sensory amplification
19. brain
20. muscular
21. intelligence
22. Genital
23a. masturbation
23b. intercourse
24. sensory
25. childhood learning
26. double standard
27. penile-vaginal
28. Performance
29a. self-concept
29b. assault
30a. communication
30b. orientation

31a. generalized
31b. situational
32. Hypoactive sexual desire
33. discrepancies
34. sexual aversion
35. Vaginal lubrication
36. sexual arousal
37a. erectile
37b. acquired
38. anorgasmia
39. generalized
40. Situational
41. Male orgasmic
42. premature
43a. Faking
43b. women
43c. men
44. Dyspareunia
45a. foreskin
45b. smegma
45c. Peyronie's
46. lubrication
47. hormones
48a. vaginal
48b. hymen
49. Vulvar vestibulitis
50a. ovaries
50b. uterine
51. endometriosis
52. Vaginismus
53. penis
54. low

Matching Answers

1. e	2. c	3. f	4. d	5. h	6. c	7. b	8. a
9. e	10. j	11. a	12. h	13. f	14. g	15. l	16. i
17. k	18. m						

Sample Multiple Choice Answers

1. d	2. d	3. d	4. a	5. a	6. d	7. a	8. b
9. d	10. b	11. b	12. d	13. d	14. d	15. c	16. c
17. a	18. c	19. d	20. b	21. d	22. b	23. a	24. d
25. c	26. b	27. a	28. c	29. a			

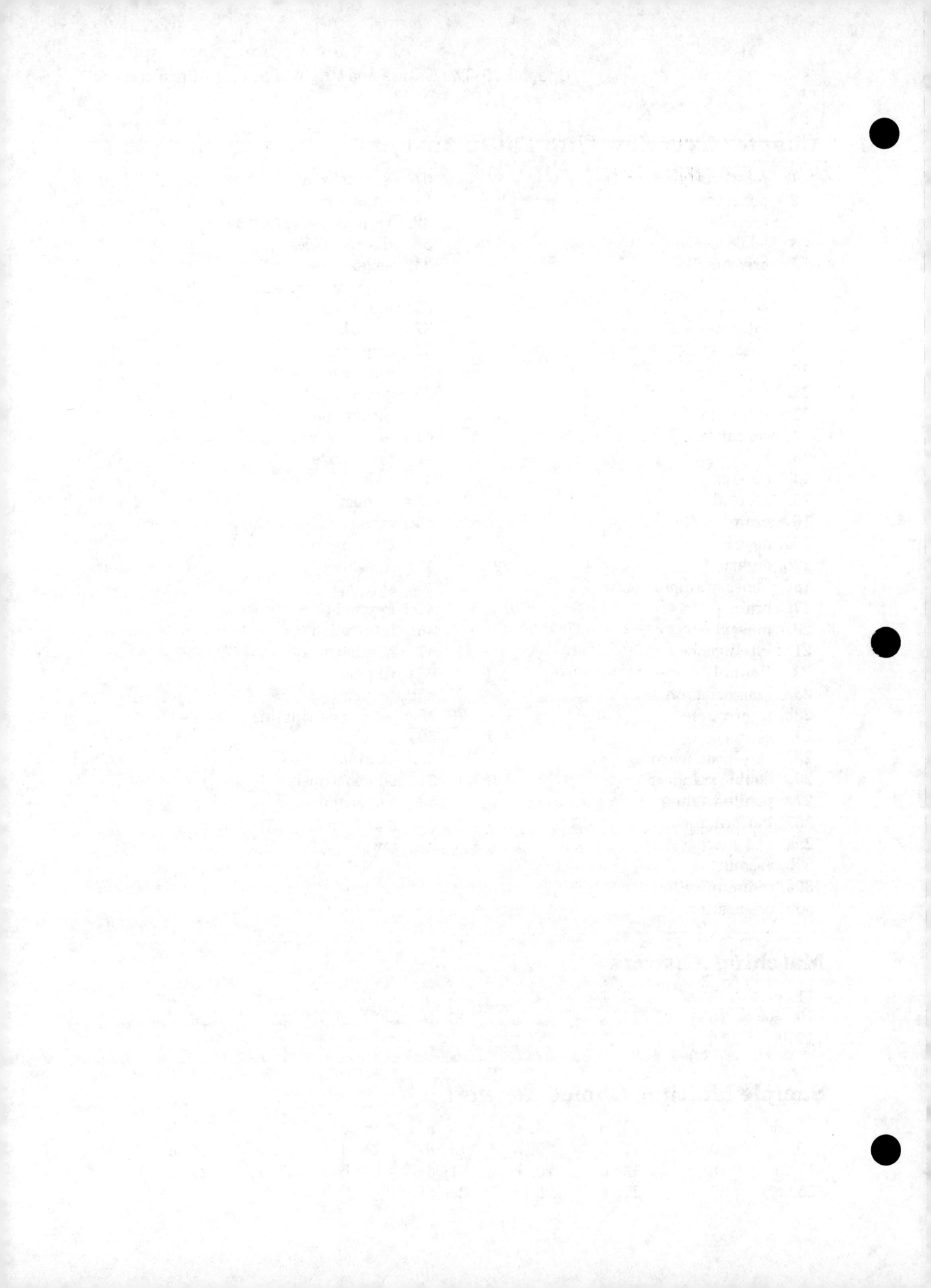

16

Sex Therapy and Enhancement

Introduction

For many people, what "sex therapy" involves is often largely unknown or misunderstood. This chapter demystifies the process by providing specific information on exactly what sex therapy entails and by describing in detail various strategies that individuals and couples may use to cope with a range of sexual difficulties. Guidelines for selecting a therapist are outlined at the end of the chapter.

Review of Key Terms and Concepts

Key terms and concepts are listed and defined below. Refer to the subject index in the back of your textbook for additional information.

1. **sensate focus** — a series of touching and communication exercises developed by Masters and Johnson, used to enhance sexual pleasure and to reduce performance pressure

2. **bridge maneuver** — a technique used to help women experience orgasm during intercourse

3. **stop-start technique** — a treatment technique for premature ejaculation, consisting of stimulating the man's penis to the point of impending orgasm and then stopping until the pre-ejaculatory sensations subside

4. **squeeze technique** — a treatment technique for premature ejaculation, whereby pressure is applied to the frenum and top side of a man's penis until the man loses the urge to ejaculate

5. **PLISSIT** — a model of sex therapy that specifies four levels of treatment: Permission; Limited Information; Specific Suggestions; and Intensive Therapy

6. **psychosexual therapy** — treatment designed to help clients gain awareness of their unconscious thoughts and feelings that contribute to their sexual problems

7. **systems therapy** — treatment that focuses on interactions within a couple's relationship and on the functions of the sexual problems in the relationship

8. **postmodern sex therapy** — the integration of systems, psychosocial and behavioral approaches in treating sexual problems

9. **EMDR (Eye Movement Desensitization and Reprocessing)** — a therapy technique that appears to stimulate rapid information and emotional processing in the brain, similar to that which occurs during REM sleep

Chapter Overview With Fill-Ins

After reading each of the major sections in the chapter, check your retention by filling in each of the blanks in the corresponding sections below. The answers are provided at the end of the chapter.

Basics of Sexual Enhancement and Sex Therapy

1. There are several procedures for improving _____ of your body and of activities that provide the most pleasurable stimulation.

2. Exercises that increase _____-_____ help us to better understand our sexual feelings and needs and how our bodies respond, which in turn makes us better able to share these feelings with a partner.

3. _____ exercises are an effective way to learn about and experience sexual response.

4. One of the primary benefits of sex therapy is that couples often develop more effective _____ skills.

5. Masters and Johnson developed a series of touching experiences called _____ _____ that can be extremely helpful in reducing the anxiety caused by goal orientation and increasing communication and closeness.

6. Finally, _____ in the presence of a partner may be a way for couples to let each other know what kind of touching they find arousing.

Specific Suggestions for Women

7. Women who wish to learn to become a)_____ may do so by seeking individual or group b)_____.

8. Therapy programs for _____ are based on progressive self-awareness exercises that a woman does at home between therapy sessions.

9. Once a woman has learned to experience orgasm through _____-_____, she shares her discoveries with her partner.

10. Other exercises involve self-stimulation with her _____ present and nondemanding manual-_____ pleasuring.

11. The use of the _____ _____ is suggested for women who wish to try experiencing orgasm during intercourse without direct clitoral stimulation.

12. Treatment for vaginismus usually begins during a a)_____ exam with the physician demonstrating the vaginal b)_____ reaction to the couple.

13. After a series of at-home relaxation and self-awareness exercises , a woman learns to insert a _____ (or a small dilator) into her vagina.

14. Eventually the woman's _____ becomes involved in the exercises, until the woman is able to experience penile-vaginal containment and, finally, thrusting with intercourse.

Specific Suggestions for Men

15. There are several approaches for learning better _____ control.

16. One approach for better ejaculatory control is to _____ more frequently.

17. Another approach is to "_____."

18. He can also alter intercourse position so there is minimal _____ tension, which is associated with a rapid sexual response cycle.

19. In addition, he can _____ with his partner in order to prolong coitus.

20. He can also consider alternatives to sexual sharing other than _____.

21. James Semans, a urologist, developed the _____-_____ technique for controlling premature ejaculation.

22. The _____ technique, while not as commonly used for premature ejaculation, can still be effective.

23. Small doses of _____ may also delay ejaculation for some men.

24. With the exception of problems that are organic in origin, _____ is the major stumbling block to erectile response.

25. Anxiety-reducing exercises are usually a)_____ _____ experiences, and initially it is suggested to not touch genitals and emphasize instead the b)_____ pleasure of touching and being touched.

26. Some men who have impaired erectile functioning as the result of a _____ problem adjust well to the absence of erection by emphasizing and enjoying other ways of sexual sharing.

27. If illness or injury leave a man unable to have erections, there are several medical treatments available: oral medications such as a)_____ and injections of b)_____ medications that dilate blood vessels and cause erection.

28. _____, a drug occasionally prescribed for hypotension, helps induce erection in some cases.

29. Devices that suction _____ into the penis and hold it there during intercourse have also been developed.

30. Another option is a surgically implanted _____ _____.

31. There are two basic types available: one is a pair of a)_____ rods placed inside the cavernous bodies of the penis, and the second type is an b)_____ device that enables the penis to be either flaccid or erect.

32. A behavioral approach is generally used in the treatment of male _____ _____, in addition to psychotherapy aimed at reducing resentment in the relationship when that plays a role in the problem.

Treating Hypoactive Sexual Desire

33. Many therapists consider desire problems the most _____ to treat.

34. Various aspects of treatment involve encouraging erotic responses through a)_____-_____ and arousing fantasies; reducing anxiety with appropriate information and b)_____ _____ exercises; improving communication; increasing skill in initiation and refusal of sexual activity; and expanding one's repertoire of affectionate and sexual c)_____.

Seeking Professional Assistance

35. The PLISSIT model of sex therapy specifies _____ levels of treatment.

36. PLISSIT is an acronym for a)_____, Limited Information, Specific b)_____, and Intensive Therapy.

37. Treatment that combines _____ techniques with the development of insight into unconscious conflicts is an important development in the sex therapy field.

38. In insight-oriented therapy or _____ therapy, the therapist provides interpretations and reflection to help clients gain awareness and understanding of the unconscious feelings and thoughts that have been contributing to their sexual problems.

39. In contrast to psychosexual therapy, _____ therapy is based on the concept that the identified problems serve important current functions in the relationship.

40. Integration of all of the above is called _____ sex therapy.

41. Finally, _____ _____ _____ _____ is a new therapy method that stimulates informational and emotional processing in the brain.

42. To locate a _____, you might ask your sexuality course instructor or health care practitioner for referrals.

43. In addition, the American Association of _____ _____, Counselors, and Therapists (AASECT) can send you the names of therapists in your area who have applied and qualified for AASECT certification.

44. Your _____ _____ _____ or friends may know therapists whom they might recommend.

45. In selecting a therapist, such considerations as specific background and training in a)_____ _____, your goals, the therapists' approach, your comfort level with the therapist, and b)_____ of therapy sessions are all important considerations to take into account.

Sample Short Answer Test Questions

1. List the four procedures that provide the basis for much of sex therapy.

2. Describe how modern sex therapy can conflict with the values of various cultures.

3. Describe sensate focus. What is its purpose?

4.   Describe the "sexological exam" exercise. What is its purpose?

5.   For what is the back-to-chest position used?

6.   What is the bridge maneuver? When is it used?

7.   Briefly describe the treatment program for women with vaginismus.

8.   Why may vaginismus be difficult to treat?

9.   List five strategies that men can use when they want to delay ejaculation.

10. Compare and contrast the stop-start and squeeze techniques. Which is more commonly used?

11. When erectile difficulties are not physiologically based, what emotions most likely cause this problem?

12. List and briefly describe various medical treatments that are available for men who are permanently unable to have erections.

13. What is Rejoyn?

14. List three types of surgical treatments that are used for dealing with erectile problems.

15. What approach is used in treating male orgasmic disorder?

16. What emotion experienced by a man may contribute to male orgasmic disorder?

17. Describe the important aspects of a treatment program to reduce ejaculatory disorder.

18. How difficult is HSD to treat compared to other sexual problems?

19. What relationship problems are frequently associated with HSD?

20. List and briefly describe the four levels of the PLISSIT model of sex therapy.

21. Briefly describe each of the following:
    a. psychosexual therapy

    b. systems therapy

    c. postmodern therapy

    d. EMDR

22. What considerations might you want to take into account in selecting a therapist?

23. List four of the most common types of professional training therapists have.

Sample Multiple Choice Test Questions

Select the best alternative. Check your answers with the answer key at the end of the chapter.

1. All of the following are basic sex therapy procedures for increased body awareness and acceptance **except**
   a. self-awareness exercises
   b. sensate focus
   c. masturbation exercises
   d. the bridge maneuver

2. Which of the following statements is **false**?
   a. Among many Asians, it can be considered shameful to discuss sex.
   b. Orthodox Jews would participate in masturbation exercises in order to treat a specific sexual problem, but would not be allowed to participate in oral sex.
   c. Muslims are taught to avoid talking to their spouses about sex.
   d. In Saudi Arabia, both male sexual potency and couple fertility are considered to be primary sexual values.

3. Masters and Johnson labeled this technique and use it as a basic step in the treatment of many sexual problems.
   a. stop-start technique
   b. squeeze technique
   c. sensate focus
   d. bridge maneuver

4. Which of the following would be **most helpful** for women learning to experience orgasm with her partner, and for premature ejaculation and erectile difficulties?
   a. using the first two steps of the PLISSIT model
   b. practicing self-awareness exercises
   c. using the stop-start technique
   d. masturbating with a partner present

5. Which of the following statements concerning genital sensate focus is **true**?
   a. The back-to-chest position is recommended when a woman is experiencing genital stimulation by her partner.
   b. Having orgasm during initial sessions is discouraged.
   c. The use of lotion or oil is suggested to increase sensation.
   d. all of the above

6. The bridge maneuver involves
   a. nondemand genital pleasuring.
   b. oral clitoral stimulation in order to achieve orgasm.
   c. manual clitoral stimulation during coitus, followed by pelvic movements.
   d. using a modified rear-entry position to increase sensation for the male.

7. All of the following are parts of the treatment program for vaginismus **except**
   a. pelvic exam by physician
   b. the bridge maneuver
   c. insertion of fingers or dilators into vagina
   d. relaxation and self-awareness exercises

8. The stop-start technique
   a. is not as commonly used as the squeeze technique.
   b. has been used successfully in the treatment of ejaculatory disorder.
   c. was developed by a urologist named James Semans.
   d. all of the above

9. The _____ refers to a technique whereby a man's partner applies pressure to the glans of the penis in order to delay ejaculation.
   a. stop-start technique
   b. squeeze technique
   c. bridge maneuver
   d. Kegel exercise

10. Which of the following would be **most likely** to delay ejaculation?
    a. woman-above intercourse position
    b. man-above intercourse position
    c. having orgasms infrequently
    d. increased muscle tension during intercourse

11. All of the following are parts of the therapy program for dealing with erectile inhibition **except**
    a. sensate focus
    b. vaginal penetration as soon as the man is able to sustain an erection
    c. nondemand pleasuring
    d. vaginal penetration in the woman-above position

12. One disadvantage of the penile prosthesis in which two rods are placed inside the cavernous bodies of the penis is
    a. retrograde ejaculation.
    b. an increased number of "partial" orgasms.
    c. that the penis is always semierect.
    d. all of the above

13. Brad and Michelle are seeing a sex therapist for the erectile difficulties Brad is experiencing. Prior to the final intercourse phase of treatment, their therapist will probably advise them to
    a. practice sensate focus exercises until erections are frequent.
    b. practice stimulating, stopping, and then restimulating to experience return of the erection.
    c. focus on mutual pleasure and sensuality rather than worrying about intercourse goals.
    d. all of the above

14. Which of the following statements concerning male orgasmic disorder is **false**?
    a. Treatment for this difficulty usually begins with sensate focus.
    b. This problem is experienced exclusively by heterosexual men.
    c. Behavioral exercises combined with psychotherapy is the usual treatment approach.
    d. Therapy to reduce resentment toward partner may be part of the treatment.

15. Which of the following statements concerning HSD is **true**?
    a. It is a fairly uncomplicated problem to treat.
    b. Treatment consists of a straightforward behavior modification program.
    c. The dysfunctional partner is typically the focus of treatment and is seen on a one-to-one basis until the problem is resolved.
    d. A power imbalance in the relationship may contribute to HSD.

16. Regarding the selection of a therapist, which of the following statements is **true**?
    a. Most sex therapy is done on an individual basis, as opposed to working with couples.
    b. It is preferable to work with a same-sex therapist.
    c. A basic criterion to use is the amount and type of training a therapist has had.
    d. all of the above

17. Rita and Sebastian are seeing a sex therapist in which their treatment involves participating in behavioral exercises at home, reflecting on the unconscious thoughts and feelings that might underlie their problems and becoming aware of the function that their sexual problems have served in their relationship. This type of therapy is called
    a. psychosexual therapy.
    b. insight-oriented therapy.
    c. systems therapy.
    d. postmodern therapy.

18. PLISSIT is an acronym for
    a. permission, limited intensity, self-stimulation, and intensive therapy.
    b. playtime, limited interference, sensual sharing, and intimate time.
    c. permission, limited information, specific suggestions, and intensive therapy.
    d. plenty of individuals see sex exams as inherently threatening.

19. Helping clients to appreciate their unique patterns of sexual desire and expression is part of the _____ level of treatment.
    a. permission
    b. limited information
    c. increased self-esteem
    d. intensive therapy

Critical Thinking/Personal Reflection

1. What kinds of sexual problems have you or a partner experienced? How have you dealt with it? Based on what you have read in the text, would you have done anything differently now?

2. There are various suggestions and exercises presented in this chapter to enhance sexual sharing for men and women, alone or with a partner. Which of the exercises or suggestions, if any, would you be **most** comfortable attempting? Why? **Least** comfortable? Why?

3. If you are a male, assume that, as the result of a injury, you are no longer able to have erections. Would you consider getting a penile prosthesis? Why or why not? If you are female, assume you are the partner of the above male. How would you feel about the above surgical procedure? What other options might you explore, if any?

Chapter Overview With Fill-In Answers

1. awareness
2. self-awareness
3. Masturbation
4. communication
5. sensate focus
6. masturbation
7a. orgasmic
7b. counseling
8. anorgasmia
9. self-stimulation
10a. partner
10b. genital
11. bridge maneuver
12a. pelvic
12b. spasm
13. fingertip
14. partner
15. ejaculatory
16. ejaculate
17. "come again"
18. muscle
19. communicate
20. intercourse
21. stop-start
22. squeeze
23. antidepressants
24. anxiety
25a. sensate focus
25b. sensual

26. medical
27a. Viagra
27b. vasoactive
28. Yohimbine
29. blood
30. penile prosthesis
31a. semirigid
31b. inflatable
32. orgasmic disorder
33. complicated
34a. self-stimulation
34b. sensate focus
34c. activities
35. four
36a. Permission
36b. Suggestions
37. behavioral
38. psychosexual
39. systems
40. postmodern
41. eye movement desensitization and reprocessing
42. therapist
43. Sex Educators
44. health care practitioner
45a. sex therapy
45b. cost

Sample Multiple Choice Answers

1. d	2. b	3. c	4. d	5. d	6. c	7. b	8. c
9. b	10. a	11. b	12. c	13. d	14. b	15. d	16. c
17. d	18. c	19. a					

17

Sexually Transmitted Diseases

Introduction

The probability of you, your partner, or a potential partner experiencing at least one of the sexually transmitted diseases discussed in this chapter is quite high. Consequently, recognizing the various symptoms, being aware of treatment options available, and learning effective preventive measures is an investment in your future health care.

Review of Key Terms and Concepts

Key terms and concepts are listed and defined below. Refer to the subject index in the back of your textbook for additional information.

1. **sexually transmitted diseases (STDs)** — diseases that are transmitted by sexual contact

2. **chlamydia infection** — caused by the bacterial microorganism *Chlamydia trachomatis*, it is among the most prevalent and most damaging of all STDs, and is the most common bacterial STD in the U.S.

3. **pelvic inflammatory disease (PID)** — invasive infections of the upper reproductive tract (uterus, pelvic cavity, etc.)

4. **trachoma** — a chronic, contagious form of conjunctivitis caused by chlamydia infections

5. **conjunctivitis** — inflammation of the mucous membrane that lines the inner surface of the eyelid and the exposed surface of the eyeball

6. **gonorrhea** — a sexually transmitted disease that initially causes inflammation of mucous membranes

7. **nongonococcal urethritis (NGU)** — an inflammation of the male urethral tube caused by other than gonorrhea organisms

8. **syphilis** — a sexually transmitted disease caused by a thin corkscrew-like bacterium called *Treponema pallidum* (also called a "spirochete")

9. **chancre** — a raised, red painless sore that is symptomatic of the primary phase of syphilis

10. **chancroid** — a disease characterized by smaller bumps in the genital region that eventually rupture and form painful ulcers with a discharge

11. **herpes** — a disease, characterized by blisters on the skin in the regions of the genitals or mouth, that is caused by a virus and is easily transmitted by sexual contact

12. **prodromal symptoms** — symptoms that give advance warning of impending eruption

13. **genital warts** — viral warts that appear on the genitals and are usually transmitted through vaginal, oral or oral-genital sexual interaction

14. **viral hepatitis** — a disease in which liver function is impaired by a viral infection

15. **bacterial vaginosis (BV)** — a vaginal infection, usually caused by a bacterium called *Gardnerella vaginalis*, that may be the most common form of vaginitis among women in the U.S.

16. **candidiasis** — an inflammatory infection of the vaginal tissues caused by the yeast-like fungus *Candida albicans*

17. **trichomoniasis** — a form of vaginitis caused by a one-celled protozoan called *Trichomonas vaginalis*

18. **pubic lice** — parasitic insects that primarily infest the pubic hair and are transmitted by sexual contact

19. **scabies** — an ectoparasitic infestation of tiny mites

20. **acquired immunodeficiency syndrome (AIDS)** — a catastrophic illness in which a virus invades and destroys the ability of the immune system to fight disease. The AIDS virus appears to be spread primarily through sexual contact, needle sharing among injection drug users, or less commonly, through administration of contaminated blood products.

21. **human immunodeficiency virus (HIV)** — an immune-system-destroying virus that causes AIDS

22. **viral load** — how much HIV is present in an infected person's blood

23. **primary infection (window period)** — the period of time between exposure to HIV and the appearance of HIV antibodies in the blood. Individuals are highly infectious at this time.

24. **seroconversion** — the process whereby people develop antibodies to HIV

Chapter Overview With Fill-Ins

After reading each of the major sections in the chapter, check your retention by filling in each of the blanks in the corresponding sections below. The answers are provided at the end of the chapter.

1. Diseases that can be transmitted through sexual interaction are called _____ _____ diseases.

2. A number of factors may contribute to the high incidence of STDs: increasing sexual activity among a)_____ people; multiple sexual partners; increased use of b)_____ _____ _____ and therefore, reduced use of vaginal spermicides and the c)_____ which can help protect against STDs; absence of obvious d)_____ in many of the diseases; and finally, feelings of e)_____ and embarrassment, that often may prevent people from seeking treatment or informing their partners.

Bacterial Infections

3. Chlamydia infection among is the most common _____ STD in the U.S., and also one of the most damaging of all STDs.

4. There are two general types of genital chlamydia infections in females: infections of the mucosa of the lower reproductive tract, commonly manifested as urethritis or a)_____, and infections of the upper reproductive tract, which are expressed as b)_____ _____ disease (PID).

5. In men, the organism is estimated to be the cause of approximately half of the cases of epididymitis and _____, a contagious form of conjunctivitis.

6. Another complication associated with chlamydia trachomatis is _____.

7. Trachoma is the world's leading cause of preventable _____.

8. Chlamydia infection can potentially have very serious consequences for women and/or their _____ children, and to a lesser degree, in men as well.

9. A variety of _____ are commonly used to treat chlamydia infection.

10. Gonorrhea is a very common communicable disease and is transmitted by penile-vaginal, oral-genital, or _____-_____ contact.

11. In regard to gonorrhea infection, typically more men will experience symptoms than women, although it is not uncommon for men to be _____.

12. In men, the two most common symptoms of gonorrhea are a bad-smelling, cloudy discharge from the a)_____ and burning sensations during b)_____.

13. In women who are infected with gonorrhea, the _____ may become inflamed without producing any observable symptoms; a greenish or yellowish discharge usually results, but it is not readily detected.

14. _____ complications may result in both men and women if gonorrhea is left untreated.

15. Any inflammation of the _____ that is not caused by gonorrhea is called nongonococcal urethritis (NGU).

16. In men, symptoms of NGU are similar to those of _____.

17. Women who are infected with NGU _____.

18. A single dose of doxycycline or _____ usually clears up the NGU.

19. Syphilis is caused by a thin, corkscrew-like bacterium called *Treponema pallidum* (also called a _____).

20. Syphilis is transmitted almost exclusively from open a)_____ of infected individuals to the mucous membranes or skin abrasions of sexual partners through penile-vaginal, b)_____-_____, or genital-anal contacts.

21. If untreated, syphilis can progress through _____ phases of development.

22. In the primary phase, syphilis is manifested in the form of a painless sore called a _____, which appears at the site where the spirochete organism enters the body.

23. During the secondary stage of syphilis, a _____ _____ appears on the body, which may look terrible but usually does not hurt or itch.

24. The _____ stage of syphilis may last for several years, during which time there are no observable symptoms of the disease.

25. Approximately one-third of individuals who do not obtain treatment during the first three stages of syphilis enter the _____ stage later in life.

26. The final manifestations of syphilis can occur anywhere from three to _____ years after infection and may include conditions such as heart failure, blindness, ruptured blood vessels, paralysis, skin ulcers, liver damage, and severe mental disturbance.

27. The treatment for syphilis is intramuscular injections of _____.

28. Chancroid is a bacterial infection that is widely prevalent in _____ as well as other tropical and semi-tropical regions of the world.

29. Chancroid is one of the most common causes of genital _____.

30. Although still relatively uncommon in the United States, the incidence of chancroid has _____ sharply in recent years.

31. The ulceration associated with chancroid infections is worrisome because it provides easy access for _____ infection.

Viral Infections

32. Herpes is caused by the _____ _____ virus (HSV).

33. There are _____ different herpes viruses that infect humans, but types 1 and 2 are the ones most widely transmitted through sexual contact.

34. Type 1 is of the type called "cold sores" or "fever blisters" that appear in the _____ or on the lips.

35. Type 2 usually causes lesions on and around the _____ areas.

36. Genital herpes appears to be transmitted primarily by penile-vaginal, a)_____-_____, or genital-anal sexual contact, while oral herpes may be transmitted by b)_____ or by oral-genital contact.

37. Research has shown that HSV-2 will not pass through _____ _____.

38. However, condoms may break or come off, and when women are infected with HSV-2 their _____ secretions containing the virus may wash over the male's scrotal area.

39. People may also spread the herpes virus from one part of their body to another by touching a sore and then scratching or rubbing somewhere else, a process known as _____.

40. Symptoms associated with HSV-1 and HSV-2 are quite _____.

41. One or more small, red, painful bumps, called a)_____, usually appear which rapidly develop into tiny painful b)_____ containing highly infectious virus particles.

42. The blisters rupture, and a person is highly _____ during this time.

43. About _____ days after the first appearance of the papule, the open sore forms a crust and begins to heal, a process that may take as long as 10 more days.

44. Sores on the _____ may continue to produce infectious material for as long as 10 days after the labial sores have completely healed.

45. After healing, herpes does not go away, but retreats up the nerve fibers leading from the infected site, where it may remain _____ or periodically flare up.

46. It is unlikely that _____ will experience any major physical complications of herpes.

47. Women may experience two serious, although uncommon complications associated with herpes: cancer of the a)_____ and infection of the b)_____.

48. Genital warts are caused by a virus called the _____ _____ virus (HPV).

49. The incidence of genital warts has reached _____ proportions in recent years.

50. Genital warts are primarily transmitted by vaginal, anal, or _____-_____ sexual interaction.

51. Warts may appear on the internal or external female genitals and on the shaft, glans, or _____ of the penis.

52. Research has revealed a strong association between HPV infections and a variety of _____ of the cervix, vagina, vulva, penis and anus.

53. No form of therapy has been shown to entirely eradicate _____.

54. A number of treatments focus on the removal of visible warts, but for a number of people the warts will _____.

55. Viral hepatitis is a disease in which _____ function is impaired by a viral infection.

56. There are three major types of viral hepatitis: _____ _____ (formerly called infectious hepatitis), hepatitis B (formerly called _____ hepatitis), and non-A/non-B hepatitis.

57. a)_____, which is the most common form of viral hepatitis in the United States, seems to be spread primarily through the b)_____-_____ route, which can be a problem when infected food handlers do not wash their hands properly after using the bathroom.

58. _____-_____ contact seems to be the primary mode for sexual transmission of hepatitis A.

59. Hepatitis B may be transmitted by blood or blood products, _____, vaginal secretions, and saliva.

60. Manual, oral, or penile stimulation of the _____ are practices strongly associated with the spread of hepatitis B.

61. Symptoms of viral hepatitis may vary from nonexistent to mild _____ symptoms to an incapacitating illness characterized by high fever, vomiting, and severe abdominal pain.

62. At present, there is no specific therapy available for the various types of viral hepatitis, and treatment generally consists of a)_____ _____ and adequate fluid intake to prevent b)_____.

63. _____ are available for both type A and type B hepatitis.

Common Vaginal Infections

64. a)_____ and leukorrhea are general terms applied to a variety of vaginal infections, which can be contracted through sexual and b)_____ means.

65. Factors that increase the likelihood of vaginal infection include a)_____ therapy, use of birth control pills, menstruation, pregnancy, wearing pantyhose and b)_____ underwear, douching, and lowered resistance from stress or lack of sleep.

66. _____ _____ is a vaginal infection caused by a bacterium known as *Gardnerella vaginalis*.

67. Males may harbor this organism as well as women, usually without _____.

68. The predominant symptom in women is a foul-smelling, thin discharge that resembles _____ _____ in consistency.

69. The treatment for bacterial vaginosis is metronidazole (Flagyl), and _____ may or may not be treated as well, depending on the physician.

70. Candidiasis, also referred to as moniliasis or a _____ infection, is caused by a yeastlike fungus called *Candida albicans*.

71. Symptoms are a white, clumpy discharge that looks like a)_____ _____, and often intense b)_____ and soreness of the vaginal and vulval tissues.

72. Treatment consists of vaginal _____ or cream such as clotrimazole, miconazole, etc.

73. _____ accounts for about one-fourth of all cases of vaginitis.

74. When women have symptoms, it is usually a frothy yellow or white vaginal discharge with an unpleasant _____.

75. Occasionally, men may have symptoms of penile discharge or burning sensations in their _____, but most often they are asymptomatic.

76. Both partners should be treated with metronidazole (_____).

Ectoparasitic Infections

77. _____ are parasitic organisms that live on the outer skin surfaces of humans and other animals.

78. Pubic lice, commonly called "_____", are quite common and are frequently transmitted during sexual contact when two people bring their _____ areas together.

79. Pubic lice may live away from the body for as long as _____ day(s) and may drop off onto underclothes, bedsheets, sleeping bags, etc.

80. Eggs deposited by the female louse on clothing or bedsheets may survive for _____ days.

81. Most people will start _____ if they get pubic lice, although other people experience little discomfort.

82. Treatment of pubic lice consists of a special a)_____ _____ applied to all affected areas and a special b)_____ applied for four minutes.

83. Scabies is caused by a parasitic _____ too tiny to be seen by the naked eye.

84. Scabies are highly _____ and can be transmitted sexually and nonsexually.

85. Symptoms of scabies include a)_____-_____ bumps and b)_____.

86. Scabies is treated with a topical a)_____ that is applied from the b)_____ to the toes.

Acquired Immunodeficiency Syndrome (AIDS)

87. AIDS results from infection with a virus called _____ _____ virus (HIV).

88. HIV specifically targets and destroys the body's CD4 a)_____, or "T" helper cells, which, in healthy people, stimulate the b)_____ system to fight disease.

89. The resulting impairment of the immune system leaves the body vulnerable to a variety of _____ and opportunistic infections.

90. HIV has been found in the semen, blood, a)_____ secretions, saliva, tears, urine and breast milk of infected individuals and in any other bodily fluids that may contain b)_____.

91. Most commonly, HIV enters the body through the exchange of bodily fluids during a)_____ anal or vaginal intercourse or oral-genital contact with an infected person, and via blood-contaminated needles shared by b)_____ drug users.

92. HIV can also be transmitted from an infected woman to her fetus or infant before or during a)_____ or after by b)_____.

93. The likelihood of HIV being transmitted during sexual contact depends on the viral dose — which is a direct effect of the a)_____ _____ — and the b)_____ of HIV exposure.

94. Behaviors that place one at increased risk of HIV infection include having a)_____ sexual partners, engaging in b)_____ sex, sexual contact with people known to be at high risk, and sharing drug injection equipment.

95. Within a few months of being infected with HIV, most people develop _____ to the virus.

96. Once infected with the virus, a person should be considered _____ regardless of whether clinical signs of HIV infection are present.

97. The a)_____ time for AIDS in adults (defined as the time between infection with HIV and the onset of one or more debilitating diseases associated with impairment of the immune system) typically ranges from b)_____ to c)_____ years or more.

98. Once an AIDS patient develops a life-threatening illness, the disease tends to run a fairly rapid course culminating in _____ for the majority of those afflicted.

99. Although there is still no _____ for HIV/AIDS, therapy has provided reason for optimism that HIV/AIDS progression may be delayed and ultimately eradicated.

100. The only certain way to avoid contracting HIV sexually is either to remain a)_____ or to be involved in a b)_____ relationship with one mutually faithful, uninfected partner.

101. If these conditions are not applicable, _____ sex practices (as described in detail in the chapter) would be advised for the person who takes his or her life and health seriously.

Matching

Match the STDs below with the corresponding descriptions. Each letter may be used once, twice or not at all, but choose only **one** answer for each blank.

a. bacterial vaginosis
b. candidiasis
c. trichomoniasis
d. chlamydia infection
e. gonorrhea
f. nongonococcal urethritis

g. syphilis
h. pubic lice
i. herpes
j. viral hepatitis
k. genital warts
l. chancroid

m. AIDS

_____1. The most common symptom in women is a frothy white or yellow vaginal discharge with an unpleasant odor. It is treated with the drug metronidazole (Flagyl).

_____2. This STD may be treated with a variety of topical applications, cauterization, freezing, surgical procedures, or a carbon dioxide laser.

_____3. The estimated incubation time of this disease is between 8 and 11 years.

_____4. This is the most common cause of vaginitis, and its main symptom is a flour-paste discharge that has a fishy, musty odor.

_____5. This is among the most prevalent and damaging of all STDs and may have severe consequences in men, women, and newborns.

_____6. This STD is frequently transmitted by two people rubbing pubic areas together, although it may be contracted by sleeping in an infected person's sheets or wearing his or her clothes.

_____7. One of the most notable symptoms of this STD is a yellowing of the skin as well as the whites of the eyes.

_____8. Also called a yeast infection, the white, clumpy discharge of this STD looks like cottage cheese.

_____9. Quite common in men, this STD manifests symptoms similar to those of gonorrhea infection and is commonly caused by chlamydia infections.

_____10. In rare cases, this disease may result in permanent joint damage. It is treated with cefixime or ofloxacin plus doxycycline.

_____11. The initial outbreak of these painful blister-like sores will heal, but the virus will retreat to the nerve cells where it will remain, perhaps for a lifetime.

_____12. The second stage of this disease is typically characterized by a skin rash on the body.

_____13. This is caused by the bacterium *Gardnerella vaginalis*.

_____14. This causes trachoma, the world's leading cause of preventable blindness.

_____15. This is caused by a bacterium called *Treponema pallidum*.

_____16. Excessive amounts of dairy products and sugar in one's diet may result in this condition.

_____17. Although most prevalent in Africa and other tropical areas, the incidence of this disease in the United States has increased sharply in recent years.

_____18. This, if left untreated, can result in severe mental disturbance, heart failure, paralysis, even death.

_____19. This is treated with metronidazole (Flagyl), and some men who are infected with it develop urethritis and cystitis.

_____20. When this invades the fallopian tubes, it is the primary preventable cause of female infertility and ectopic pregnancy.

Sample Short Answer Test Questions

1. In the U.S. eighty-six percent of all STDs occur among which age group?

2. What percent of the U.S. population will acquire one or more STDs by age 30–35?

3. List four factors that may contribute to the high incidence of STDs.

4. Discuss the consequences of chlamydia infection in men, women and children.

5. What are the symptoms of chlamydia infection in men and women? How is it diagnosed?

6. What other STDs commonly coexist with chlamydia infection?

7. Describe the symptoms of gonorrhea infection in men and in women.

8. If gonorrhea infection is left untreated, what complications may develop in men? In women? In both sexes?

9. What is the risk to an infant whose mother has gonorrhea? How may this be averted?

10. Explain the problem in diagnosing and treating gonorrhea.

11. Describe the symptoms of NGU in women and in men.

12. What problem sometimes exists in diagnosing NGU in men?

13. How may a pregnant woman who has syphilis transmit the disease to her unborn child? What are the effects on the infant?

14. Describe the symptoms of syphilis at each of the following stages:

a. primary

b. secondary

c. latent

d. tertiary

15. What are the symptoms of chancroid?

16. In what parts of the world is chancroid typically found? Where have outbreaks been recently?

17. Describe the two most common types of herpes viruses.

18. How may herpes viruses be transmitted?

19. What practices may help prevent the transmission of herpes?

20. Describe the symptoms of oral and genital herpes.

21. What happens to the herpes virus once it heals?

22. Describe the prodromal symptoms of herpes.

23. When is a person with herpes considered infectious?

24. What factors may trigger reactivation of the herpes virus?

25. What complications may arise from herpes infection in men? In women?

26. What drugs are effective in managing herpes? What are the advantages and drawbacks?

27. In addition to using drugs, list five ways that a person may find symptom relief from herpes.

28. Describe the incidence of genital warts in the United States

29. What are some of the complications associated with genital warts?

30. Describe some of the available treatments for genital warts.

31. What is viral hepatitis?

32. Briefly describe the two most common types of viral hepatitis and how they are transmitted.

33. List some of the symptoms of viral hepatitis.

34. How is viral hepatitis treated?

35. Describe the normal chemical balance of the vaginal environment. What factors may increase the likelihood of a vaginal infection?

36. Briefly summarize the cause, symptoms, and treatment alternatives for the three vaginal infections listed below:

	Cause	Symptoms	Treatment
a. bacterial vaginosis			
b. candidiasis			
c. trichomoniasis			

37. In what ways might an individual contract pubic lice? What is the treatment?

38. List four groups of people most at risk for contracting scabies.

39. What are the symptoms of scabies?

40. What year was the first AIDS case reported in the U.S.? Based on available evidence, when was evidence of HIV first noted worldwide?

41. When is HIV infection diagnosed as AIDS?

42. Describe the incidence of AIDS in men and women from 1992–1996. What factors account for this?

43. According to the World Health Organization, how many people worldwide are infected with HIV? What percentage of these people live in Africa?

44. Why is the rate of HIV infection higher for women than men in most nations?

45. What is one reason why the HIV epidemic is escalating in Thailand? What percent of Thailand's female sex workers are HIV infected?

46. In what bodily fluids has the AIDS virus been isolated?

47. The likelihood of HIV being transmitted during sexual contact depends on what two factors?

48. List two time periods when an HIV infected person would tend to have a higher viral load.

49. List reasons why HIV is transmitted more easily from men to women during intercourse.

50. How common is the transmission of HIV during fellatio? Cunnilingus?

51. List at least six common symptoms of HIV infection.

52. After being infected with HIV, how soon do most people test positive for the antibodies?

53. Name the two blood tests that are most commonly used to screen for HIV infection.

54. List two key issues involving HIV/AIDS and the law.

55. In February 1997, what did New York become the first state to do?

56. What is the incubation period for AIDS in adults?

57. Specifically, what does triple drug therapy consist of?

58. Despite initial optimism, list six drawbacks of triple drug therapy.

59. The risk of contracting HIV is higher in individuals that have what other STDs?

60. What three STDs show the **highest** association with HIV infection?

61. Aside from abstinence and monogamy, list at least five suggestions for reducing your risk of exposure to HIV.

62. List eight guidelines for STD prevention.

Sample Multiple Choice Test Questions

Select the best alternative. Check your answers with the answer key at the end of the chapter.

1. In the U.S., 86% of all STDs occur among which of the following age groups?
   a. 12–20-year-olds
   b. 15–29-year-olds
   c. 18–35-year-olds
   d. 21–38-year-olds

2. According to the text, one of the factors contributing to the high incidence of STDs is
   a. the lack of quality health care.
   b. the decreasing quality of latex condoms.
   c. the use of birth control pills.
   d. infections that are increasingly resistant to treatment.

3. *Gardnerella vaginalis*
   a. causes bacterial vaginosis.
   b. is not as common as trichomoniasis.
   c. is treated with vaginal suppositories.
   d. is characterized by a white, clumpy discharge that looks like cottage cheese.

4. The fishy odor of the vaginal discharge that is symptomatic of this infection can be especially pungent after intercourse.
   a. bacterial vaginosis
   b. candidiasis
   c. trichomoniasis
   d. pesce vaginalis

5. Wearing pantyhose and having a diet high in sugar are two factors that may make a woman susceptible to
   a. bacterial vaginosis.
   b. candidiasis.
   c. trichomoniasis.
   d. chlamydia infection.

6. _____ is characterized by a frothy, white or yellow discharge that has an unpleasant odor and is treated with metronidazole (Flagyl). Long-term infection may increase susceptibility to cervical cancer.
   a. Bacterial vaginosis
   b. Chlamydia infection
   c. Candidiasis
   d. Trichomoniasis

7. Chlamydia infection, if left untreated, may result in all of the following in women **except**
   a. urethritis
   b. cervicitis
   c. pelvic inflammatory disease
   d. clitoral adhesions

8. Chlamydia causes trachoma, the world's leading cause of
   a. cervical cancer.
   b. liver damage.
   c. preventable blindness.
   d. testicular cancer.

9. Which of the following statements regarding chlamydia infection is **false**?
   a. Chlamydia salpingitis is the primary preventable cause of female infertility.
   b. If left untreated, it may invade the upper reproductive tract, resulting in symptoms that include chronic pelvic pain, nausea and vomiting.
   c. It is treated with doxycycline, azithromycin, or ofloxacin.
   d. It is a viral infection.

10. If gonorrhea is left untreated in men, which of the following complications would be **least** likely to occur?
    a. epididymitis
    b. prostatic abscesses
    c. sterility
    d. penile abscesses

11. Men who contract NGU often manifest symptoms similar to those of a _____ infection.
    a. herpes
    b. gonorrhea
    c. syphilitic
    d. yeast

12. The incidence of syphilis in the United States
    a. has gradually been decreasing, except in several poor inner-city areas.
    b. has stayed approximately the same since 1960.
    c. has gradually been increasing.
    d. has increased dramatically in the last five years, especially in several poor inner-city areas.

13. During the latent stage of syphilis
    a. the infectious organisms continue to multiply.
    b. the infected individual is highly contagious after the first year has elapsed.
    c. a skin rash may develop.
    d. a person may experience heart failure, blindness, and even death.

14. The most common treatment for syphilis is
    a. penicillin.
    b. Flagyl.
    c. a blood transfusion.
    d. azidothymidine.

15. Which of the following statements concerning pubic lice is **false**?
    a. They are commonly called "crabs".
    b. They may survive on sheets and clothing.
    c. They are treated with metronidazole (Flagyl).
    d. In terms of symptoms, people may itch or feel little or no discomfort.

16. Which of the following statements concerning herpes is **false**?
    a. HSV-1 usually infects the mouth or lips but may infect the genitals as well.
    b. HSV-2 will not pass through latex condoms.
    c. During the prodromal phase, the herpes blisters begin to crust over and heal.
    d. There are eight different types of herpes viruses that infect humans.

17. Which of the following statements concerning herpes is **true**?
    a. The herpes virus may be eliminated by taking the drug acyclovir, also known as Zovirax.
    b. Being under emotional stress may trigger a herpes outbreak.
    c. One example of a prodromal symptom is a high level of anxiety.
    d. all of the above

18. A possible complication of a herpes infection in both men and women is
    a. damage to the joints if left untreated.
    b. sterility.
    c. severe eye infection.
    d. memory loss and disorientation.

19. All of the following are possible complications of herpes infections in women **except**
    a. ovarian cancer
    b. infection of the newborn
    c. severe eye infection
    d. cervical cancer

20. A suggestion for symptom relief from herpes is to
    a. drink large quantities of cranberry juice.
    b. wash frequently and dry the genital area with a blow dryer.
    c. apply a heating pad to the infected area to help minimize discomfort.
    d. keep the infected area moist with a topical lubricant to minimize drying and cracking.

21. A yellowing of the whites of the eyes is one of the most notable signs of
    a. third stage syphilis.
    b. trichomoniasis.
    c. HIV infection.
    d. viral hepatitis.

22. _____ is the most common form of viral hepatitis in the United States.
    a. Hepatitis A
    b. Hepatitis B
    c. Hepatitis non-A/non-B
    d. Hepatitis C

23. The incidence of genital warts has been
    a. increasing dramatically.
    b. increasing slowly.
    c. stabilizing over the past five years.
    d. decreasing slowly.

24. Podophyllin is one of the treatments for
    a. viral hepatitis.
    b. candidiasis.
    c. genital warts.
    d. pubic lice.

25. AIDS was first reported in the U.S. in _____, although recent evidence suggest that it was present in Africa as early as the _____.
    a. 1973; mid 1950s.
    b. 1977; mid 1960s.
    c. 1981; late 1940s.
    d. 1985; late 1950s.

26. Human immunodeficiency virus
    a. has been in the saliva and breast milk of infected individuals.
    b. can easily be transmitted via saliva exchange.
    c. can be contracted as a result of donating blood.
    d. can be transmitted through casual contact (hugging, shaking hands, etc.).

27. The Western blot
    a. is one of the standard blood tests that is initially given to individuals to detect the presence of HIV antibodies.
    b. is a more costly blood test that is able to detect a silent HIV infection.
    c. is a type of Rorschach test that is administered to AIDS patients for clinical diagnosis and assessment.
    d. is a recently discovered drug therapy for AIDS patients that has not yet been approved by the FDA.

28. The time between infection with HIV and the onset of AIDS is referred to as
    a. the latent stage.
    b. reverse transcription.
    c. the incubation period.
    d. the prodromal phase.

29. HIV is diagnosed as AIDS
    a. seven years after initial infection with HIV has occurred.
    b. eleven years after initial infection with HIV has occurred.
    c. when the person infected with HIV develops a debilitating illness such as pneumonia or cancer.
    d. when the person infected with HIV has a specified number or less of T helper cells in his or her blood.

30. All of the following are recommended suggestions for minimizing the possibility of contracting sexually transmitted diseases **except**
    a. washing the genitals before or after sexual contact
    b. inspecting your partner's genitals
    c. routine postcontact antibiotic therapy
    d. routine medical evaluations

31. In one survey of 400 college students, _____% of men and _____% of women said they would falsely claim that they had tested negative for HIV.
    a. 5; 12
    b. 10; 10
    c. 10; 2
    d. 20; 4

32. With which of the following STDs would a condom be **least** effective?
    a. herpes
    b. gonorrhea
    c. bacterial vaginosis
    d. chlamydia

Critical Thinking/Personal Reflection

1. Prior to reading this chapter, what changes, if any, have you noticed in your sexual attitudes and behaviors over the past two to three years as a result of what you have read and heard concerning sexually transmitted diseases? Based on what you have read in the chapter, do you anticipate further changes in your sexual attitudes and behavior? If so, what do you think they will be? Give specific examples.

2. Assume that you have been sexually involved with a new partner for six months and things seem to be going well. At this point, your partner confides that he/she has genital herpes. Because the outbreaks are infrequent (approximately once a year) and because your partner is aware of health concerns and takes proper precautions, she/he made the decision to not share this information with you in the early stages of the relationship for fear of your reaction. Your partner has brought the subject up now because he/she has just begun experiencing prodromal symptoms and wants to abstain from genital sex for a while, so it is mandatory that this discussion not be postponed any further. What would be your reaction to this? How would you feel? What would you say and/or do? Do you think your partner's decision to refrain from discussing this with you six months ago was justified? Why or why not?

3.   Have you or your partner ever contracted any of the sexually transmitted diseases discussed in this chapter? If so, what actions were taken — medically and insofar as your relationship was concerned? Based on what you have read and learned more recently, how would you have handled that situation(s) differently, if at all? Give specific examples.

4.   Review the list of prevention guidelines in the text. Which of these do you or have you used with comfort? Which of these would you like to include in your repertoire? Which of these would you find difficult to implement, if any? Why?

Chapter Overview With Fill-In Answers

1. sexually transmitted
2a. young
2b. birth control pills
2c. condom
2d. symptoms
2e. guilt
3. bacterial
4a. cervicitis
4b. pelvic inflammatory
5. nongonococcal urethritis
6. trachoma
7. blindness
8. newborn
9. drugs
10. genital-anal
11. asymptomatic
12a. penis
12b. urination
13. cervix
14. Severe
15. urethra
16. gonorrhea
17. asymptomatic
18. azithromycin
19. spirochete
20a. lesions
20b. oral-genital
21. four
22. chancre
23. skin rash
24. latent
25. tertiary
26. 40
27. benzathine penicillin G
28. Africa
29. ulcers
30. increased
31. HIV
32. herpes simplex
33. eight
34. mouth
35. genital
36a. oral-genital
36b. kissing
37. latex condoms
38. vaginal
39. autoinoculation
40. similar
41a. papules
41b. blisters
42. contagious
43. ten
44. cervix
45. dormant
46. men
47a. cervix
47b. newborn
48. human papilloma
49. epidemic
50. oral-genital
51. foreskin
52. cancers
53. HPV
54. recur
55. liver
56a. hepatitis A
56b. serum
57a. Hepatitis A
57b. fecal-oral
58. Oral-anal
59. semen
60. anus
61. flu-like
62a. bed rest
62b. dehydration
63. vaccines
64a. Vaginitis
64b. nonsexual
65a. antibiotic
65b. nylon
66. Bacterial vaginosis
67. symptoms
68. flour paste
69. male
70. yeast
71a. cottage cheese
71b. itching
72. suppositories
73. Trichomoniasis
74. odor
75. urethras
76. Flagyl
77. Ectoparasites
78a. crabs
78b. pubic
79. one

80. several
81. itching
82a. cream rinse
82b. shampoo
83. mite
84. contagious
85a. pimple-like
85b. itching
86a. scabicide
86b. neck
87. human immunodeficiency
88a. lymphocytes
88b. immune
89. cancers
90a. vaginal
90b. blood
91a. unprotected
91b. intravenous

92a. birth
92b. breastfeeding
93a. viral load
93b. routes
94a. multiple
94b. unprotected
95. antibodies
96. contagious
97a. incubation
97b. 8
97c. 11
98. death
99a. cure
99b. triple drug
100a. celibate
100b. monogamous
101. safer

Matching Answers

1. c	2. k	3. m	4. a	5. d	6. h	7. j	8. b
9. f	10. e	11. i	12. g	13. a	14. d	15. g	16. b
17. l	18. g	19. a	20. d				

Sample Multiple Choice Answers

1. b	2. c	3. a	4. a	5. b	6. d	7. d	8. c
9. d	10. d	11. b	12. a	13. a	14. a	15. c	16. c
17. b	18. c	19. a	20. b	21. d	22. a	23. a	24. c
25. c	26. a	27. a	28. c	29. d	30. c	31. d	32. a

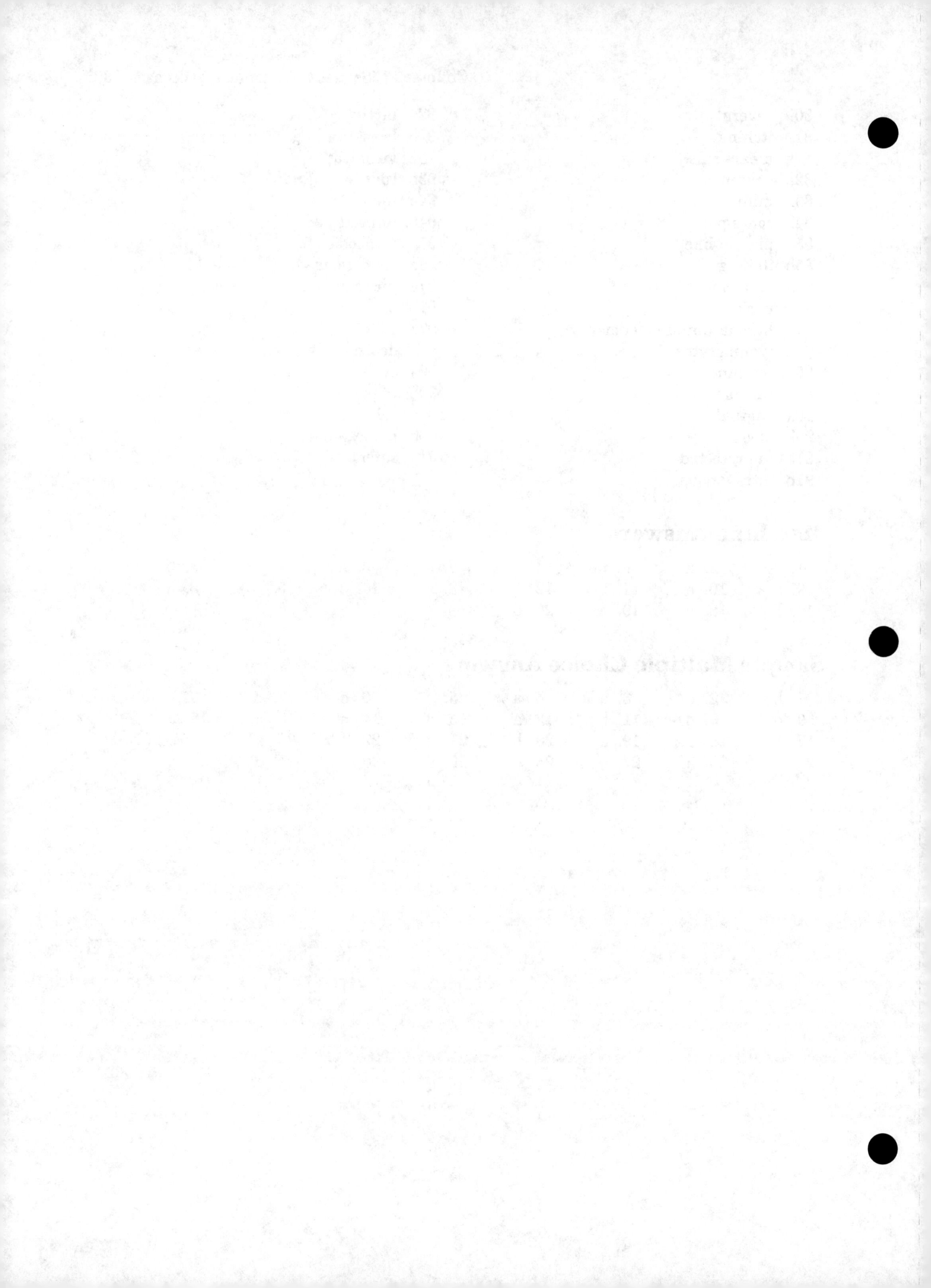

18

Atypical Sexual Behavior

Introduction

In this chapter, the authors use the label "atypical sexual behavior" to refer to the paraphilias, or the more uncommon types of sexual expression. Some of us have engaged in milder forms of some of the behaviors described, although to merit the labels discussed here one must usually engage in the behavior as a primary means of sexual arousal and expression. Being an unwilling recipient of some of these behaviors would be very upsetting and offensive to many people, which is why many of these behaviors are illegal.

Review of Key Terms and Concepts

Key terms and concepts are listed and defined below. Refer to the subject index in the back of your textbook for additional information.

1. **paraphilia** — term used to describe uncommon types of sexual expression in the psychological and psychiatric literature

2. **atypical sexual behavior** — term the authors use to describe sexual behavior that is not typically expressed by the majority of people in American society; clinical term is paraphilia

3. **erotosexual differentiation** — the development of sexual arousal in response to various kinds of images or stimuli

4. **fetishism** — obtaining sexual excitement primarily or exclusively from an inanimate object or a particular part of the body

5. **symbolic transformation** — the process by which an individual may learn to associate sexual arousal with objects that belong to an emotionally significant person

6. **transvestism** — deriving sexual arousal from wearing clothing of the other sex

7. **sadomasochism** — the association of sexual expression with pain

8. **sexual sadism** — the act of obtaining sexual arousal through giving physical or psychological pain

9. **sexual masochism** — the act of obtaining sexual arousal through receiving physical or psychological pain

10. **bondage** — deriving sexual pleasure from being bound, tied up or otherwise restricted

11. **autoerotic asphyxia** — the enhancement of sexual excitement and orgasm by pressure-induced oxygen deprivation

12. **klismaphilia** — a very unusual variation of sexual expression in which an individual obtains sexual pleasure from receiving enemas

13. **coprophilia** — a sexual paraphilia in which a person obtains sexual arousal from contact with feces

14. **urophilia** — a sexual paraphilia in which a person obtains sexual arousal from contact with urine

15. **exhibitionism** — the act of exposing one's genitals to an unwilling observer

16. **voyeurism** — the act of obtaining sexual gratification by observing people who are undressed or engaged in sexual interaction without their consent

17. **frotteurism** — a fairly common paraphilia in which a person obtains sexual pleasure by pressing or rubbing against another in a crowded public place

18. **zoophilia (bestiality)** — a paraphilia in which a person has sexual contact with animals

19. **necrophilia** — a rare sexual paraphilia in which a person obtains sexual gratification by viewing or having intercourse with a corpse

20. **psychotherapy** — a noninvasive procedure involving verbal interaction between a client and therapist designed to improve a person's adjustment to life

21. **cognitive therapies** — approaches to therapy that are based on the premise that most psychological disorders result from distortions in cognitions or thoughts

22. **behavior therapy** — therapy based on the assumption that maladaptive behavior has been learned and can therefore be unlearned

23. **aversive conditioning** — a behavior therapy method that substitutes a negative response for positive responses to inappropriate stimuli

24. **systematic desensitization** — behavior therapy technique that pairs slow, systematic exposure to anxiety-inducing situations with relaxation training

25. **orgasmic reconditioning** — a behavior therapy technique in which a client is instructed to switch from paraphilic to healthy fantasies at the moment of masturbatory orgasm

26. **satiation therapy** — a technique for reducing arousal to inappropriate stimuli by first masturbating to orgasm while imagining appropriate stimuli and then continuing to masturbate while fantasizing about paraphilic images

27. **antiandrogen drugs** — drugs that may block inappropriate sexual arousal patterns by lowering testosterone levels

28. **social skills training** — training designed to teach socially inept clients the skills necessary to initiate and maintain satisfying relationships

29. **nymphomania** — a term, which most professionals refrain from using because of its pejorative nature, that refers to a woman who is dominated by insatiable sexual needs

30. **satyriasis (Don Juanism)** — a term, which most professionals refrain from using because of its pejorative nature, that refers to a man who is dominated by insatiable sexual needs

Chapter Overview With Fill-Ins

After reading each of the major sections in the chapter, check your retention by filling in each of the blanks in the corresponding sections below. The answers are provided at the end of the chapter.

What Constitutes Atypical Sexual Behavior?

1. The term _____ is a relatively non-judgmental term used to describe uncommon types of sexual expression.

2. The authors also use the term _____ sexual behavior to refer to sexual behavior that is not typically expressed by most people in our society.

3. A key distinguishing characteristic of paraphilias is whether or not they involve an element of _____,

Noncoercive Paraphilias

4. Fetishism occurs when an individual becomes sexually aroused by focusing on an a)_____ object or a part of the human b)_____.

5. Fetishism is only applicable when a person focuses on these objects to the _____ of everything else.

6. For some people, fetish objects serve as substitutes for _____ contact and are dispensed with if a partner becomes available.

7. A common way that fetishism is developed is by a kind of _____ conditioning, in which some object or body part becomes associated with sexual arousal.

8. This association typically happens by incorporating the object or body part, often through fantasy in a a)_____ sequence where the reinforcement of b)_____ strengthens the fetishistic association.

9. Only rarely does fetishism develop into an offense that might harm someone, although _____ is the most frequent serious offense to be associated with fetishism.

10. The term transvestism applies to behaviors whereby an individual obtains sexual excitement from putting on the _____ of the other sex.

11. Some people prefer to don the a)_____ garb of the other sex; more commonly, a person becomes aroused by wearing only b)_____ garment (e.g., panties or brassiere).

12. In the majority of cases, it appears that a)_____ are attracted to transvestism, although some isolated cases of b)_____ transvestism have been reported.

13. Several studies indicate that cross-dressing occurs primarily among married men with predominantly _____ orientations.

14. A recent national survey of 372 male cross-dressers reported that although a majority of these men were heterosexual, a significant portion (more than 30%) classified themselves as _____, _____ or not sexually active with another person.

15. Data suggest that most wives only _____ rather than support the cross-dressing of their husbands.

16. Like fetishism and some other atypical sexual behaviors, the development of transvestism often reveals a pattern of _____.

17. Occasionally, transvestism is the behavior of the heterosexual male who is striving to explore the _____ side of his personality.

18. Sexual sadism is the act of obtaining sexual arousal through _____ physical or psychological pain.

19. Sexual masochism is the act of obtaining sexual arousal through _____ physical or psychological pain.

20. Sadomasochistic behavior is the association of sexual expression with _____.

21. Many people enjoy some form of _____ interaction during sexual sharing, for which the label sadomasochism seems inappropriate.

22. People with a)_____ tendencies may be aroused by such things as being whipped, cut, pierced with needles, bound, spanked, humiliated, or forced to do filthy or b)_____ service.

23. There are some indications that people with sadistic tendencies are _____ common than their masochistic counterparts.

24. Many people in contemporary Western societies view sadomasochism in a very _____ light.

25. Several researchers maintain that the traditional model of sadomasochism as a _____ condition is misleading because it is based on a limited sample of individuals.

26. Some theorists have suggested that such activity has definite a)_____ value, heightening sexual arousal by means of increased blood pressure, muscle tension and b)_____.

27. Baumeister has theorized that sexual masochism may represent an attempt to escape from high levels of _____-_____.

28. Clinical studies of sadomasochism participants sometimes reveal early experiences that may have established a connection between a)_____ and b)_____.

29. a)_____ _____ is the enhancement of sexual excitement and orgasm by pressure-induced oxygen b)_____, a very dangerous activity that sometimes results in c)_____.

30. It has been suggested that the above may be a highly unusual variant of sexual _____ in which participants act out ritualized bondage themes.

31. Klismaphilia is when an individual obtains sexual satisfaction from receiving _____.

32. Case histories of these individuals reveal that, as children, they were frequently given enemas by concerned and affectionate a)_____, and they learned to associate loving attention with the erotic pleasure of b)_____ stimulation.

33. Coprophilia and urophilia refer to activities in which people obtain sexual arousal from contact with a)_____ and b)_____, respectively.

Coercive Paraphilias

34. Often called a)_____ _____, exhibitionism refers to behavior where an individual (usually male) exposes his genitals to an b)_____ observer (usually an adult woman or female child).

35. Based on limited available data, it would appear that most people who exhibit themselves are adult males in their a)_____ or b)_____ , and over one-half are or have been c)_____.

36. They are often shy, nonassertive people who feel inadequate and suffer from problems with _____.

37. The majority of men who engage in exhibitionism _____ their illegal behaviors to exposing themselves.

38. However, a minority of men may progress to more serious offenses, such as rape and
_____ _____.

39. In the past several years, there has been a trend toward _____ as an alternative to incarceration for exhibitionism.

40. The best response to exhibitionism is to calmly _____ it and to report such acts to proper authorities.

41. The characteristics of people who make obscene phone calls seem to be similar to those of people who engage in _____.

42. According to research, these individuals are usually a)_____, they often feel inadequate and insecure, and when relating to the other sex, they frequently show greater b)_____ and hostility than people who engage in exhibitionism.

43. Advice for dealing with people who make obscene phone calls includes: do not overreact — gently hang up the phone and continue with what you were doing; _____ the phone if it rings again; feign _____; set the phone down and never return.

44. You may also choose to get a a)_____ number or subscribe to service called b)_____-_____ offered by your telephone company.

45. Voyeurism refers to deriving pleasure from looking at the a)_____ bodies or sexual activities of others, usually b)_____, without their consent.

46. To qualify as atypical sexual behavior, voyeurism must be preferred to a)_____ _____ with another, or indulged in with some b)_____, or both.

47. Most people inclined toward voyeurism have some of the same characteristics as people who expose themselves: poorly developed _____ skills and strong feelings of inferiority, especially toward potential sexual partners.

48. Voyeurs tend to be men in their early _____, and occasionally they will progress to other crimes, but that is typically not the case.

49. a)_____ may be a fairly common paraphilia that goes largely unnoticed in that it involves an individual, usually a male, who obtains sexual pleasure by pressing and rubbing against a fully-clothed b)_____ in a crowded public place like an c)_____, bus, or subway.

50. The man may achieve arousal and a)_____ during this act, and more commonly, he incorporates the mental images of his actions into b)_____ fantasies at a later time.

51. Zoophilia, also called _____, involves sexual contact between humans and animals.

52. Sexual contact with animals is commonly a _____ experience of young people to whom a sexual partner is inaccessible or forbidden.

53. True zoophilia exists only when sexual contact with animals is _____ regardless of what other forms of sexual outlet are available.

54. Necrophilia is when a person obtains sexual gratification by viewing or having intercourse with a _____.

55. Necrophilia appears to occur exclusively among _____.

56. Due to problems associated with gaining access to a)_____ bodies, some men with necrophilic tendencies limit their contact to b)_____ who pose as corpses.

Treatment of Coercive Paraphilias

57. _____ has generally not been proven very effective in treating coercive paraphilia.

58. Psychologists who use _____ therapies, which attempt to alter the person's distorted thoughts that lead to the problematic behavior, have reported limited success in using this approach to treat paraphilias.

59. A type of behavior therapy called a)_____ _____ substitutes a negative response for a positive response to an b)_____ stimulus situation.

60. Another type of behavior therapy used in the treatment of paraphilias, called a)_____ _____ is based on the premise that people cannot be both relaxed and b)_____ at the same time.

61. Two other behavior therapies, a)_____ _____ and b)_____ therapy are also used to treat paraphilias.

62. Antiandrogen drugs that lower a)_____ levels have been used most effectively to treat sex offenders when their use is combined with psychotherapy or b)_____ therapy.

63. The idea that people may become dominated by insatiable sexual needs has been around for a long time, exemplified by the term _____, applied to women, and _____, or Don Juanism, applied to men.

64. The concept of _____ sexuality achieved heightened legitimacy through several books written by Patrick Carnes.

65. According to Carnes, many of the people who engage in many atypical as well as victimization behaviors are manifesting the outward symptoms of psychological a)_____, in which the feelings of b)_____, anxiety, loneliness, and worthlessness are temporarily relieved through a sexual c)"_____" not unlike the high achieved by drugs or alcohol.

66. Carnes suggests that the addiction cycle progresses through four phases: preoccupation, a)_____ behaviors, expression of the sexual act, and b)_____.

67. Although Carnes' conception of the sexual addict has received considerable attention, many sexologists do not believe that it should be a distinct category because it is rare and also similar to other _____ disorders, such as gambling and eating disorders.

68. According to sexologist Eli Coleman, a person manifesting excessive sexual behaviors, often suffers from feelings of a)_____, b)_____, c)_____, and d)_____.

69. Professional _____ programs as well as a number of _____-_____ groups for compulsive or addictive sexual behaviors have emerged throughout the nation.

Matching

Match the terms below with the appropriate descriptions. Each term may be used more than once, but choose only **one** answer for each blank.

a. exhibitionism
b. voyeurism
c. sadomasochism
d. fetishism
e. transvestism
f. zoophilia

g. necrophilia
h. klismaphilia
i. coprophilia
j. urophilia
k. frotteurism
l. autoerotic asphyxia

_____1. engaging in this activity may intensify sexual excitement and orgasm in a similar way that inhaling amyl nitrate intensifies orgasm.

_____2. sexual arousal from contact with urine

_____3. female partners of men who engage in this activity tend to tolerate, rather than support it

_____4. burglary is the most frequent serious offense to be associated with this

_____5. a recent survey of 975 men and women reported occasionally engaging in a form of this activity with a partner

_____6. obtaining sexual pleasure from rubbing against a fully clothed person (usually female) in a crowded place

_____7. some professionals believe that this behavior is more common among women than we suspect because they can engage in this behavior without detection

_____8. this activity may often result in death

_____9. obtaining sexual gratification by having sex with a corpse

_____10. also called bestiality

_____11. Baumeister has hypothesized that this behavior may be an attempt to escape from high levels of self-awareness

_____12. sexual arousal from contact with feces

_____13. many professionals link this behavior with fetishism

_____14. men who engage in this are usually in their early 20s, and they have similar characteristics to men who expose themselves

_____15. obtaining sexual pleasure from receiving enemas

_____16. this behavior increases blood pressure, muscle tension and hyperventilation more so than other sexual activities, resulting in greater arousal from a physiological standpoint

Sample Short Answer Test Questions

1. Define paraphilia.

2. What is John Money's explanation for why atypical sexual expression is more prevalent among men instead of women?

3. Distinguish between coercive and noncoercive paraphilias and list three examples of each.

4. List and briefly describe two ways in which fetishism may develop.

5. With what more serious offense may fetishism be associated?

6. Distinguish between transvestism and transsexualism.

7. Making reference to gender, sexual orientation and relationship status, describe the person who would be most likely to engage in transvestism.

8. According to various research studies, how do wives of men who engage in transvestism respond to this behavior?

9. According to a recent survey of 975 men and women, what percentage reported engaging in some form of sadomasochistic activity with a partner?

10. According to the same survey described above, what percentage of respondents engaged in bondage?

11. Why is the medical model of sadomasochism as a pathological condition being questioned?

12. List four reasons why people might choose to engage in sadomasochistic activity.

13. Describe Baumeister's theory of the function that sexual masochism serves.

14. Briefly describe the following noncoercive paraphilias:
    a. autoerotic asphyxia

    b. klismaphilia

    c. coprophilia and urophilia

15. Characterize the typical person who engages in exhibitionism.

16. Briefly describe some of the explanations for exhibitionistic behavior.

17. According to Gene Abel's 1981 research, what histories of other types of atypical sexual behaviors were found among rapists?

18. Describe the characteristics of people who make obscene phone calls.

19. What are some suggestions for dealing with obscene phone calls? For people who exhibit themselves?

20. Briefly characterize the person who engages in voyeuristic behavior.

21. Briefly describe the following coercive paraphilias:

    a. frotteurism

    b. zoophilia

    c. necrophilia

22. List and briefly describe four types of behavior therapy that are used to treat coercive paraphilias.

23. Name two therapeutic approaches for treating coercive paraphilias that have had limited success.

24. What drugs are sometimes used to treat coercive paraphilias? Exactly how do they work?

25. According to Patrick Carnes, what is sexual addiction?

26. List and briefly describe the four phases of sexual addiction as suggested by Patrick Carnes.

    a.

    b.

    c.

    d.

27. Why do some sexologists such as Eli Coleman disagree with the label "sexual addiction?"

Sample Multiple Choice Test Questions

Select the best alternative. Check your answers with the answer key at the end of the chapter.

1. Paraphilias are **best** defined as _____ sexual behaviors.
    a. illegal
    b. noncoital
    c. uncommon
    d. perverted

2. A person who becomes sexually aroused by exposing his genitals to a stranger is engaging in
    a. voyeurism.
    b. exhibitionism.
    c. fetishism.
    d. coprophilia.

3. Which of the following groups of adjectives would **best** describe a person who engages in exhibitionism?
    a. relatively young, shy, nonassertive
    b. relatively young, antisocial, aggressive
    c. middle-aged to older, potentially violent, hostile
    d. relatively young, self-confident, reckless

4. According to Abel's research, approximately _____ percent of the rapists on his sample had histories of other types of variant sexual behavior.
    a. 25
    b. 50
    c. 75
    d. 90

5. Which of the following statements concerning men who expose themselves is **false**?
    a. They are usually in their 20s or 30s.
    b. The majority of those men go on to commit more serious offenses.
    c. They usually have feelings of inadequacy and insecurity.
    d. The majority of these men were raised in environments characterized by oppressive attitudes toward sexuality.

6. The characteristics of people who make obscene phones calls are similar to those who engage in
    a. fetishism.
    b. masochism.
    c. sadism.
    d. exhibitionism.

7. Watching X-rated movies or reading sexually explicit magazines is a mild form of _____, in which many people participate.
    a. exhibitionism
    b. frotteurism
    c. voyeurism
    d. masochism

8. A person who obtains sexual gratification from covertly observing people who are nude or engaging in sex is called a/an
    a. fetishist.
    b. sadist.
    c. voyeur.
    d. exhibitionist.

9. Obtaining sexual arousal through giving or receiving pain is called
    a. klismaphilia.
    b. frotteurism.
    c. fetishism.
    d. sadomasochism.

10. Rubin's survey of 975 men and women revealed that _____ occasionally engaged in a form of sadomasochistic activity with a partner.
    a. 5%
    b. 15%
    c. 25%
    d. 35%

11. Which of the following statements concerning sadomasochism is **false**?
    a. Any kind of physical or mental pain will sexually arouse a person with masochistic tendencies.
    b. One survey of 975 men and women revealed that 25% of the respondents engaged in some type of bondage during sex.
    c. It appears that masochism is more common than sadism.
    d. A majority of people who engage in sadomasochistic activities may prefer one role or the other, but are comfortable in either role.

12. Among the majority of individuals that Weinberg and his colleagues interviewed, sadomasochism was definitely a _____ activity.
    a. nonconsensual
    b. consensual
    c. severely humiliating
    d. severely painful

13. Sadomasochistic activity may result in all of the following **except**
    a. increased blood pressure
    b. hyperventilation
    c. increased muscle tension
    d. facial tics

14. Which of the following statements regarding autoerotic asphyxia is **false**?
    a. It is a fairly common paraphilia.
    b. The purpose of engaging in this behavior is to enhance sexual arousal by reducing the supply of oxygen to the brain.
    c. It may be a type of sexual masochism.
    d. It may result in death.

15. Fetishism is **best** defined as
    a. obtaining sexual gratification, primarily or exclusively, from an inanimate object or part of the body.
    b. cross-dressing for purposes of sexual arousal.
    c. cross-dressing to make your appearance correspond with your sexual orientation.
    d. being dependent on pornography for sexual gratification.

16. The development of fetishism is often an example of
    a. operant conditioning.
    b. classical conditioning.
    c. cultural conditioning.
    d. tactile conditioning.

17. Which of the following statements concerning transvestism is **true**?
    a. It exists primarily when people cross-dress to make their appearance correspond to their gender identity.
    b. It occurs primarily among unmarried homosexual men.
    c. People who cross-dress are usually gender dysphoric.
    d. Although most people who engage in transvestism are men, there are some cases of female transvestism that have been reported.

18. Anthropologist Robert Munroe has noted that _____ tends to appear more often in cultures where men assume more economic responsibility than women.
    a. transvestism
    b. transsexualism
    c. fetishism
    d. homosexuality

19. Which of the following statements concerning transvestism is **true**?
    a. Most people who engage in transvestism are likely to seek therapy at some point.
    b. The practice of transvestism can be successfully altered with therapy.
    c. One explanation for the development of transvestism is that it is a heterosexual male's attempt to explore the feminine side of his personality.
    d. The majority of people who engage in transvestism have a bisexual or homosexual orientation.

20. Which of the following statements concerning zoophilia is **true**?
    a. According to Kinsey, approximately the same number of men and women reported having had sexual contact with animals.
    b. The animals most frequently involved in sex with humans are horses, rabbits, and hamsters.
    c. It is commonly a transitory experience of young people for whom a sexual partner is not available.
    d. Males who engage in this activity usually have contact with household pets.

21. The term "necrophilia" refers to
    a. being dependent on violent pornography for sexual arousal.
    b. obtaining sexual gratification by having intercourse with a corpse.
    c. being sexually aroused by a person who is an amputee.
    d. obtaining sexual gratification from contact with feces.

22. When a person becomes sexually aroused from contact with feces, it is called
    a. coprophilia.
    b. klismaphilia.
    c. frotteurism.
    d. naturophilia.

23. Which of the following statements is **true**?
    a. Don Juanism is one term for men who have insatiable sexual needs.
    b. The final phase of Carnes' cycle of sexual addiction is the sexual act itself.
    c. The term "satyriasis" is used to refer to a man who is bisexual.
    d. There are six phases in Carnes' sexual addiction cycle.

24. Eli Coleman and others believe that excessive sexual activity reflects _____ rather than addiction.
    a. sexual dysfunction
    b. sexual compulsion
    c. a hormonal imbalance
    d. optimal health

Critical Thinking/Personal Reflection

1. After reading this chapter, how have your attitudes changed, if at all, toward any of the sexual behaviors discussed?

2. Which of the atypical sexual behaviors discussed in the chapter do you find most acceptable? Least acceptable? Why?

3. Which of the atypical sexual behaviors discussed should be illegal? Under what circumstances? Why?

4. Have you experienced any of the paraphilias mentioned in the chapter or been a victim of any of the coercive paraphilias that are described? If so, how have your personal experiences — or the ways in which you dealt with them — compared to the information presented in the text?

Chapter Overview With Fill-In Answers

1. paraphilia
2. atypical
3. coercion
4a. inanimate
4b. body
5. exclusion
6. human
7. classical
8a. masturbation
8b. orgasm
9. burglary
10. clothes
11a. entire
11b. one
12a. men
12b. female
13. heterosexual
14a. bisexual
14b. homosexual
15. tolerate
16. conditioning
17. feminine
18. giving
19. receiving
20. pain
21. aggressive
22a. masochistic
22b. degrading
23. less
24. negative
25. pathological
26a. neurophysiological
26b. hyperventilation
27. self-awareness
28a. sex
28b. pain
29a. Autoerotic asphyxia
29b. deprivation
29c. death
30. masochism
31. enemas
32a. mothers
32b. anal
33a. feces
33b. urine
34a. indecent exposure
34b. involuntary
35a. 20s
35b. 30s

35c. married
36. intimacy
37. limit
38. child molestation
39. therapy
40. ignore
41. exhibitionism
42a. male
42b. anxiety
43a. ignore
43b. deafness
44a. unlisted
44b. call-trace
45a. naked
45b. strangers
46a. sexual relations
46b. risk
47. sociosexual
48. 20s
49a. Frotteurism
49b. female
49c. elevator
50a. orgasm
50b. masturbation
51. bestiality
52. transitory
53. preferred
54. corpse
55. men
56a. dead
56b. prostitutes
57. Psychotherapy
58. cognitive
59a. aversive conditioning
59b. inappropriate
60a. systematic desensitization
60b. anxious
61a. orgasmic reconditioning
61b. satiation
62a. testosterone
62b. behavior
63a. nymphomania
63b. satyriasis
64. compulsive
65a. addiction
65b. depression
65c. high
66a. ritualistic
66b. despair

67. compulsive
68a. shame
68b. unworthiness
68c. inadequacy
68d. loneliness
69a. treatment
69b. self-help

Matching Answers

1. l	2. j	3. e	4. d	5. c	6. k	7. e	8. l
9. g	10. f	11. c	12. i	13. e	14. b	15. h	16. c

Sample Multiple Choice Answers

1. c	2. b	3. a	4. b	5. b	6. d	7. c	8. c
9. d	10. c	11. a	12. b	13. d	14. a	15. a	16. b
17. d	18. a	19. c	20. c	21. b	22. a	23. a	24. b

19

Sexual Victimization

Introduction

There is a growing awareness of the high incidence of sexual victimization that occurs in our society. Men and women who survive rape, childhood sexual abuse, and sexual harassment are becoming more willing to speak out regarding their experiences, and our society is being forced to confront some of the cultural patterns that condone and even support sexual victimization. This chapter presents current research on both the perpetrators and victims of the coercive behaviors listed above and includes strategies for reducing the risk of rape, preventing child sexual abuse, and dealing with sexual harassment.

Review of Key Terms and Concepts

Key terms and concepts are listed and defined below. Refer to the subject index in the back of your textbook for additional information.

1. **rape** — sexual intercourse that occurs without consent as a result of actual or threatened force

2. **statutory rape** — intercourse with a person under the age of legal consent

3. **age of consent** — varies from state to state and ranges from age 14 to age 18; having sexual intercourse with a person under the age of consent is statutory rape

4. **stranger rape** — rape of a person by an unknown assailant

5. **acquaintance rape (date rape)** — forced sexual assault by a friend, acquaintance or date

6. **anger rape** — rape that is characterized by the use of physical violence far in excess of the amount necessary to force sexual submission

7. **power rape** — rape in which the primary goal is to exert control over another human being

8. **sadistic rape** — rape in which power or anger, or both, may be eroticized

9. **sexual gratification rape** — rape in which the primary goal is sexual gratification; most acquaintance rapes probably fit into this category

10. **Rohypnol** — a powerful tranquilizer that, when combined with alcohol, may dramatically reduce inhibitions, produce unconsciousness, and total amnesia for events that occur while a person is under its influence

11. **rape trauma syndrome** — the emotional repercussions women experience following rape or attempted rape

12. **acute phase** — the first phase of rape trauma which begins immediately following the rape and may last up to several weeks; it includes a range of emotional and physical symptoms

13. **long-term reorganization phase** — the second phase of rape trauma which may last for up to several years; it includes a range of fearful and/or negative feelings and behaviors

14. **child sexual abuse** — sexual contact of any kind between an adult and a child (inappropriate touching, oral-genital stimulation, coitus, etc.)

15. **pedophilia (child molestation)** — nonrelative child sexual abuse

16. **incest** — sexual contact between two people who are related, one of whom is often a child

17. **sexual harassment** — unwanted sexual advances from individuals in the workplace or an academic setting

Chapter Overview With Fill-Ins

After reading each of the major sections in the chapter, check your retention by filling in each of the blanks in the corresponding sections below. The answers are provided at the end of the chapter.

Rape

1. The legal definition of rape varies from state to state; however, most laws define rape as sexual intercourse that occurs under a)_____ or b)_____ forcible compulsion that overcomes the earnest resistance of the victim.

2. a)_____ rape refers to intercourse with a person who is under the age of b)_____.

3. _____ rape is the rape of a person by an unknown assailant.

4. _____ rape, or date rape, is committed by someone known to the victim.

5. Estimates of the percentage of rapes that women victims report to the police or other agencies range from _____ to _____ percent.

6. Various contemporary surveys indicate that anywhere from _____ to _____ percent of women have experienced rape or attempted rape.

7. There are a number of false beliefs about rape: 1) the belief that women can always successfully a)_____ a rape attempt is false for several reasons; 2) the distorted perception that some men have that women want to be b)_____ into sexual activity, even to the extent of being raped; 3) the notion that many women "cry rape" is inaccurate; 4) although some women do have rape c)_____, in which they have control of the situation and they risk no threat of physical d)_____, it is a false belief that "all women want to be raped," as many novels and films suggest; and finally, 5) many women think "it could never happen to me," which is again inaccurate because any female is a potential e)_____.

8. Many men incarcerated for rape offenses appear to have a strong tendency toward _____ that is often reflected in their act of rape.

9. The above fact, along with certain assumptions concerning male-female relationships, resulted in a number of feminist writers taking the position that rape is not a)_____ motivated, but rather an act of b)_____ and domination.

10. However, recent research has made it clear that while this may be the case, rape is frequently motivated by a desire for _____ gratification as well.

11. Research has indicated that mere exposure to a)_____ materials may not be the critical factor in increasing men's aggressiveness toward women, but rather the b)_____ nature of the material may have harmful effects on men's attitudes toward sex and women.

12. Besides the different socialization processes that often distinguish rapists from nonrapists, other characteristics that have been linked to men who rape include: a tendency to embrace traditional a)_____ roles; b)_____ -_____ personalities which may make them c)_____ to others' feelings; d)_____ toward women; and e)_____ use.

13. The authors differentiate among a)_____ types of rapes and rapists: b)_____ rape, power rape, c)_____ rape and sexual gratification rape.

14. A majority of rapes are committed by someone who is _____ to the woman.

15. A number of recent studies provide solid evidence of the _____ of sexual coercion in dating situations.

16. A powerful tranquilizer drug called a)_____ ("roofies") has been used with increasing frequency to facilitate b)_____ conquest or c)_____ victims who are then sexually molested or raped.

17. Numerous examples of wartime rape reveal how it is used in that context to dominate, a)_____ and b)_____ women.

18. Wartime rape can also serve the purpose of destroying a)_____ integrity, forcing communities to leave, thereby achieving the goal of b)"_____ _____."

19. The emotional repercussions women experience following rape have been labeled _____ _____ syndrome.

20. There are usually two phases of rape trauma: the _____ phase and the long-term reorganization phase.

21. Women often find that supportive counseling, either individually or in _____, can help them deal with the aftermath of rape.

22. It is estimated that 5 to10 percent of rapes committed annually in the United States involve _____ victims, although this statistic is probably low.

23. It appears that the majority of men who are raped are both Caucasian and a)_____, and that the majority of perpetrators are b)_____ _____.

Sexual Abuse of Children

24. _____ sexual abuse is defined as an adult engaging in sexual contact of any kind with a child.

25. Most researchers distinguish between nonrelative child sexual abuse, referred to as a)_____ or child molestation, and b)_____, which is sexual contact between two people who are related (one of whom is often a child).

26. Although incest occurs at all a)_____ levels, it appears to occur with greater frequency in families disrupted by severe marital conflict, b)_____ abuse, alcoholism, unemployment, and emotional illness.

27. Although a)_____-_____ and first cousin incest is most common,
    b)_____-_____ incest is more likely to be reported to authorities.

28. It is difficult to accurately estimate the incidence of _____ or pedophilia for a
    number of reasons.

29. However, numerous reports and surveys indicate the _____ of child sexual
    abuse is startling.

30. A recent survey that combined data from fourteen U.S. studies and two Canadian studies
    indicated that approximately _____ percent of women and _____ percent of men had
    been sexually abused as children.

31. There is increasing evidence that child sexual abuse can have severely damaging long-
    term consequences such as: difficulty in forming a)_____ relationships,
    especially with men; b)_____ difficulties; low self-esteem, guilt, shame, and
    depression; a sense of alienation from others; a lack of trust in others; revulsion at being
    c)_____; drug and alcohol abuse; obesity; elevated d)_____ rates; and
    predisposition to being e)_____ in other ways.

32. The pedophile offender is most commonly a a)_____ who is shy, lonely, poorly
    informed about b)_____, and is often very moralistic or c)_____.

33. These offenders have often been _____ themselves during their own childhood.

34. The man who engages in an incestuous relationship with his own child _____
    many of the characteristics of the pedophile.

Preventing Child Sexual Abuse

35. The following list, drawn from the writings of a number of child abuse specialists, offers
    some suggestions for a)_____ child sexual abuse: 1) present prevention-oriented
    material to boys and girls when they are still very b)_____; 2) keep the
    discussion and concepts c)_____; 3) avoid making a discussion of child sex
    abuse d)_____; 4) carefully explain the differences between okay and not-okay
    touches; 5) encourage children to believe they have e)_____; 6) encourage
    children to tell someone right away if an adult has touched them inappropriately; 7)
    discuss some of the strategies adults might use to entice children; 8) discuss some of the
    strategies for getting away from f)_____ situations; 9) encourage children to
    state clearly to the offender that they will g)_____ a responsible adult about
    what went on; and 10) discuss the h)_____ aspects of touch and sexuality
    between two adults who care for each other.

Sexual Harassment

36. The definition of sexual harassment is "any unwanted sexual attention of a sexual nature
    from someone at the a)_____ or in an b)_____ setting."

37. In 1980, the Equal Employment Opportunity Commission issued guidelines derived from
    the a)_____ _____ Act that emphasize that both verbal and physical
    harassment are b)_____.

38. Two kinds of sexual harassment are a)"_____ _____ _____" and
    "_____ or offensive environment."

39. A number of studies have indicated that sexual harassment is extremely _____
    in the workplace.

40. A survey of more than 24,000 federal employees found that _____ percent of the women and _____ percent of the men had been sexually harassed.

41. Other surveys of women indicate an even _____ incidence.

42. In recent years sexual harassment involving members of the a)_____ sex has become an increasing issue in the workplace and in America's b)_____.

43. A person who quits or is fired as a result of sexual harassment faces the prospect of severe a)_____ difficulties, as well as a variety of adverse emotional, b)_____, and psychological effects.

44. The text outlines _____ guidelines for dealing with sexual harassment in the workplace.

45. Sexual harassment may also take place in an _____ environment.

46. The authors advise students to _____ sexual harassment if they encounter it — as opposed to dropping the class or dropping out of school — so that the inappropriate actions may be curtailed.

Sample Short Answer Test Questions

1. List five common false beliefs about rape and briefly describe why the beliefs are inaccurate.

    a.

    b.

    c.

    d.

    e.

2. Of 114 imprisoned rapists, what percentage did not see themselves as rapists?

3. Briefly describe the Peruvian rape law that women activists are attempting to repeal.

4. What has been the problem with some of the past studies on men who rape?

5. In addition to having power and control over women, what motivates some men to rape women?

6. Briefly summarize the results of Peggy Reeves Sanday's research.

7. What are some of the characteristics of a rape-prone society?

8. Describe the relationship between sexually violent media and some rapists' behaviors. Cite research to support your answer.

9. What are the effects of sexually violent media versus sexually degrading media?

10. In general, what are some of the characteristics of men who rape?

11. What were the results of Gene Abel's study of rapists who had never been identified by the criminal justice system?

12. List and briefly characterize the four types of rapes and rapists.

13. What are some reasons for engaging in unwanted sexual acts where physical force is not used?

14. According to one study of 610 females, what were some of the reasons given for saying no when they meant yes?

15. What is Rohypnol? What are the effects of taking it — with and without alcohol?

16. List four reasons why rape is often prevalent during war times.

17. List at least five strategies for reducing the risk of stranger rape.

18. List five strategies for reducing the risk of acquaintance rape.

19. What can a woman do if she has been raped?

20. List and briefly describe the two phases of rape trauma syndrome.

21. What types of sexual problems were most common among rape survivors? Least common?

22. List at least four suggestions for how a man might effectively respond to his partner after she has been raped.

23. In what situations and by whom may men be raped?

24. In reference to a 1997 survey of adult male sexual assault, list at least three of the key findings.

25. Explain why men might get erections and women might lubricate and be orgasmic while they are being sexually molested.

26. Describe some of the family conditions associated with incest.

27. What is the most common type of incest?

28. How may a father manipulate his daughter into sexual contact with him?

29. Explain some of the difficulties estimating how prevalent child abuse really is.

30. How common is incest in Europe as compared to the United States?

31. Describe some of the long-term effects of sexual abuse on the child and what factors influence the severity of these effects?

32. List some of the sex differences regarding the impact of childhood sexual abuse.

33. Describe the profile of the person who sexually abuses children.

34. How may offenders who have not been prosecuted for sexual assault differ from those who have?

35. Briefly summarize the controversy surrounding the issue of recovered memories of child sexual abuse.

36. List at least five suggestions for preventing child abuse.

37. List and briefly describe the two kinds of sexual harassment.

38. In a study of 24,000 federal employees, what percent of men and women surveyed had been sexually harassed?

39. List at least three forms that sexual harassment can take.

40. Describe some of the emotional, physical, and financial effects of sexual harassment.

41. Summarize the issues that make same-sex harassment especially problematic.

42. List at least three options for dealing with sexual harassment in the workplace.

43. How does sexual harassment in the academic environment differ from sexual harassment in the workplace?

44. What do the authors suggest that students do if they experience sexual harassment?

Sample Multiple Choice Test Questions

Select the best alternative. Check your answers with the answer key at the end of the chapter.

1. _____ refers to intercourse with a person who is under the age of consent.
   a. Power rape
   b. Stranger rape
   c. Statutory rape
   d. Pedophilia

2. One reason that the notion that "women can always successfully resist rape if they really want to" is false is that
   a. the assailant has the elements of surprise and intimidation on his side.
   b. men are usually physically larger and stronger than women.
   c. a woman's shoes and clothing may inhibit her ability to escape.
   d. all of the above

3. Peggy Reeves Sanday's research indicated that American women are _____ as likely to be raped as are women in certain other societies.
   a. five times
   b. fifty times
   c. one hundred times
   d. several hundred times

4. According to Malamuth, which of the following is the **best** predictor of a man's inclination to engage in rape?
   a. his own experience of sexual abuse as a child
   b. his perception of peer group acceptance of rape
   c. the type of athletic activities he participated in
   d. the nature and extent of his moral or religious training

5. Which of the following statements concerning sexual gratification rape is **false**?
   a. It is likely to be impulsive.
   b. The majority of date rapes fit into this category.
   c. Power and anger are usually eroticized in this type of rape.
   d. This is probably the most common kind of rape.

6. All of the following are listed as characteristics of men who rape **except**
   a. self-centered personality
   b. anger toward women
   c. recovering drug addict
   d. adheres to traditional gender roles

7. All of the following were reasons men and women gave for engaging in unwanted sex acts where physical force was not used **except**
   a. being turned on by partner's actions and later regretting it
   b. a desire to be popular
   c. partner questioning one's sexuality
   d. easier to comply than resist

8. Which of the following is a characteristic of the acute phase of rape trauma syndrome?
    a. reacting in a controlled or expressive manner
    b. frequent changes in place of residence
    c. refraining from sexual contact
    d. sexual difficulties

9. One long-term study of rape survivors revealed that _____ percent avoided sexual contact for six months to a year after the assault.
    a. 20
    b. 40
    c. 60
    d. 80

10. A woman may report having various sexual problems during the _____ phase of rape trauma syndrome.
    a. acute
    b. reorganization
    c. primary
    d. adjustment

11. The **best** explanation for why a man might have an erection while he was being sexually assaulted is that
    a. he has probably had prior "rape fantasies" that are now becoming a reality.
    b. he probably has some underlying masochistic desires.
    c. he was sexually attracted to his assailant.
    d. sexual responses can occur in situations that cause high levels of anxiety.

12. The profile of the pedophile who is prosecuted typically includes all of the following **except**
    a. someone with good interpersonal skills.
    b. a religious or moralistic person.
    c. sexually victimized themselves as children.
    d. alcoholic.

13. Which of the following patterns appears to be a precursor to rape and other deviant sexual acts?
    a. masturbating to deviant sexual fantasies
    b. conflicts regarding gender identity
    c. a history of interpersonal as well as sexual dysfunction
    d. conflicts regarding sexual orientation

14. All of the following are examples of incestuous behavior **except**
    a. sexual contact between mother and son
    b. a 21-year-old man having intercourse with an unrelated 16-year-old girl
    c. sexual contact between uncle and niece
    d. sexual contact between first cousins

15. Which of the following statements concerning brother-sister incest is **false**?
    a. It is the most common form of incest.
    b. It is not uncommon for siblings to look favorably upon their experiences.
    c. It is frequently not reported or discovered.
    d. The effects of coercive sibling sexual abuse are often perceived to be much more devastating then they really are.

16. Father-daughter incest
    a. usually involves physical force on the part of the father.
    b. may bring the daughter special recognition or privileges.
    c. usually begins in late adolescence.
    d. is most common.

17. All of the following were listed as characteristics of men who engage in incest and are prosecuted for it **except**
    a. violent
    b. emotionally immature
    c. devoutly religious
    d. unemployed

18. All of the following were suggestions given for preventing child sexual abuse **except**
    a. Avoid complicated discussions and keep explanations simple.
    b. Carefully explain the differences between okay and not-okay touches.
    c. Encourage children to believe that they have rights.
    d. The best time to initiate discussions with children is at about age eight

19. Approximately _____ percent of child sex abuse victims are younger than age seven.
    a. 10
    b. 25
    c. 40
    d. 60

20. Which of the following statements is **false**?
    a. A survey of 24,000 federal employees found that 42 percent of the women and 15 percent of the men surveyed had been sexually harassed.
    b. Sexual harassment includes physical and verbal harassment.
    c. An increasing number of larger companies are establishing programs that clarify for their employees exactly what sexual harassment is.
    d. According to the EEOC guidelines, there are four basic types of sexual harassment.

21. If you are a victim of sexual harassment on campus, it is suggested that you
    a. drop the class.
    b. find another faculty advisor.
    c. report the harassment.
    d. transfer to another school.

22. Janelle's coworker constantly makes lewd remarks about her body and makes other sexist comments or derogatory sexual remarks in her presence. This is called _____ harassment.
    a. quid pro quo
    b. hostile or offensive environment
    c. corporal
    d. verbal

Critical Thinking/Personal Reflection

1. Think of specific films, television programs, novels, and media images that perpetuate and support the "rape culture" discussed in the text. Give specific examples of these. How do these messages and role models influence relationships between the sexes?

2. Have you personally experienced any of the various types of sexual victimization discussed in this chapter? If so, how have you dealt with those experiences? What kind of personal or professional help have you sought, if any? How closely have your experiences paralleled the information presented in the text?

3. Has anyone close to you (partner, family member or friend) experienced any of the types of sexual victimization discussed in this chapter? If so, how did you respond/react to the person's experience? If you had it to do over again, would you respond differently? If so, how?

4. What kind of "child sexual abuse prevention" information did you receive when you were growing up, if any? If you could recreate that part of your history, what kinds of information and/or examples would have been helpful to you, and at what age(s)?

Chapter Overview With Fill-In Answers

1a. actual
1b. threatened
2a. Statutory
2b. consent
3. Stranger
4. Acquaintance
5. 8; 16
6. 19; 30
7a. resist
7b. coerced
7c. fantasies
7d. harm
7e. victim
8. violence
9a. sexually
9b. power
10. sexual
11a. erotic
11b. violent
12a. gender
12b. self-centered
12c. insensitive
12d. anger
12e. alcohol
13a. four
13b. anger
13c. sadistic
14. known
15. prevalence
16a. Rohypnol
16b. sexual
16c. incapacitate
17a. humiliate
17b. control
18a. cultural
18b. ethnic cleansing
19. rape trauma
20. acute
21. groups
22. male
23a. heterosexual
23b. heterosexual men
24. Child

25a. pedophilia
25b. incest
26a. socioeconomic
26b. spouse
27a. brother-sister
27b. father-daughter
28. incest
29. prevalence
30. 22; 9
31a. intimate
31b. sexual
31c. touched
31d. suicide
31e. victimized
32a. male
32b. sexuality
32c. religious
33. victimized
34. shares
35a. preventing
35b. young
35c. simple
35d. frightening
35e. rights
35f. dangerous
35g. tell
35h. pleasurable
36a. workplace
36b. academic
37a. Civil Rights
37b. illegal
38a. quid pro quo
38b. hostile
39. common
40. 42; 15
41. greater
42a. same
42b. courts
43a. financial
43b. physical
44. six
45. academic
46. report

Sample Multiple Choice Answers

1. c	2. d	3. d	4. b	5. c	6. c	7. d	8. a
9. b	10. b	11. d	12. a	13. a	14. b	15. d	16. b
17. a	18. d	19. b	20. d	21. c	22. b		

20

Sex For Sale

Introduction

This chapter examines two topics in which sex and money converge: pornography and prostitution. The controversial social and legal aspects of each are explored.

Review of Key Terms and Concepts

Key terms and concepts are listed and defined below. Refer to the subject index in the back of your textbook for additional information.

1. **pornography** — visual and written materials of a sexual nature that are used for purposes of sexual arousal

2. **obscene** — a term that implies a personal or societal judgment that something is offensive

3. **prostitution** — the exchange of sexual services for money

4. **streetwalker** — a type of female prostitute who services male customers; she solicits customers on the street or in bars

5. **call girl** — a type of female prostitute who is at the top of the prostitution hierarchy; she generally earns more than other types of prostitutes and also provides social services to her customers

6. **brothel** — a house in which a group of prostitutes works

7. **gigolos** — men who provide sexual services for women in exchange for money and gifts

8. **hustler** — a male prostitute who caters to homosexual men; he makes contact with his customers on the streets or in gay bars

9. **call boy** — a male prostitute who caters to homosexual men; he earns more money than hustlers, and provides social as well as sexual services to his customers

10. **kept boy** — a male prostitute who is partially or fully supported by an older male

11. **peer-delinquent prostitutes** — male prostitutes who work in small groups and use homosexual prostitution as a vehicle for assault and robbery

12. **pimps** — men who "protect" prostitutes (usually streetwalkers) and live off their earnings

13. **COYOTE** — the prostitutes' union (Cast Off Your Old Tired Ethics) which acts as a collective voice for prostitutes' concerns

Chapter Overview With Fill-Ins

After reading each of the major sections in the chapter, check your retention by filling in each of the blanks in the corresponding sections below. The answers are provided at the end of the chapter.

Pornography

1. Pornography is defined as _____, or written materials of a sexual nature that are used for the purposes of sexual arousal.

2. The legal controversies related to pornography have centered on four issues: the evaluation of what is a)_____; the constitutional right of b)_____ _____; regulations concerning the _____ of sexually explicit materials; and the extent to which pornography c)_____ against women.

3. In the late 1960s, President Johnson appointed a Commission on Obscenity and Pornography to study the effects of _____ _____ materials.

4. The commission found that after pornography was legalized in Denmark in the late 1960s, sales of pornography to Danes _____ in the years after legalization.

5. The commission noted that legalization and increased availability of pornography did not result in an increase of reported _____ _____, although a cause-and-effect relationship is difficult to establish.

6. After analyzing current research, the 1970 commission concluded that no significant, long-lasting changes in behavior were evident in college-student volunteer research subjects after being exposed to _____.

7. On the basis of this information, the commission recommended _____ all laws prohibiting access to pornography for adults.

8. However, both President Nixon and the U.S. Senate _____ these recommendations.

9. The 1986 U.S. Attorney General's Commission on Pornography (the Meese Commission) reached drastically different conclusions, and concluded that a)_____ pornography b)_____ sexually aggressive behavior toward women and that c)_____ pornography fostered accepting attitudes toward rape and has some causal relationship to sexual violence.

10. Many of the Meese Commission's conclusions and recommendations have generated considerable _____.

11. The distinction between _____ and dissemination of pornography is a long-standing legal issue.

12. The regulation of pornography in _____ has been a critical censorship issue and will probably continue to be.

13. Research has shown that exposure to pornography can increase acceptance of male a)_____ and female b)_____.

14. One study found that after repeated exposure to pornography, men and women became less satisfied with the a)_____ appeal and b)_____ performance of their partners.

Prostitution

15. Prostitution refers to the exchange of sexual services for _____.

16. Although prostitution has existed throughout history, the significance and meaning of prostitution have _____ in different times and societies.

17. Customers of prostitutes are usually white, middle-aged, middle-class, and _____, and they patronize prostitutes for various _____.

18. No single theory can explain the motivation for being a prostitute, although studies have found that prostitutes have experienced a _____ to _____ percent incidence of childhood sexual abuse.

19. _____ is a concern with prostitution.

20. In parts of _____, sex with prostitutes is a primary mode of _____ transmission.

21. In Kenya, a study found that _____ percent of 1000 prostitutes tested in Nairobi were infected with HIV.

22. In a study of New York streetwalkers, HIV rates were _____ percent.

23. Most teenage prostitutes come from unstable, problem-ridden families; approximately _____ percent have been victims of sexual abuse.

24. There are several different types of female prostitutes who service male customers: a)_____, women who work in b)_____ or massage parlors, and call girls.

25. Men who provide sexual services for women in exchange for money and gifts are called _____.

26. Male prostitutes who cater to other men can be classified into different groups: hustlers, call boys, _____ boys, and peer-delinquent prostitutes.

27. Some male prostitutes consider themselves to be a)_____; they have concurrent female sexual partners and usually return to a b)_____ lifestyle after a brief career in prostitution.

28. Most men and women who sell sexual services view their work as an _____ opportunity.

29. However, pimps, the _____ justice system, referral agents, and hotel operators all benefit financially from prostitution as well.

Sample Short Answer Test Questions

1. Why is a contemporary definition of pornography difficult to establish?

2. List and briefly describe the three categories of sexually explicit materials that are currently being researched.

    a.

    b.

    c.

3. List the three criteria used by the Supreme Court for evaluating obscenity.

4. Freedom of speech is guaranteed under which constitutional amendment?

5. Briefly summarize the findings of President Johnson's Commission on Obscenity and Pornography regarding the following:

    a. the effects of legalization of pornography in Denmark

    b. how imprisoned sex offenders' exposure to pornography compared to other prison inmates and non-prison populations

    c. the effects of exposure to pornography on college students

    d. The Commission's recommendations

6. What were the conclusions of the 1986 U.S. Attorney General's Commission on Pornography Report?

7. List some of the criticisms of the report's conclusions and recommendations.

8. What year were sexually explicit materials banned in China? How are offenders punished?

9. How is dissemination of pornography regulated?

10. Why are some people opposed to laws establishing pornography as a form of sexual discrimination?

11. What did one research study find in states that had higher rates of nonviolent, soft-core pornography?

12. What were the results of the 1988 study in which men and women were repeatedly exposed to pornography?

13. Briefly summarize the research findings on the effects of degrading pornography.

14. Briefly summarize the researching findings of the effects on violent pornography.

15. Briefly summarize the role of prostitution in:
    a. ancient Greece

    b. medieval Europe

    c. England during the Victorian era

16. Characterize the customers of female prostitutes.

17. Briefly state the arguments for maintaining the status of prostitution as a criminal offense.

18. List several arguments for the legalization of prostitution.

19. List several arguments for the decriminalization of prostitution.

20. What is COYOTE?

21. Compare the problem of AIDS and prostitution in Africa and the United States. What percent of prostitutes in Kenya were infected with HIV?

22. What percentage of teenage prostitutes have been victims of sexual abuse?

23. List and briefly describe the three types of female prostitutes who service male customers:

a.

b.

c.

24. Briefly describe the following:

    a. gigolos

    b. hustlers

    c. call boys

    d. kept boys

    e. peer-delinquent prostitutes

    f. pimps

25. List and briefly describe four different groups of people that benefit financially from prostitution:

    a.

    b.

    c.

    d.

26. In what countries is the "sex tourism" industry most proliferate? Which countries supply most of the clientele?

27. What does an economics professor from Thailand have to say regarding the earnings of the sex trade vs. the agricultural industry?

Sample Multiple Choice Test Questions

Select the best alternative. Check your answers with the answer key at the end of the chapter.

1. The legal controversies about pornography center on what is to be legally defined as
    a. erotic.
    b. obscene.
    c. degrading and humiliating.
    d. violent.

2. Current federal law regarding obscene materials prohibits all of the following **except**
    a. broadcasting obscene materials.
    b. private possession of obscene materials.
    c. mailing obscene materials.
    d. importing obscene materials.

3. Most pornography dissemination statutes stem from
    a. the Comstock Act.
    b. the West Coast Society for the Suppression of Vice.
    c. the John Birch Society.
    d. COYOTE.

4. Which of the following findings and/or recommendations regarding the 1970 commission report on pornography was **true**?
    a. Legalization and increased availability of pornography in Denmark caused an increase in the sale of pornography to Danes.
    b. Imprisoned sex offenders had more exposure to pornography than other prison inmates or non-prison populations.
    c. Significant, long-lasting changes in behavior were evident in college students who were exposed to pornography.
    d. President Nixon and the U.S. Senate rejected the commission's recommendation.

5. Central to both violent and degrading pornography is the depiction of
    a. aggression or brutality.
    b. people who are there out of a sense of shared pleasure.
    c. unequal balance of power.
    d. degradation and humiliation.

6. One study of college students and the general population found that after repeated exposure to pornography
   a. women and men became more innovative in their sexual interaction with their partners.
   b. men became sexually more demanding and women became more submissive.
   c. women and men became less satisfied with the physical appeal and sexual performance of their partners.
   d. women and men found their partners to be more sexually attractive.

7. One study of college students who were shown 4 video segments, one which included an X-rated video that was both highly romantic and highly explicit, found that
   a. women rated the video as most amusing but men did not.
   b. men rated the video as most amusing but women did not.
   c. neither men or women rated the video as most arousing.
   d. both men and women rated the video as most arousing.

8. One reason that researchers criticized the Meese Commission's report on pornography is that
   a. it ignored the detrimental effects of violence, whether accompanied by sexually explicit materials or not.
   b. it focused on sexually explicit materials that were violent and ignored the effects of materials that were degrading and humiliating.
   c. it ignored the results of the Denmark study.
   d. it was a sophisticated rehash of the 1970 Commission report and reached similar conclusions without taking into account the results of more recent research.

9. Which of the following statements concerning prostitution is **true**?
   a. There are times throughout history when it flourished and other times when it was nonexistent.
   b. In medieval Europe, it was viewed in an extremely negative light.
   c. Customers of prostitutes are typically young, single, blue-collar workers.
   d. The significance of prostitution has varied in different times and societies.

10. A common pattern in the backgrounds of female prostitutes is a history of
    a. sexual abuse.
    b. being raised in a single-parent family.
    c. early experimentation with drugs and alcohol.
    d. excessive masturbation.

11. Approximately _____ percent of teenage prostitutes have been victims of sexual abuse.
    a. 35
    b. 55
    c. 75
    d. 95

12. This type of female prostitute is usually managed by a "madam".
    a. woman who works in a brothel
    b. call girl
    c. kept girl
    d. streetwalker

13. _____ often work in small groups and use homosexual prostitution as a vehicle for assault and robbery.
    a. Streetwalkers
    b. Peer-delinquent prostitutes
    c. Hustlers
    d. Gigolos

14. When laws against prostitution are enforced,
    a. the customer is most likely to be punished.
    b. the prostitute is most likely to be punished.
    c. both the prostitute and the customer receive equal punishment.
    d. the pimp is most likely to be punished.

15. Regulation in terms of licensing and taxation would most likely occur if prostitution were
    a. legalized.
    b. institutionalized.
    c. decriminalized.
    d. litigated.

Critical Thinking/Personal Reflection

1. How would you describe your exposure to violent pornography, degrading pornography and erotica? What is your subjective assessment of the ways in which violent pornography, degrading pornography, and erotica affect intimate relationships between men and women, if at all?

2. Do you think prostitution should be legalized, decriminalized, or remain illegal? Why? Consider the ramifications of your decision in the community in which you live. What kinds of issues would be important to take into account?

Chapter Overview With Fill-In Answers

1. visual
2a. obscene
2b. free speech
2c. dissemination
2d. discriminates
3. sexually explicit
4. decreased
5. sex offenses
6. pornography
7. repealing
8. rejected
9a. violent
9b. caused
9c. degrading
10. controversy
11. possession
12. cyberspace
13a. dominance
13b. servitude
14a. physical
14b. sexual

15. money
16. varied
17a. married
17b. reasons
18. 46; 60
19. AIDS
20a. Africa
20b. HIV
21. 85
22. 35
23. 95
24a. streetwalkers
24b. brothels
25. gigolos
26. kept
27a. heterosexual
27b. heterosexual
28. economic
29. criminal

Sample Multiple Choice Answers

| 1. b | 2. b | 3. a | 4. d | 5. c | 6. c | 7. d | 8. a |
| 9. d | 10. a | 11. d | 12. a | 13. b | 14. b | 15. a | |

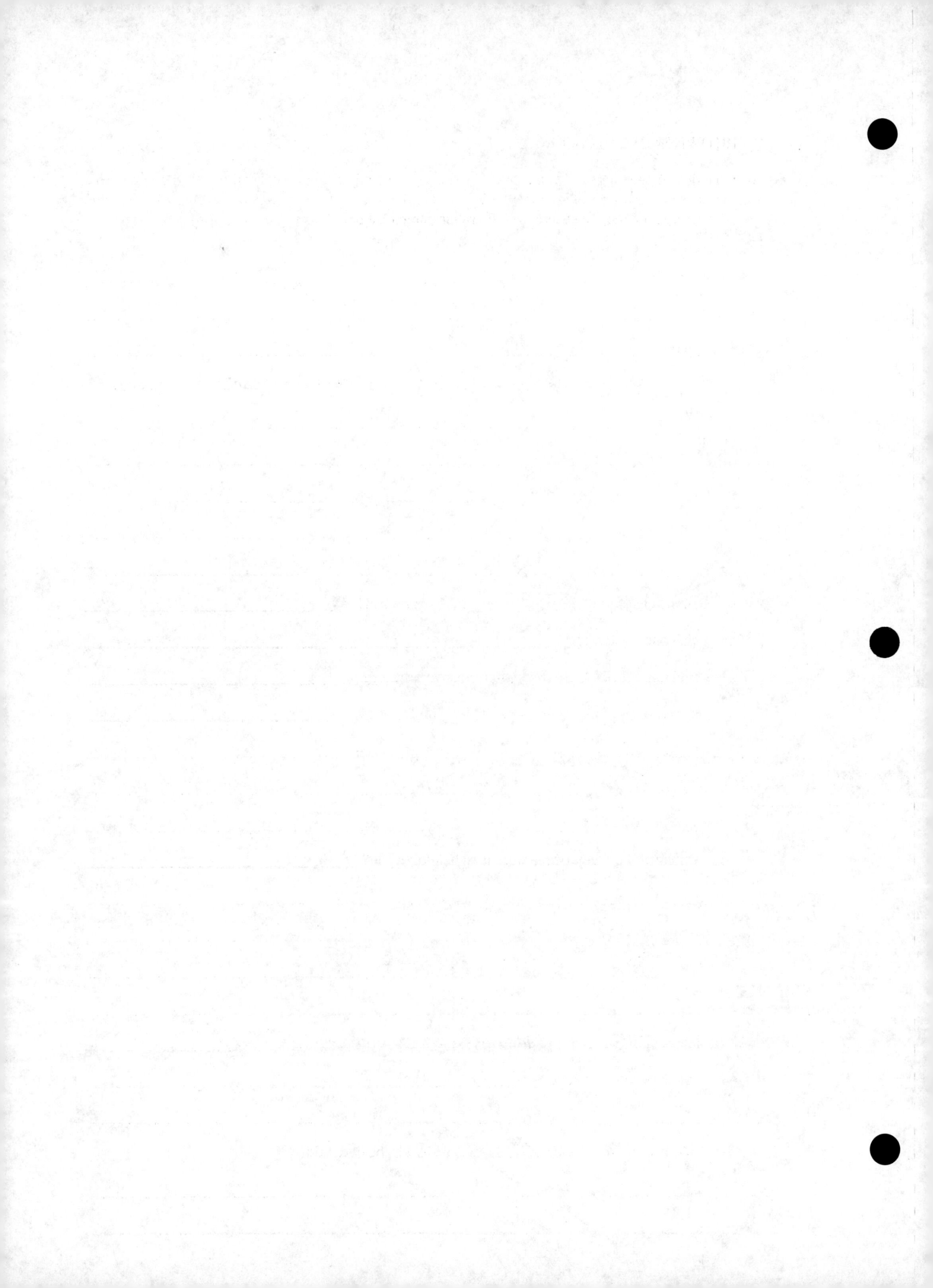

TO THE OWNER OF THIS BOOK:

I hope that this study guide has been helpful for you in your study of human sexuality. In order to improve future editions of this material, your feedback is essential. I would appreciate it if you would take the time to respond to the following questions and return the completed questionnaire to me. Thank you for your help!

School and address: _____

Department: _____

Instructor's name: _____

1. What did you like most about the *Study Guide for Crooks and Baur's Our Sexuality*, Seventh Edition?

_____

_____

2. What did you like least about it? _____

_____

_____

3. Were all of the chapters of the book assigned for you to read? _____

   If not, which ones weren't? _____

4. Did you find that the *Study Guide* promoted active learning? _____

5. Which sections of the *Study Guide* were most helpful to you? _____

_____

   Why were they helpful? _____

_____

6. Which sections of the *Study Guide* were least helpful to you? _____

_____

   Why were they not helpful? _____

_____

_____

7. Was the material in the *Study Guide* consistent with that in the textbook? _____

   If it was not, please describe: _____

_____

8. Do you have any other suggestions for us to consider for the next edition? _____

_____

_____

Optional:

Your name: _____   Date: _____

May Brooks/Cole quote you, either in promotion for *Study Guide for Crooks and Baur's Our Sexuality,* Seventh Edition, or in future publishing ventures?

Yes: _____   No: _____

Sincerely,

Lauren Kuhn